P9-DOE-686

Christianity According to the Bible

Ron Rhodes

HARVEST HOUSE PUBLISHERS

EUGENE, OREGON

CHRISTIANITY ACCORDING TO THE BIBLE
Copyright © 2006 by Ron Rhodes
Published by Harvest House Publishers
Eugene, Oregon 97402
www.harvesthousepublishers.com

Rhodes, Ron.
  Christianity according to the Bible / Ron Rhodes
    p. cm.
  Includes bibliographical references.
  ISBN-13: 978-0-7369-1724-7 (pbk.)
  ISBN-10: 0-7369-1724-1 (pbk.)
  1. Christian life—Biblical teaching. 2. Christianity. 3. Bible. I. Title.
  BS680.C47R46 2006
  230—dc22
                                                    2006002117

Printed in the United States of America

06 07 08 09 10 11 12 / LB-CF / 10 9 8 7 6 5 4 3 2 1

*With appreciation for my brothers
and sisters at Frisco Bible Church*

Frisco, Texas

Acknowledgments

Heartfelt thanks go to Bob Hawkins Jr. and Steve Miller at Harvest House Publishers for their helpful insights on the structure and content of this book. Thanks also to my wife, Kerri, and two children, David and Kylie, who make the sun rise each morning for me.

Contents

Christianity According to the Bible

Have you ever wondered if the Christianity you believe in is the genuine, bona fide Christianity of the Bible? Have you ever pondered the possibility that even though most of your Christian beliefs are biblical, others may find more support in other traditions? Have you ever secretly asked whether your view of salvation is rooted more in the official position of your denomination than the Bible? I've thought a lot about such questions as I've researched this book.

In fact, the more research I do, the stronger my conviction becomes that today's Christianity has been tainted—at least to some degree—by modern culture. For example, many people consider Sunday to be a sacred day and Monday through Saturday to be secular days, but no such distinction existed in biblical times. Christianity wasn't just a Sunday thing (though corporate worship did take place that day) but rather a seven-day-a-week thing. Every day was an opportunity to live for and glorify God.

And when people hear the word *church* today, they often think of buildings located throughout the city where Christians meet. In biblical days the word primarily referred to the people of God, and the meeting place was secondary.

Moreover, when people think of successful churches these days, they think of churches with lots of money and strong membership roles. In the first century, a church was successful if it featured consistent and accurate teaching of God's Word, prayer, worship, and growth in holiness among members. Tragically, church members today give few indications of being morally different from nonattenders. For example, many Christians openly attend R-rated movies with nudity, and divorces are just as common among Christians as among non-Christians.

The truth of the matter is that America is very religious but biblically ignorant. We talk a lot about God, prayer, heaven, and angels, and we are one of the most churchgoing nations on earth. However, many people—professing Christians included—cannot name the four Gospels. Quite a few cannot identify more than two or three of the twelve disciples or name even half of the Ten Commandments. A surprising number of people don't know who preached the most famous sermon in history—the Sermon on the Mount. (It was Jesus.) Many assume the phrase "God helps those who help themselves" is from the Bible. (It's not. In fact, God helps the helpless.) A 2005 Barna poll indicates that approximately 25 percent of people claiming to be born again rely on means other than God's grace to get to heaven, thereby indicating an unbiblical view of salvation.[1]

America has increasingly become a biblically illiterate nation. I say this not to sound preachy, to condemn, or to make anybody feel guilty. I mention it to make the very important point that *Christianity and Christian doctrine may include more (and less) than many of us realize.* If many of us are ignorant of some of the primary people and teachings of the Bible, might our concept of Christianity also be shallow and even unbiblical at points? This concern motivated me to write *Christianity According to the Bible.*

This book gets to the heart of what Christianity is all about based on the one book that really matters, the Bible—God's direct special revelation to humankind. Let's bypass the spin, hype, and false caricatures and let the Bible speak for itself regarding what Christianity is and what it is not. If you are interested in liberation from false ideas about Christianity and Christian teachings, then this book is for you. It will "tell it like it is" and provide you with the real thing—the *real Christianity* and *real biblical teachings*. Join me on an exciting journey through the Scriptures so that we can separate fact from fiction on the revolutionary, life-changing truth of Christianity.

What Is a Christian?

In my childhood and through my teenage years, I thought I was a Christian because I attended church regularly. For years I participated in various church activities, sang in the church choir, and went through all the right motions. I even participated in a confirmation ceremony at my church—an event that supposedly confirmed my status as a Christian. I had no idea at the time that I really wasn't a Christian.

Like so many other people today, I was under the illusion that a Christian is merely a church attender or perhaps a person who is fairly consistent in living by a Christian code of ethics. In this line of thinking, people can look forward to a destiny in heaven as long as their good deeds outweigh their bad deeds by the time they die.

Only years later did I realize that the mere act of attending church does not make a person a Christian. At the most basic level, a Christian is a person who has a personal relationship with Jesus Christ. This relationship begins the moment you place faith in Christ for salvation (Acts 16:31). When you believe in Jesus (John 3:16), you start an eternal relationship with Him. (It's eternal because it lasts the rest of your life on earth and then continues forever in heaven after you die.) It is a blessed relationship in which the Christian has the profound privilege of spiritually walking with Jesus on a daily basis, trusting

Him to meet each and every need. From a biblical perspective, then, Christianity is not so much a religion as it is a relationship.

We must keep in mind that being a Christian is more than just knowing *about* Jesus Christ. Becoming a Christian involves faith in Christ, and this faith leads to genuine fellowship with Him. "Our fellowship," explained the apostle John, "is with the Father and with his Son, Jesus Christ" (1 John 1:3).

Amazingly, the New Testament uses the word *Christian* only three times—most significantly in Acts 11:26. (The other two verses are Acts 26:28 and 1 Peter 4:16.) What did this label mean to those to who wore it?

In Acts 11:26, we are told simply and straightforwardly, "The disciples were called Christians first at Antioch." This would have been around AD 42, about a decade after Christ died on the cross and rose from the dead. Earlier, the followers of Jesus had called themselves "believers" (Acts 5:14 NASB), "brothers" (Acts 15:1,23), and "disciples" (Acts 9:26). But now, in Antioch, they are called Christians.

What does the term mean? Among the ancients, the -*ian* ending meant "belonging to the party of." Herodians belonged to the party of Herod. Caesarians belonged to the party of Caesar. Christians belonged to Christ. And Christians were loyal to Christ, just as the Herodians were loyal to Herod and Caesarians were loyal to Caesar (Matthew 22:16; Mark 3:6; 12:13).

The significance of the name *Christian* was that people saw these followers of Jesus as a distinct group. They were distinct from Judaism and from all other religions of the ancient world. We might loosely translate the term *Christian* to mean "one who belongs to Christ," "Christ-one," or perhaps "Christ-follower." *Christians are people who believe in Christ and who have a personal relationship with Him.*

Imagine a conversation between two residents of Antioch regarding these committed followers of Jesus. One might ask, "Who are these people?" The other person could answer, "Oh, these are the people who are always talking about Christ—they are the Christ-people, the Christians."

Those who have studied the culture of Antioch have noted that the Antiochans were well-known for making fun of people. They may have called the early followers of Jesus *Christians* to deride or ridicule them. History reveals that by the second century, Christians adopted the title as a badge of honor. They took pride (in a healthy way) in following Jesus. They had a genuine relationship with the living, resurrected Christ, and they were utterly faithful to Him, even in the face of death.

That the followers of Jesus were first called Christians in Antioch is highly significant. This city was made up of a mixture of Jews and Gentiles, and people of both backgrounds were followers of Jesus. What brought these believers unity was not their race, culture, or language. Rather, their unity came from their relationship with Jesus. Christianity crosses all cultural and ethnic boundaries.

What Is Christianity?

So Christianity—at its most basic level—is a personal relationship with Jesus. As J.I. Packer put it so well, "The essence of Christianity is neither beliefs nor behavior patterns. It is the reality of communion here and now with Christianity's living founder, the Mediator, Jesus Christ."[2] Indeed, "Christianity is a kind of love affair with our loving Lord and Savior, and the more days we turn into spiritual Valentine's Days by talking to the Lord about our relationship with Him…the richer and more joyful the relationship itself will become."[3]

In the New Testament, the early Christians never referred to their collective movement as *Christianity* even though the term *Christian* was used with greater frequency as the movement grew. By the time of Augustine (AD 396-430), the term *Christianity* appears to have become widespread. It progressively became a term describing a movement of people who had a personal relationship with and commitment to Jesus Christ.

Great Christians throughout the centuries have recognized that Christianity most fundamentally involves a personal relationship with Jesus.

- Devotional writer Oswald Chambers (1874–1917) said, "Christianity is not devotion to work, or to a cause, or a doctrine, but devotion to a person, the Lord Jesus Christ."[4]

- Evangelist Billy Graham said, "Christianity isn't only going to church on Sunday. It is living twenty-four hours of every day with Jesus Christ."[5]

- Bible scholar Stephen Neill said, "Christianity is not the acceptance of certain ideas. It is a personal attitude of trust and devotion to a person."[6]

- Theologian John R.W. Stott said, "A Christian is, in essence, somebody personally related to Jesus Christ."[7]

Why do I focus so much attention on the relational aspect of Christianity? Simply because a personal relationship with Jesus is the heart and soul of Christianity. Christianity is essentially Christ. The person and work of Jesus Christ are the rock upon which Christianity is built. If He is not who He said He is, and if He did not do what He said He came to do, the foundation of Christianity is undermined and the whole superstructure collapses.

Take Christ from Christianity, and you disembowel it. Nothing is left. Christ is the heart and center of Christianity. All else is mere circumference. Christianity is not primarily concerned with following Jesus' philosophy of life or imitating His ethic. Christianity is first and foremost concerned with personally relating to Him.

From a scriptural perspective, to know Jesus is to know God (John 8:19). To see Jesus is to see God (John 12:45). To believe in Jesus is to believe in God (John 12:44). To receive Jesus is to receive God (Mark 9:37). To honor Jesus is to honor God (John 5:23). To worship Jesus is to worship God (Revelation 4–5). A relationship with Jesus is the most important relationship you can have.

As you read this book, you will see—as I came to see years ago—that the Bible is predominantly a Jesus book. Jesus affirmed to some Jews, "You diligently study the Scriptures because you think that by them you possess eternal life. These are the Scriptures that testify about me, yet you refuse to come to me to have life" (John 5:39-40). The Jews to whom Jesus spoke knew the shell of the Bible but were neglecting the kernel within it. The Book is not what saves; the Savior of the Book does. Jesus Himself affirmed that the Old Testament Scriptures were "concerning himself" (Luke 24:27), were "written about me" (verse 44; Hebrews 10:7), and "testify about me" (John 5:39).

Jesus Is the Heart of Christianity

If a relationship with Jesus is the heart of Christianity, then the major doctrines (or teachings) of Christianity—including the doctrines of God, man, salvation, the church, angels, and the afterlife—must be tied directly to Christ. Christ is the thread that runs through each of these doctrines. He ties the whole Bible together. Let's take a look at how that works.

Jesus is God. We'll talk a lot about God in this book. And a book about Christianity *should* talk a lot about God. One thing we'll see is that Jesus Himself *is* God. In fact, the Bible refers to Him as both "God" (Hebrews 1:8) and "Lord" (Matthew 22:43-45). Jesus also has all the attributes (or characteristics) of God. For example, He's all-powerful (Matthew 28:18) and all-knowing (John 2:24-25). Jesus does things that only God can do—such as creating the entire universe (John 1:3) and raising people from the dead (John 11:43-44). Moreover, the people who came to know Him worshipped Him as God (Matthew 14:33; John 20:28).

Jesus is at the very heart of the doctrine of God.

Jesus is the Creator of the universe. The Old Testament presents God Almighty as the Creator of the universe (Isaiah 44:24). The New

Testament, however, portrays Jesus as the agent of creation (Colossians 1:16). This confirms for us that Jesus Himself is God.

So when we look at the universe around us, we see the handiwork of Jesus Christ. He's the one who made it. We catch a glimpse of His majesty and glory as we look at the starry sky above.

Jesus is at the very heart of the doctrine of creation.

Jesus created humankind. Jesus didn't create just the universe, He also created humankind (John 1:3). In the Genesis account we read that when the Lord created Adam, He declared Adam's loneliness to be "not good" (Genesis 2:18). The Lord created man to have relationships. He created man as a social being. And since man is a social being, for him to be alone is not good.

You and I were created with a need not only for fellowship with other humans (as Adam had a need for Eve) but also for fellowship with God. We are restless and insecure until a relationship with God becomes our living experience. Christ came into the world as a man to make that experience a reality for all who believe in Him.

Jesus is at the very heart of the doctrine of man.

Jesus is the ultimate revelation of God. God has revealed Himself to humankind in many ways. For example, God reveals His majesty and glory in the universe around us (Psalm 19). And because Christ Himself created the universe, the revelation in the universe is His doing.

God has also revealed Himself through the mouths of the prophets. First Peter 1:11 tells us that the Spirit of Christ spoke through all the prophets in biblical times. So the revelation that came through them is Christ's doing.

The Bible reveals that the ultimate revelation of God was Jesus Himself. Jesus—as eternal God—took on human flesh so He could be God's fullest revelation to humankind (Hebrews 1:2-3). Jesus was a revelation of God not only in His person (as God) but in His life and teachings as well. By observing the things Jesus did and said, we learn a great deal about God.

Jesus is at the very heart of the doctrine of revelation.

Jesus is the Savior. Man's sin against God posed a problem for God. How could He remain holy and just and at the same time forgive the sinner and allow the sinner into His presence? God's ineffable purity cannot tolerate sin. His eyes are too pure to behold evil. So how can the righteous God deal in a just way with the sinner and at the same time satisfy His own compassion and love by saving him from doom?

The answer is Jesus. Jesus came as our beloved Savior and died on the cross on our behalf (Matthew 20:28). Jesus our Savior "gave himself as a ransom for all men" (1 Timothy 2:6). Those who believe in Him are forgiven of their sins, and their relationship with God is instantly restored (Acts 16:31).

Jesus is at the very heart of the doctrine of salvation.

The Holy Spirit glorifies Jesus. Just before His crucifixion, Jesus met with the disciples in the upper room and gave them some final words of encouragement. During this time, He spoke to them about the coming of the Holy Spirit.

A primary ministry of the Holy Spirit is to glorify Christ and to make known the things of Christ (John 14:26). The Spirit testifies about Christ (John 15:26). The Spirit does not seek to make Himself prominent but rather seeks to exalt Jesus Christ.

Jesus is at the heart of the doctrine of the Holy Spirit.

Jesus is the head of the church. The church is a company of people who have one Lord and who share together in one gift of salvation in the Lord Jesus Christ.

In Matthew 16:18 Jesus affirmed to Peter, "I will build *my* church." The church is not created by a pastor or priest or body of elders. It is not owned by a denomination. Christ Himself builds the church. The church is His alone.

Christ not only owns the church, He is also the head of it (Ephesians 5:23). Moreover, Scripture says that Christ bought the church with His own blood on the cross (Acts 20:28).

Jesus is at the very heart of the doctrine of the church.

JESUS CHRIST
The Heart of Our Salvation

Here are just a few of the blessings that accompany the salvation we have in Jesus Christ:

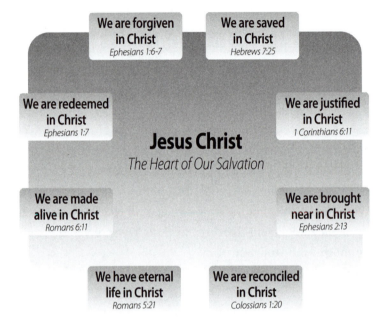

We are forgiven
in Christ
Ephesians 1:6-7

We are saved
in Christ
Hebrews 7:25

We are redeemed
in Christ
Ephesians 1:7

We are justified
in Christ
1 Corinthians 6:11

Jesus Christ
The Heart of Our Salvation

We are made
alive in Christ
Romans 6:11

We are brought
near in Christ
Ephesians 2:13

We have eternal
life in Christ
Romans 5:21

We are reconciled
in Christ
Colossians 1:20

The angels worship and serve Jesus. Jesus created the angels (Colossians 1:16). An angel announced Jesus' (human) birth to Mary (Luke 1:26-28) and to Joseph (Matthew 1:20). Angels proclaimed Jesus' birth to the shepherds in the field (Luke 2:9-15). Angels ministered to Jesus during His infancy (Matthew 2:13,19-20). The angels worshipped Jesus (Hebrews 1:6).

Angels also ministered to Jesus during His ministry (Matthew 4:1-11) and just before the crucifixion (Luke 22:43). An angel rolled away the stone following Jesus' resurrection from the dead (Matthew 28:1-6).

Angels appeared when Jesus ascended back into heaven (Acts 1:9-11). When Jesus comes again, angels will accompany Him (Matthew

JESUS IS THE HEART OF CHRISTIANITY

A relationship with Jesus is the very heart of Christianity.

Jesus is also the heart of every major doctrine (or teaching) of Christianity, as the chart below illustrates. Truly, Christianity without Christ is like a chest without a treasure, a frame without a portrait.

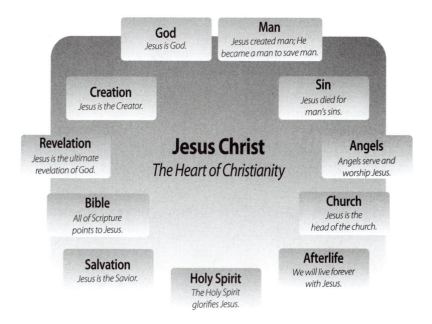

16:27). These angels will worship and exalt Jesus for all eternity (Revelation 5:11-14).

Jesus is at the very heart of the doctrine of angels.

Jesus made eternal life possible for us. Because of Jesus, you and I can go to heaven. Those who believe in Jesus receive eternal life and will live forever with Him (John 3:16-17; Acts 16:31).

Can anything be more sublime and more utterly satisfying for the Christian than to enjoy the sheer delight of unbroken fellowship with Christ in heaven and to have immediate and completely unobstructed access to Him? (See 2 Corinthians 5:6-8.) We will see our beloved Lord face-to-face in all His splendor and glory. We will gaze on His countenance and bask in His resplendent beauty forever.

Jesus is at the very heart of the doctrine of the afterlife.

The heart of the matter. You can easily see that Jesus is a thread that runs through the entire Bible. Who could deny that a relationship with Jesus is the heart of Christianity? Christianity without Christ is like a chest without a treasure.

My friend, my deepest desire and prayer for you when you finish this book is not only that you will have a better understanding of the major doctrines of Christianity (and an increased understanding of modern cultural distortions of them) but also that your personal relationship with Jesus will soar to new heights of intimacy. That, after all, is what true Christianity is all about.

Discussion Questions

1. Has your view of Christianity been influenced by extra-biblical traditions? How so?

2. Why might America be so biblically illiterate even though it is the most churchgoing nation on earth?

3. Summarize the most important elements of what it means to be a Christian.

4. What are some differences between Christianity and what we might called "churchianity"?

5. Summarize how Jesus is the very heart of Christianity.

1

God Communicates to Us

Authentic Christianity, as opposed to cultural (man-made) religion, is based on divine revelation. God did not create man and then leave him to grope around in the dark, trying to discover his Creator. God has always been the aggressor in making Himself known. He has always taken the initiative in revealing Himself to humankind. He does this through *revelation.*

Revelation makes good sense when you consider that God is our Father. Loving parents would never deliberately keep out of their children's sight so that the children grew up without knowing of the parents' existence. That would be the height of cruelty. Likewise, to create us and then not communicate with us would not be in character for a loving heavenly Father.

The word *communication* brings to mind someone coming to us to tell us about himself—telling us what he knows, opening up his mind to us, asking for our attention, and seeking a response.[1] That is what divine revelation is all about. God has come to us to tell us about Himself, tell us what He knows, open His mind to us, ask for our attention, and seek a response from us.

God has revealed Himself in two primary ways—through *general* revelation and *special* revelation. Let's take a brief look at both of these.

General Revelation and Special Revelation

General revelation refers to revelation that is available to all persons of all times. For example, God reveals Himself to everyone through the world of nature (Psalm 19).

By observing nature, we can detect something of God's existence and discern something of His divine power and glory. We might say that the whole world is God's kindergarten to teach us the ABCs of the reality of God. And since Jesus Christ is the one who created the physical universe (Colossians 1:16), the revelation of God in the universe is Christ's doing.

The great French theologian John Calvin wrote about this:

> Men cannot open their eyes without being compelled to see God. Upon his individual works he has engraved unmistakable marks of his glory. This skillful ordering of the universe is for us a sort of mirror in which we can contemplate God, who is otherwise invisible.[2]

Of course, we can only learn so much from general revelation. For example, general revelation does not tell us anything about God's cure for man's sin problem. It doesn't tell us the gospel message. (These kinds of things require *special* revelation.) But general revelation does give us enough information about God's existence that if we reject it and refuse to turn to God, God is justified in bringing condemnation against us (Romans 1:20).

Special revelation refers to God's specific and clear revelation through His mighty acts in history, the person and work of Jesus

Christ, and His message spoken through Old Testament prophets (like Isaiah and Daniel) and New Testament apostles (like Paul and Peter). Let's take a brief look at each of these.

God's Revelation in History

If a personal God really did create humankind, then we would naturally expect that He would reveal Himself among us in the outworking of human history. And indeed, God *has* manifested Himself historically.

God is the *living* God, and He has communicated knowledge of Himself through the ebb and flow of historical experience. The Bible is first and foremost a record of God's interactions with Abraham, Isaac, Jacob, the twelve tribes of Israel, the apostles Paul, Peter, and John, and many others in biblical times.

God's greatest revelatory act in the Old Testament was Israel's deliverance from bondage in Egypt. God, through Moses, inflicted ten plagues on the Egyptians—plagues that showed His awesome power (Exodus 7–12). God's demonstration of power was all the more impressive because the Egyptians believed their many false gods could protect them from such plagues.

Whenever God performed miracles and orchestrated events, He always talked about them. He never left a miracle or event to speak for itself. Nor did he leave people to infer whatever conclusions they wanted to draw from the event. God made sure that when a significant event occurred, a prophet was on hand to interpret it.

For example, Moses was present to record everything related to the Exodus. Jeremiah and Ezekiel were on hand to record all that happened during Israel's time of exile. Haggai, Zechariah, and Malachi were present to preserve a record of the Israelites' return from exile. And the apostles testified about Jesus' life and death. God has revealed Himself, and He has always made sure His actions were adequately recorded!

Here's an important fact we should pay close attention to. First

Peter 1:10-11 tells us that the Spirit of Christ was the one who spoke through the mouths of all the prophets who wrote the Bible. This means that the revelation that came through the prophets *was Christ's doing!* From the very beginning, Christ has been providing revelation about God (John 1:18).

God's Ultimate Revelation in Jesus Christ

The only way for God to be able to fully do and say all that He wanted was to actually leave His eternal residence and enter the arena of humanity. This He did in the person of Jesus Christ. Jesus was Immanuel—"God with us" (Matthew 1:23). He was God's ultimate special revelation, God's show and tell.

Why did Jesus have to come as God's fullest revelation? Because God is a Spirit. And because He is a Spirit, He is invisible. With our natural senses, we can't perceive anything about Him except what we can detect in general revelation.

Not only that, but man is also spiritually blind and deaf. Since man's fall in the Garden of Eden, man has lacked true spiritual perception (1 Corinthians 2:14). So humankind was in need of special revelation from God in the worst sort of way.

Jesus—as eternal God—took on human flesh so He could be God's fullest revelation to man (Hebrews 1:2-3). Jesus was a revelation of God not just in His person (as God) but in His life and teachings as well. By observing the things Jesus did and the things Jesus said, we learn a great deal about God. Jesus revealed and demonstrated...

- God's awesome power (John 3:2)
- God's incredible wisdom (1 Corinthians 1:24)
- God's boundless love (1 John 3:16)
- God's unfathomable grace (John 1:14,17)

These verses show why Jesus told a group of Pharisees, "When a man believes in me, he does not believe in me only, but in the one who sent me" (John 12:44). Jesus likewise told His disciple Philip that "anyone who has seen me has seen the Father" (John 14:9). Jesus was the ultimate revelation of God!

God's Revelation in the Bible

Another key means of special revelation is the Bible. In this one book, God has provided everything He wants us to know about Him and how we can have a relationship with Him.

God is the one who caused the Bible to be written. Through it He speaks to us today just as He spoke to people in ancient times when those words were first given. We are to receive the Bible as *God's words to us* and revere and obey it as such. As we submit to the Bible's authority, we place ourselves under the authority of the living God.

The Scriptures are...

> God preaching, God talking, God telling, God instructing, God setting before us the right way to think and speak about him. The Scriptures are God showing us himself: God communicating to us who he is and what he has done so that in the response of faith we may truly know him and live our lives in fellowship with Him.[3]

The Inspiration of the Bible

Amazingly, the Bible's authors were from all walks of life—kings, peasants, philosophers, fishermen, physicians, statesmen, scholars, poets, and farmers. These individuals lived in different cultures, had vastly different experiences, and often were quite different in character. Yet despite these differences, we can see the Bible's remarkable continuity from Genesis to Revelation.

How could this be? How did God accomplish this? We call the process *inspiration.*

When we say the Bible is inspired, we mean that God superintended the human authors so that, using their own individual personalities (and even their writing styles), they composed and recorded without error His revelation to man. Because of inspiration we can rest assured that what the human authors wrote was precisely what God wanted written.

The Greek word we translate as *inspiration* literally means "God-breathed." Because Scripture is breathed out by God, it is true and has no errors. We can put this in the form of a logical argument: The first premise of our argument is that God is true (Romans 3:4). The second premise is that God breathed out the Scriptures (2 Timothy 3:16). Our conclusion, then, is simple: Therefore, the Scriptures are true (John 17:17).

The Holy Spirit Is the Agent of Inspiration

Second Peter 1:21 tells us that "prophecy never had its origin in the will of man, but men spoke from God as they were carried along by the Holy Spirit."

Even though God used people—His prophets and apostles—to write down His Word, they were all literally "borne along" by the Holy Spirit. This means the authors were not the originators of God's message. God did not permit the will of sinful human beings to misdirect or erroneously record His message. Rather, "God *moved* and the prophet *mouthed* these truths; God *revealed* and man *recorded* His word."[4]

The Greek word for "carried along" in 2 Peter 1:21 is used in an interesting way in Acts 27:15-17. In that passage, we read about a group of experienced sailors who could not navigate their ship because the wind was so strong. The ship was being driven, directed, and carried along by the wind. This is similar to the Spirit's driving, directing, and carrying the human authors of the Bible as He wished. So "carried along" in 2 Peter 1:21 is a strong word, indicating the Spirit's complete superintendence over the human authors. Yet just as the sailors were active on the ship (though the wind, not the sailors, ultimately controlled the ship's movement), so also were the human authors active in writing as the Spirit directed.

As a direct result of the Holy Spirit's superintendence over the human authors, the Scriptures are inerrant. Bible scholar Edward J. Young, in his book *Thy Word Is Truth,* explains inerrancy this way: "The Scriptures possess the quality of freedom from error. They are exempt from the liability to make mistakes, and are incapable of error. In all their teachings they are in perfect accord with the truth."[5]

Because the written revelation from God has been recorded under the Spirit's superintendence and is the very breath of God, the Bible is therefore authoritative—just as authoritative as God Himself. We cannot separate the authority of Scripture from the authority of God. This means that what the Bible affirms (or denies), it affirms (or denies) with the very authority of God. For this reason, theologian John Calvin said, "We owe to Scripture the same reverence which we owe to God."[6]

Are All Holy Books the Same?

Despite the strong evidence for the Bible's uniqueness, I often encounter people today who espouse the politically correct view that the Bible is *not* unique because it teaches the same kinds of things that we find in the Muslim Koran and the Hindu Vedas. They suggest that all these holy books are essentially the same and only superficially different. The truth of the matter is that these books are essentially different and only superficially the same.

An honest examination of the contents of these books quickly reveals that the differences between them are so substantive that if one of them is correct, the others must necessarily be wrong. (The evidence is on the Bible's side.) Consider the doctrine of God, the most fundamental doctrine of any holy book. According to the Christian Bible, Jesus revealed one personal God who is triune in nature (Mark 12:29; John 4:24; 5:18-19). In the Muslim Koran, Muhammad taught that God is one but *is not* a Trinity. Confucius wrote about many gods. The Hindu Vedas also point to many gods, though they refer to a single impersonal god that underlies them all. Zoroaster's writings promote religious dualism—the belief in both a good god and a bad god. Buddha taught that God was essentially irrelevant. Clearly, these various religious leaders and their holy books present completely contradictory views of the nature of God.

We should not ignore the radical and irreconcilable differences between the Bible, the Vedas, the Koran, and other so-called holy books. If the Bible truly is God's Word, as I have sought to demonstrate, then these other holy books *cannot* be God's Word.

Historical Support for the Bible

One of the big theological movements in the second half of the twentieth century involved "the quest for the historical Jesus." In this quest, many critics—such as those affiliated with the Jesus Seminar (composed of extremely liberal Christian scholars)—have undermined the Bible as a historical document. They have concluded that we cannot trust what the Bible says about Jesus, especially regarding His identity and His teachings.

The truth is that significant historical support exists for the Bible— the Old *and* the New Testaments—including archaeological support, manuscript support, and extra-biblical support (that is, support from documents outside the Bible). Let us briefly consider the facts.

Archaeological Support

The word *archaeology* literally means "study of ancient things." Biblical archaeology, then, involves a study of ancient things related to biblical people, places, and events. Archaeological finds produced by both Christian *and* non-Christian scholars have proved the Bible's accuracy and reliability over and over again. This includes verification for numerous customs, places, names, and events that the Bible mentions.

The Hittites. For many years the existence of the Hittites, a powerful people who lived during the time of Abraham (Genesis 23:10-20), was questioned because no archaeological digs had uncovered anything about them. Today the critics are silenced. Abundant archaeological evidence for the existence of the Hittites during the time of Abraham has been uncovered. The University of Chicago even offers a doctorate in Hittite Studies.

Handwriting during the time of Moses. Critics once claimed that Moses could not have written the first five books of the Bible (Genesis, Exodus, Leviticus, Numbers, and Deuteronomy) because handwriting had not yet been invented. However, archaeological discoveries of ancient inscriptions now conclusively prove that handwriting did exist in Moses' lifetime.

Sodom and Gomorrah. Critics once claimed that Genesis 10, 13–14, and 18–19 are full of myth because Sodom and Gomorrah never existed. These critics have now been silenced by abundant archaeological evidence of the existence of these cities.

Many other archaeological evidences support the Bible. Fossil graveyards around the world attest to the universal flood of Noah's day. Archaeologists have discovered the grave of Abraham's wife, Sarah, as well as illustrations of Hebrew slaves making bricks for the cities of Pithom and Rameses in Egypt. Plenty of archaeological finds point to David and Solomon and their respective empires. Many people believe the actual house of Joseph (Jesus' father) has been discovered in Nazareth, as well as the tomb of Lazarus, whom Jesus raised from the dead. Other discoveries include the grave box of Caiaphas the high priest, the synagogue in Capernaum where Jesus often taught, the Pool of Siloam (John 9:7), and Jacob's Well (John 4:12). A stone discovered at a Roman theater in Caesarea bears the name of Pontius Pilate.

Bible scholar Donald J. Wiseman is correct in his assessment that "the geography of Bible lands and visible remains of antiquity have been gradually recorded until today more than 25,000 sites within this region and dating to Old Testament times, in their broadest sense, have been located."[7] Nelson Glueck, a specialist in ancient literature, did an exhaustive study that led to this conclusion: "It can be stated categorically that no archaeological discovery has ever controverted a biblical reference."[8] Well-known scholar William F. Albright, following a comprehensive study, concluded that "discovery after discovery has established the accuracy of innumerable details, and has brought increased recognition of the value of the Bible as a source of history."[9]

What About the New Testament Gospels?

In my travels, I often encounter people—influenced by the Jesus Seminar—who claim the New Testament Gospels are man-made documents and therefore contain historical errors. The evidence, however, supports the historical accuracy of the four Gospels. Let's consider Luke as an example.

Modern archaeologists who have studied the Gospel of Luke say Dr. Luke's writings are accurate, erudite, and eloquent, approaching classical Greek. At the very outset of his Gospel, Luke is careful to emphasize that he based his work on reliable, firsthand sources (Luke 1:1-4). He wanted to preserve the truth about Jesus in an ordered and accurate way. Archaeologists have occasionally thought Luke might be wrong about a particular issue, but further research has always vindicated Luke.[10]

Sir William Ramsay was a skeptic when he began his 30-year study on Luke. Reversing his initial skepticism, he concluded that "Luke is a historian of the first rank; not merely are his statements of fact trust-worthy…this author should be placed along with the very greatest of historians."[11] Ramsey noted that Luke's critics are "pre-archaeological." Luke, who also gave us the book of Acts, wrote about one-fourth of the New Testament—more than any other writer, including Paul!

In support of Luke's accuracy, classical scholar and historian Cohn Hemer painstakingly identified 84 facts in the final 16 chapters of Luke's book of Acts that have been archaeologically verified.[12] Since

Luke has a proven track record on these 84 points, he should be given the benefit of the doubt on other issues he speaks of that have not yet been archaeologically verified. Luke's critics have an uphill battle.

Manuscript Support

We also have extensive manuscript evidence that points to the reliability of the Bible. We presently possess 5686 partial and complete manuscript copies of the New Testament. These manuscript copies are very ancient and are available for inspection. Here are a few highlights about them:

- The Chester Beatty papyrus (P45) dates to the third century AD and contains the four Gospels and the book of Acts (chapters 4–17). (P stands for papyrus.)
- The Chester Beatty papyrus (P46) dates to about AD 200 and contains ten Pauline epistles (all but the pastorals) and the book of Hebrews.
- The Chester Beatty papyrus (P47) dates to the third century AD and contains Revelation 9:10–17:2.
- The Bodmer papyrus (P66) dates to about AD 200 and contains the Gospel of John.
- The Bodmer papyrus (P75) dates to the early third century and contains Luke and John.
- The Sinaiticus uncial manuscript dates to the fourth century and contains the entire New Testament.
- The Vaticanus uncial manuscript dates to the fourth century and contains most of the New Testament except part of Hebrews (9:14 to the end), the pastoral epistles, Philemon, and Revelation.

If one adds into the mix over 10,000 Latin Vulgate manuscripts and at least 9300 other early versions—including Ethiopic, Slavic, Armenian, and other versions—the total approximates 25,000 manuscripts that cite portions of the New Testament. This far exceeds the number of manuscripts of other ancient documents, which, in most cases, is fewer than ten.

We also have about 86,000 quotations of the New Testament from the early church fathers and several thousand lectionaries (church-service books containing Scripture quotations used in the early centuries of Christianity). In fact, even if we did not have a single manuscript copy of the Bible, the early church fathers provide enough quotations of the New Testament for scholars to reconstruct all but 11 verses of the entire New Testament from material written within 150 to 200 years of the time of Christ.

The Dead Sea Scrolls provide further evidence. In these scrolls, discovered at Qumran in 1947, we have Old Testament manuscripts dating from 150 BC—about a thousand years earlier than the other Old Testament manuscripts previously in our possession. A comparison of the two sets of manuscripts shows that they are essentially the same, with very few changes. The fact that manuscripts separated by a thousand years are essentially the same indicates the incredible accuracy of the Old Testament's manuscript transmission.

Extra-biblical Support

Both Christian and secular extra-biblical references that date very close to the time of Christ lend support to the accuracy of the Bible. Christian sources include these:

1. *Clement.* Clement was a leading elder in the church at Rome. In his epistle to the Corinthians (c. AD 95), he cites portions of Matthew, Mark, and Luke, and he introduces them as Jesus' actual words.[13]

2. *Papias.* Papias, the bishop of Hierapolis in Phrygia and author of *Exposition of Oracles of the Lord* (c. AD 130), cites all four Gospels. He specifically says that John's Gospel contains Jesus' words.[14]

3. *Justin Martyr.* Justin Martyr, the foremost apologist of the

second century (AD 140), considered all four Gospels to be Scripture.

4. *The Didache.* The Didache, an ancient manual of Christianity from the end of the first century or the beginning of the second, cites portions of the three synoptic Gospels and refers to them as Jesus' words. This manual quotes extensively from Matthew's Gospel.

5. *Polycarp.* Polycarp, a disciple of the apostle John, quotes portions of Matthew, Mark, and Luke, and he refers to them as Jesus' words (c. AD 150).

6. *Irenaeus.* Irenaeus, a disciple of Polycarp (c. AD 170), quotes from 23 of the 27 New Testament books, omitting only Philemon, James, 2 Peter, and 3 John.[15]

Secular extra-biblical sources also mention various aspects of Jesus' life, thus lending support to the Bible. These include ancient historians such as Tacitus, Jewish sources such as Josephus and the Talmud, and government officials such as Pliny the Younger. Let us consider a few details:

Josephus. Josephus, a Jewish historian born in AD 37, wrote toward the end of the first century. In *The Antiquities* (book 20, chapter 9; and book 18, chapter 3), Josephus corroborates that Jesus was the leader of Christians, that He did wonderful works, and that He was a martyr (by crucifixion) for the Christian cause.[16]

The Talmud. We find some references to Jesus in the Talmud, a collection of ancient rabbinic writings on Jewish law and tradition that constitute the basis of religious authority in Orthodox Judaism. Of course, the Jewish leaders were against Jesus, so the Talmud's references are understandably unflattering. Keeping Jewish hostility in mind, we see that the Talmudic text indicates that Jesus was born of an adulteress (a Jewish attempt at explaining away the virgin birth), that He practiced sorcery (an attempt to explain away His miracles), and that He was crucified "on the eve of the Passover."[17]

Pliny the Younger. Pliny the Younger (AD 62-113) was a Roman governor whose personal correspondence to his friend Trajan refers to Christians he arrested. In Pliny's writings we find extra-biblical corroboration that Christians met for worship on a "certain fixed day" (Sunday), worshipped Jesus, changed their behavior as a result of their commitment to Christ, and celebrated the Lord's Supper with "food of an ordinary and innocent kind."[18]

Tacitus. The Roman historian Tacitus (AD 56-117) provides extra-biblical evidence that Christians derived their name from a historical person named Jesus Christ ("Christus"). He "suffered the extreme penalty"—a reference to Roman crucifixion. Tacitus mentions that the crucifixion occurred during the reign of Tiberius at the hands of Pontius Pilatus. Tacitus also makes reference to "a most mischievous superstition," possibly a reference to the resurrection.[19]

Thallus. In AD 52, Thallus made reference to the darkness that engulfed the land at the time of Christ's resurrection. We do not possess actual copies of Thallus' work, but other people's writings preserve some of his words. In AD 221 Julius Africanus quoted Thallus: "'On the whole world there pressed a most fearful darkness, and the rocks were rent by an earthquake, and many places in Judea and other districts were thrown down.' This darkness Thallus, in the third book of his *History,* calls, as appears to me without reason, an eclipse of the sun."[20]

Clearly, this extra-biblical evidence provides significant information that corroborates the New Testament record. Taken in conjunction with the archaeological and manuscript evidence, we must conclude that the claim that the New Testament Gospels are not historically reliable is groundless.

My primary goal in this chapter has been to demonstrate that God communicates with His people. Because the Bible, which records God's revelation to man, is under constant attack in our day, I have provided a strong case for the inspiration of the Bible with substantive historical evidence that supports the Bible's trustworthiness. This is critically important because throughout the rest of the book, I will build my discussion of Christian doctrines on the foundation of the Bible.

Discussion Questions

1. How has God revealed Himself throughout history? What is significant about these methods of communication?

2. What do you think are the most significant evidences for the trustworthiness of the Bible?

3. How many evidences can you think of that prove that not all holy books are the same?

The Right Way to Interpret the Bible

Y ou can make the Bible say just about anything you want it to say."

"That's just your interpretation. Other interpretations are just as legitimate."

"The Bible means different things to different people."

"You shouldn't take the Bible literally. If you do, you'll end up with some warped viewpoints."

People make such comments because they buy into some popular cultural lies about the Bible and Christianity. Remarks like these have found their way into movies, TV shows, newspapers, magazines, and books, and they keep resurfacing year after year. We might wonder if somebody is perpetually running a negative PR campaign, trying to convince the masses in our culture that Bible words and topics don't really have clear and specific definitions and interpretations. (They do.)

But wait a minute. The more I think about it, the more I think that somebody *really is* running such a negative PR campaign—Satan. Consider the facts: When Satan tempted Eve in the Garden of Eden, he did so by undermining her confidence in God's Word ("Did God really say…?" [Genesis 3:1]). When Satan tempted Jesus in the desert, he likewise distorted the Word of God (Matthew 4:6). First Timothy 4:1 refers to "things taught by demons"—doctrines based on a twisted reading of Scripture. This emboldens me to suggest that one of Satan's methods today is to undermine confidence in God's Word and cause people to misinterpret it. If he conditions the culture against the Bible, he deals a major blow to Christianity.

We do well to focus some attention on the proper way to interpret the Bible. I will zero in on some well-established principles that will help us read the Bible accurately.

When the *Plain* Sense Makes *Good* Sense, Seek *No Other* Sense

A plain reading of Genesis indicates that when God created Adam in His own image, He gave Adam the gift of intelligible speech. This enabled him to communicate objectively and verbally with his Creator and with other human beings (Genesis 1:26; 11:1,7). Scripture shows that God sovereignly chose to use human language as a medium of revelational communication, often through the "thus saith the Lord" pronouncements of the prophets (see the KJV rendering of Isaiah 7:7; 10:24; 22:15; 28:16; 30:15; 49:22; 51:22; 52:4).

If God created language so He could communicate with human beings and so human beings could communicate with each other, then we can expect Him to use language and expect man to use it in its normal and plain sense. This view of language is a prerequisite to understanding not only God's spoken word but His written Word (Scripture) as well.

So I begin with a simple but profound principle of Bible interpretation: When the *plain*, literal sense of Scripture makes *good* sense, seek *no other* sense. For example, when God says in His Word that

He loves us so much that He sent His Son to die for us (Romans 5:8), let's accept that literally and give thanks to God for it. When God says in His Word that His gift of salvation comes only by faith in Christ (Acts 16:31), let's accept that literally and respond accordingly. Likewise, when God says in His Word that those who reject this gift will spend eternity in hell (Matthew 25:41), we need to accept that literally without trying to spin biblical Christianity into a "kinder and gentler," culturally acceptable religion.

Submit All "Preunderstandings" to Scripture

Theological "preunderstandings"—doctrinal opinions we have previously formed—should not bias our interpretation of Scripture. The International Council on Biblical Inerrancy addresses this issue: "We affirm that any preunderstandings which the interpreter brings to Scripture should be in harmony with scriptural teaching and subject to correction by it. We deny that Scripture should be required to fit alien preunderstandings, inconsistent with itself."[1] The point of this affirmation is to avoid interpreting Scripture through an alien grid or filter that obscures or negates its true message. It acknowledges that a person's preunderstanding can affect his or her understanding of a text. So to avoid misinterpreting Scripture, students must be careful to examine their presuppositions in the light of Scripture.

We must frankly admit that personal, theological, denominational, and political prejudices influence all interpreters to some degree. None of us approaches Scripture in a purely objective state. For this reason, preunderstandings must harmonize with Scripture and be subject to correction by it. Only preunderstandings that are compatible with Scripture are legitimate.

Graham Stanton, a professor of New Testament studies at King's College London, suggests that...

> the interpreter must allow his own presuppositions and his own pre-understandings to be modified or even completely reshaped by the text itself. Unless this is allowed to

happen, the interpreter will be unable to avoid projecting his own ideas on to the text…The text may well shatter the interpreter's existing pre-understanding and lead him to an unexpectedly new vantage point from which he continues his scrutiny of the text."[2]

Pay Close Attention to the Context

We must read each statement in Scripture in its proper context. Every word in the Bible is part of a sentence, every sentence is part of a paragraph, every paragraph is part of a book, and every book is part of the whole of Scripture. As Bible scholar Bernard Ramm has noted, "The entire Holy Scripture is the context and guide for understanding the particular passages of Scripture."[3] The interpretation of a specific passage must not contradict the total teaching of Scripture on a point. Individual verses do not exist as isolated fragments but as parts of a whole. The exposition of these verses, therefore, must exhibit them in right relation both to the whole and to each other. Scripture interprets Scripture. As J.I. Packer put it so well, "If we would understand *the parts,* our wisest course is to get to know *the whole.*"[4]

In this spirit the Westminster Confession affirms, "The infallible rule of interpretation of Scripture is *the Scripture itself;* therefore, when there is a question about the true and full sense of any Scripture, it must be searched and known by other places that speak more clearly."[5]

Matthew 5:48 quotes Jesus as saying, "Be perfect, therefore, as your heavenly Father is perfect." Some people have wrongly concluded from this verse that a person must attain sinless perfection before he or she can be saved. But what does the context reveal?

This verse is embedded in a section of Scripture dealing not with sin and salvation but with the law of love. The Jewish leaders of Jesus' day taught that we should love those who are near and dear to us (Leviticus 19:18) but hate our enemies. Jesus refuted this idea, instructing us to love even our enemies. After all, Jesus said, God's love extends to all people (Matthew 5:45). Since God is our righteous standard, we should seek to be as He is in this regard. We are to be "perfect" (or complete) in loving others as He is perfect. The context, then, helps us to understand the verse rightly.

Determine the Genre

The Bible contains a variety of literary genres, and each one has certain peculiar characteristics that we must recognize in order to interpret the text properly. Biblical genres include history (Acts), the dramatic epic (Job), poetry (Psalms), wise sayings (Proverbs), and apocalyptic writings (Revelation). An incorrect genre judgment will lead one far astray when interpreting Scripture. A parable, for example, should not be treated as history, nor should poetry or apocalyptic literature (both of which contain many symbols) be treated as straightforward narrative. For example, the Psalms refer to God as a Rock (Psalm 18:2; 19:14). Of course, this is a symbol of God's sturdiness: God is our rock-solid foundation. The Psalms often use such metaphors.

The wise interpreter allows his knowledge of genres to guide his approach to each individual biblical text. It helps him accurately determine what the biblical author was intending to communicate to the reader.

I must emphasize that even though the Bible contains a variety of literary genres and many figures of speech, the biblical authors most often employed literal statements to convey their ideas. Where they use a literal means to express their ideas, the Bible student must employ a corresponding literal approach to explain them. A literal method of interpreting Scripture gives to each word in the text the same basic meaning it would have in normal, ordinary, customary usage. Without such a method, communication between God and man would be impossible.

Consult History and Culture

The interpreter of Scripture must seek to step out of his Western mind-set and into a first-century Jewish mind-set, paying special attention to such things as Jewish marriage rites, burial rites, family practices, farm practices, business practices, monetary system, methods of warfare, slavery, treatment of captives, and religious practices. Armed with such detailed historical information, interpreting the Bible correctly becomes a much easier task because we better understand the world of the biblical writers. Here's an example:

The apostle John writes, "If anyone comes to you and does not bring this teaching [about Christ], do not take him into your house or welcome him" (2 John 10). Some have wrongly concluded from this verse that when cultists ring our doorbells, we should never invite them into our houses to witness to them. By consulting biblical history and culture, we find a more balanced understanding of the verse.

In the early days of Christianity, believers had no centralized church buildings to congregate in. Rather, they met in small house-churches. Luke pictures the early Christians "breaking bread from house to house" (Acts 2:46; 5:42 NASB) and gathering to pray in the house of Mary, the mother of Mark (Acts 12:12). Paul also recognized that churches met in houses (Romans 16:5; 1 Corinthians 16:19; Colossians 4:15). Church buildings did not appear before the end of the second century.

In 2 John 10, John is apparently warning against (1) allowing a false teacher into the church, and (2) giving this false teacher a platform from which to teach. Seen in this way, this prohibition guards the purity of the church. To extend hospitality to a false teacher would imply that the church accepted or approved of his or her teaching. This should never be. The historical context clears up the mystery regarding the correct meaning of 2 John 10.

Interpret the Difficult Verses in Light of the Clear Verses

Interpreting the difficult verses in light of the clear verses of Scripture will keep you on track. The clearer we are on the clear verses, the easier we can make sense of the difficult verses.

For example, Paul writes in Philippians 2:12, "Continue to work out your salvation with fear and trembling." Some people have taken this to mean that salvation hinges on our works. But other *clear* verses of Scripture make this conclusion impossible. Ephesians 2:8-9, for example, affirms this: "For it is by grace you have been saved, through faith—and this not from yourselves, it is the gift of God—not by works, so that no one can boast." Works obviously can have no part in salvation.

So how should we understand Philippians 2:12? In this case, we again consult history to clear up the mystery. The church at Philippi was plagued by (1) rivalries and individuals with personal ambition (Philippians 2:3-4; 4:2), by (2) the teaching of Judaizers, who said circumcision was necessary for salvation (3:1-3), by (3) the teaching that a person could attain sinless perfection in this life (3:12-14), and by (4) individuals who took excessive liberty in how they lived their lives, ignoring or going against God's law (3:18-19). Because of such problems, this church as a unit was in need of "salvation"—that is, salvation in the temporal, experiential sense, not in the eternal sense.

"Salvation" in this context is referring to the community of believers in Philippi and not to individual believers. We are to understand this salvation in a corporate sense. The Greek word for "work out" is a compound verb that indicates achievement or bringing to a conclusion. Paul was calling the Philippians to solve the church's problems, thus bringing corporate "salvation" or deliverance to a state of final achievement. Paul would not permit things to continue as they were. The problems must be solved. The Philippians were to work it out to the finish.

To review, a proper understanding of Philippians 2:12 involves two interpretive principles: (1) Interpret the difficult verses in light of the clear verses, and (2) consult history and culture.

Interpret the Old Testament in Light of the New Testament

God gave revelation to humankind progressively throughout Old and New Testament times. He didn't just give His entire revelation for

JESUS CHRIST
The Heart of the Bible

Jesus affirmed that the Scriptures were "concerning himself" (Luke 24:27), were "written about me" (verse 44); Hebrews 10:7), and "testify about me" (John 5:39).

all time to our first parents, Adam and Eve, or to Moses, the lawgiver. Rather, as the centuries slowly passed, God provided more and more revelation that became progressively full so that by the time the New Testament was complete, God had told us everything He wanted us to know. This is why we should always interpret the Old Testament in view of the greater light of the New Testament.

The activity of the preincarnate Christ in Old Testament times provides a good example. In the Exodus account we see God sustaining His people during the wilderness sojourn. But the greater light of the New Testament is more specific, informing us that Christ (as God) sustained His people in the wilderness (1 Corinthians 10:1-4). By approaching the Old Testament through the greater light of the

New Testament, we see things in the Old Testament we wouldn't otherwise see.

Distinguish Between the Descriptive and the Prescriptive

When reading the Bible, ask this key question: Is the Bible verse in question merely descriptive, or is it prescriptive? In other words, is the verse merely describing something that took place in biblical times, or is it prescribing something that Christians should be doing for all time?

This principle is illustrated in Acts 2:3-4, where we see tongues of fire fall on those who were baptized on the Day of Pentecost. Scholars believe this passage of Scripture is descriptive, not prescriptive. (That means we shouldn't expect to see fire every time the Holy Spirit is active among His people.)

Realize That Some Biblical Truths Are Explicit and Others Are Implicit

Explicit things are "fully and clearly expressed; leaving nothing implied"; implicit things are "implied or understood though not directly expressed."[6] Explicit truth from the Bible, then, refers to truth that is fully and clearly expressed in the Bible, such as the truth that God created the heavens and the earth (as explicitly stated in Genesis 1:1). Implicit truth from the Bible, by contrast, refers to truth that is implied in the Bible but not directly stated, such as the truth that the Father, the Son, and the Holy Spirit are a Trinity—three persons in one Godhead.

Serious students of doctrine collect bits of scriptural evidence from throughout the entire Bible. They compare, classify, and correlate these bits of evidence and then draw theological inferences from them. The doctrine of the Trinity emerges from following such a procedure. Various bits of data about God from throughout the Bible clearly imply the doctrine of the Trinity.

This implicit doctrine is just as legitimate as explicit doctrines in the Bible because it is solidly backed by facts of Scripture: There is only one God (Deuteronomy 6:4); the Father is God (Romans 1:7); Jesus is God (Titus 2:13); the Holy Spirit is God (Psalm 139:7-9); the Father, the Son, and the Holy Spirit are persons; and the Father, the Son, and the Holy Spirit are distinct from each other—for example, the Father and Son *know* each other (Matthew 11:27), and the Holy Spirit is called *another* comforter (John 14:16). Taken together, these facts provide solid proof for the doctrine of the Trinity.

Distinguish Between Promises and Principles

We must be cautious to distinguish between promises and principles in the Bible. Many wisdom sayings in the book of Proverbs, for example, are not intended to be promises. The book of Proverbs is a wisdom book and contains maxims of moral wisdom.

The word *proverb* literally means "to be like," or "to be compared with." A proverb, then, is a form of communicating truth by using comparisons or figures of speech. The proverbs, in a memorable way, crystallize and condense the writers' experiences and observations about life and provide principles that are generally (but not always) true. The reward of meditating on these maxims or wisdom sayings is, of course, wisdom. But these maxims were never intended as Bible promises.

We might be tempted to find a promise in these words from Proverbs 22:6: "Train a child in the way he should go, and when he is old he will not turn from it." I know of parents who have claimed this verse as a promise and have done everything they could to bring their children up rightly and in the fear of the Lord. But in some cases, the children have ended up departing from Christianity and going astray in life. The parents of these children became disillusioned and wondered what they did wrong. But Proverbs 22:6 was never intended to be a promise. Like other wisdom sayings in the book of Proverbs, this verse contains a principle that is generally true. But a general principle always involves some exceptions to the rule. (Keep in mind that God the Father is a perfect parent, but His children, Adam and Eve, certainly went astray.)

Since God is the ultimate author of Scripture (2 Timothy 3:16), shouldn't we do everything in our power to make sure we understand it rightly? After all, God's Word helps us live optimally during our time on earth and ensure eternal life in God's presence following the moment of death. Join me in resolving to make every effort to correctly understand every verse.

Discussion Questions

1. What would you say to a person who tells you, "That's just your interpretation of the Bible—other interpretations are just as legitimate"?

2. What preunderstandings do you have that might influence the way you interpret Scripture? Do you want to adjust or even toss out any of them?

3. Can you think of any incorrect interpretations of the Bible you once held that you later corrected by following principles of proper Bible interpretation?

4. Are you presently struggling with any difficult verses? How might the principles in this chapter help you come to a correct understanding of them?

Our God Is
an Awesome God

What were we made for? To know God!" said J.I. Packer in his modern classic, *Knowing God.* "What aim should we set ourselves in life? To know God...What is the best thing in life, bringing more joy, delight, and contentment, than anything else? Knowledge of God."[1]

We read in Scripture, "This is what the LORD says: 'Let not the wise man boast of his wisdom or the strong man boast of his strength or the rich man boast of his riches, but let him who boasts boast about this: that he understands and knows me'" (Jeremiah 9:23-24).

When God created Adam, He declared Adam's loneliness to be "not good" (Genesis 2:18). God made man as a social being. Man was not created to be alone. He was created to enter into and enjoy relationships with others.

Man's most important relationship is with God Himself. Our hearts have a hunger that none but God can satisfy, a vacuum or void that only God can fill. God created us with a built-in need for fellowship with Him. And we are restless and insecure until this becomes our living experience.

Certainly many people have tried (and will continue to try) to fill the inner void with other things—human relationships, power, prestige, and the like. But until a person comes into the relationship with God that he was created for, the void will remain ever present.

Scripture shows the first man and woman entering into intimate fellowship with God in a very direct way. We read that on one particular day Adam and Eve "heard the sound of the LORD God as he was walking in the garden in the cool of the day" (Genesis 3:8). I believe this statement implies that God entered the garden on a regular basis. It seems natural to assume that God came into the garden frequently for the sole purpose of fellowshipping with the first man and woman. How blessed those times must have been!

We can enjoy getting to know God today as well. I must, however, make an important qualification. I'm not talking about mere intellectual knowledge *about* God. I'm talking about personally and intimately knowing God. This is what authentic Christianity is all about.

Knowing God includes a whole lot more than just knowing some things about Him. A person could have all the right facts in his head without ever tasting in his heart the reality of what he has studied.

Knowing God in the biblical sense is a matter of personal involvement. It involves personal commitment to God's desires, to His interests, to His concerns, and to fellowshipping with Him. In short, our aim should be not just to understand the attributes of God intellectually but to enlarge our personal acquaintance with Him.

Getting to Know God

Our relationship with God begins the very moment we trust in Christ (who Himself *is* God) for salvation (Acts 16:31). But, of course, coming to know God is not possible with just a single encounter. Knowing God involves a relationship not just of commitment but of time. Only with loving involvement together do people come to actually know each other.

That principle is true in human relationships. The only way to get to know a person is to spend time with him or her. And as we spend time with that person, we come to understand what he or she likes and dislikes.

So it is with God. The more time we spend with Him, the more intimately we come to know Him. And the more intimately we know Him, the more we understand what He likes and dislikes. We understand, for example, that living in unrepentant sin displeases Him and that seeking righteousness brings Him great pleasure.

Relationships also involve communication. Can you imagine a newlywed husband and wife who never speak to one another? That wouldn't make sense. Intimate relationships thrive on communication.

We communicate with God by prayer. Through prayer we talk to God, interact with Him, make requests of Him, verbalize our hurts and our joys to Him, and ask for help (Philippians 4:6). And He hears us.

The first-century Christians knew and understood God in these ways. They spent time with Him, they came to understand how He would respond to specific circumstances, and they communicated with Him. They had a relationship of intimacy with God—and this same kind of relationship is available to each of us through the person of Jesus Christ.

God is the same today as He was yesterday (Hebrews 13:8), so how can we rest content unless we experience the same level of intimate communion with Him that the first-century believers had? How can we *not* be disturbed if our experience of knowing God falls woefully short of what the early Christians experienced?

The fact is, you and I today *can* enjoy a wonderfully intimate relationship with God. We may not see Him with our physical eyes, but He is here, walking with us side by side as a shepherd accompanies his sheep.

In a way, you and I have an advantage as we know God today because we have His completed Word (the Bible). During New Testament times, the Gospels and epistles were not yet written and distributed. The disciples and followers of Christ learned about God gradually over a period of years, but you and I have all of God's Word available to us in the pages of Scripture. What a wonderful privilege we have!

This Bible reveals numerous wonderful things about God that help us know Him. Rejoice with me in the awesome wonder of our God as we ponder scriptural truths about Him.

The One True God

God is completely unique. This must be our starting point. The one true God of Scripture is the only God.

Way back during the time of Moses, God affirmed, "See now that I myself am He! There is no god besides me" (Deuteronomy 32:39). The God of the Bible is without rival.

Isaiah 44:6 emphasizes the same truth: "This is what the LORD says—Israel's King and Redeemer, the LORD Almighty: I am the first and I am the last; apart from me there is no God." Isaiah 46:9 likewise quotes God as saying, "I am God, and there is no other; I am God, and there is none like me."

God Is a Spirit

The Scriptures tell us that God is Spirit (John 4:24). A spirit does not have flesh and bones (Luke 24:39), so we should not think of God as a physical being. (At the same time, of course, we need to keep in mind that when Jesus became a man in order to reveal God, He took on human flesh. So, Jesus—from the moment He became a man—*did* have a physical body.)

Because God is a Spirit, He is invisible. He cannot be seen. First Timothy 1:17 refers to God as "the King eternal, immortal, invisible, the only God." Colossians 1:15 speaks of "the invisible God." John 1:18 tells us, "No one has ever seen God [the Father], but God the

One and Only [Jesus Christ], who is at the Father's side, has made him known." When Jesus became a man, He became a visible revelation of the invisible God.

If God is a Spirit, how are we to interpret the many references in Scripture to God's face, ears, eyes, hands, strong arm, and so on? The ancients often described God metaphorically in anthropomorphic (human) language because they considered Him very much alive and active in human affairs. To the men and women of the Old Testament, God was real. They knew Him as a person. And the clearest, most succinct way they could express their view of God and their interaction with Him was in the language of human personality and activity—not in cold metaphysical jargon.

However, we are not to take such language in a woodenly literal sense. When Moses spoke to God face-to-face (Exodus 33:11), this doesn't mean Moses saw a divine face with eyes, ears, a nose, and a mouth. Rather it means that Moses spoke to God in His direct presence and in an intimate way.

The Bible often uses metaphorical language to describe God and His ways. For example, Psalm 91:4 says, "He will cover you with his feathers, and under his wings you will find refuge." Are we to take this literally, envisioning God as sort of a giant bird with wings and feathers? Of course not. This is simply metaphorical language that communicates spiritual truth.

The Living God

Some people today choose to believe God is a distant deity who is not too involved with earthly affairs. They are called *deists.* But the Bible often refers to God as "the living God" (for example, Deuteronomy 5:26; 1 Samuel 17:26-36; Psalm 84:2). The living God is truly among His people (Joshua 3:10).

In his wonderful book *The Living God,* Bible scholar R.T. France explains how real God seemed among the ancients:

Watch the hand of this living God intervening, in answer to His people's prayers, working miracles, converting thousands, opening prison doors, and raising the dead, guiding His messengers to people and places they had never thought of, supervising the whole operation and every figure in it so as to work out His purpose in the end. Is it any wonder they prayed, constantly, not in vague generalities, but in daring specific requests? To them, God was real; to them He was the living God.[2]

God's Names

In the ancient world, a name was not a mere label as it is today. A name was considered to reveal certain characteristics about the person. Indeed, knowing a person's name amounted to knowing his essence.

We learn much about God from the names the Bible ascribes to Him. These names are not man-made; God Himself used these names to describe Himself. They are *characteristic* names, each one making known something new about Him. Here are just a few of God's names in Scripture:

God is Yahweh. The Old Testament name *Yahweh* is connected with the Hebrew verb "to be" and conveys the idea of eternal self-existence (Exodus 3:14-15). Yahweh never came into being at a point in time, for He has always existed. He was never born. He will never die. He does not grow older, for He is beyond the realm of time. Yahweh is the eternal one.

God is Elohim. Elohim is a common name for God in the Old Testament, used about 2570 times, and literally means "strong one." Elohim is portrayed in the Old Testament as the powerful and sovereign governor of the universe, ruling over the affairs of humankind (Isaiah 54:5; Jeremiah 32:27; Nehemiah 2:4).

God is El Shaddai. El in Hebrew refers to "Mighty God." But *Shaddai* qualifies this meaning and adds something to it (Genesis

17:1-21). Many scholars believe *Shaddai* is derived from a root word that refers to a mother's breast. This name, then, indicates not only that God is a mighty God but also that He is full of compassion, grace, and mercy.

God is Yahweh-Nissi—"the Lord Our Banner." Israel could not defeat her enemies in her own strength. She was weak in the face of her mighty foes. But her battles were actually the Lord's because He was Israel's banner—her source of victory (Exodus 17:15). This name indicates that God is the one who seeks to fight our battles.

God is the Lord of Hosts. This title pictures God as the sovereign commander of a great heavenly army of angels (Psalm 89:6,8). It should give every Christian a supreme sense of security to know that this heavenly army—headed by the Lord of hosts—is committed to watching over us (Psalm 91:11-12).

God Is Immanent and Transcendent

Many people in our churches today emphasize God's immanence—the idea that He is here and among us. God certainly is immanent, but too often this idea is emphasized to the exclusion of God's transcendence.

The phrase *transcendence of God* refers to God's otherness or separateness from the created universe and from humanity. The God of the Bible is both transcendent *and* immanent, high above His creation but at the same time intimately involved with His creatures.

Many Bible verses speak of God's transcendence and immanence. For example, Deuteronomy 4:39 affirms, "Acknowledge and take to heart this day that the LORD is God in heaven above and on the earth below." In Isaiah 57:15 God states, "I live in a high and holy place, but also with him who is contrite and lowly in spirit, to revive the spirit of the lowly and to revive the heart of the contrite." In Jeremiah 23:23-24 God asks, "'Am I only a God nearby,' declares the LORD, 'and not a God far away? Can anyone hide in secret places so that I cannot see him?' declares the LORD."

The Perfections of God

I often hear people today speak of God's love. Certainly this is one of God's prime attributes. However, some people have a concept of God that focuses almost exclusively on this attribute, seemingly blind to the reality that God is also characterized by absolute holiness that manifests itself in wrath toward sin. This points to the need for a full and balanced understanding of the attributes or perfections of God. Let's consider some of God's perfections and the ramifications they have for us.

God Is Eternal

One theologian describes God as "the eternal without beginning, He who is above the whole course of time, He who in harmony beyond explanation possesses unity and life, the Father, the Son, and the Holy Spirit, the basis of eternity, the Living One, the only God."[3]

God transcends time altogether. He is above the space-time universe. As an eternal being, He has *always* existed. He is the King eternal (1 Timothy 1:17), who alone is immortal (6:16). He is the Alpha and Omega (Revelation 1:8) and is the first and the last (Isaiah 44:6; 48:12). He exists from eternity (Isaiah 43:13 NASB) and from everlasting to everlasting (Psalm 90:2). He lives forever from eternal ages past (Psalm 41:13; 102:12,27; Isaiah 57:15).

Some people believe that because God is involved in temporal affairs on earth, He Himself must be a temporal being and not an eternal being. Such a view is unbiblical. Indeed, Scripture reveals that God acts *within* the realm of time but *from* the realm of eternity. God is eternal, but He does temporal things. God's *acts* take place within time, but His *attributes* remain beyond time.[4]

A comforting ramification of God's eternal nature is the absolute confidence that God will never cease to exist. He will always be there for us. We are assured of His continued providential control of our lives.

God Is Love

God isn't just characterized by love; He is the very personification of love (1 John 4:8). Love permeates His being. And God's love does not depend on our lovability. God loves us despite the fact that we are fallen in sin (John 3:16). (God loves the *sinner* without condoning the *sin*.)

This is important for us to remember, especially when we're acutely aware of our failures. Sometimes we may feel so guilty that we're convinced we are unworthy of God's love. In fact, we might feel like worms before God. But this feeling is not rooted in God's actual feelings toward us. He loves us even when we are unlovable.

God Is Everywhere-Present

God is everywhere-present. This does not mean that God in His divine nature is diffused throughout space as if part of Him is here and part of Him is there. Rather God in His whole being is in every place. No one can go anywhere that God is not (Psalm 139:7-8; Jeremiah 23:23-24; Acts 17:27-28; Hebrews 1:3). Please note that while God is omnipresent (Psalm 139:7-9), He is not pantheistically one with the universe. He remains eternally distinct from creation and from humankind (Numbers 23:19; Ecclesiastes 5:2; Hebrews 11:3).

How comforting to know that wherever we go, we can never escape the presence of our beloved God. Because He is everywhere-present, we can be confident of His real presence with us at all times. We will always know the blessing of walking with Him in every trial and circumstance of life.

God Is All-Knowing

Denying that God is all-knowing is fashionable in some Christian circles today. In theological systems known as process theology and open theism, the future is radically open, for we are not directed toward a predetermined end. In this view, God does not foreknow future events. At any moment in time, He knows as much as *can* be known, embracing the past up to the present moment, but His knowledge continues to grow as unforeseen events unfold.

Such a view is contrary to the Bible. Because God transcends time—because He is above time—He can see the past, present, and future in a single intuitive act. "God's knowledge of all things is from the vantage point of eternity, so that the past, present, and future are all encompassed in one ever-present 'now' to Him."[5]

God knows all things, both actual and possible (Matthew 11:21-23). He knows all things past (Isaiah 41:22), present (Hebrews 4:13), and future (Isaiah 46:10). Because He knows all things, His knowledge cannot increase or decrease. Psalm 147:5 affirms that God's understanding "has no limit." His knowledge is infinite (Psalm 33:13-15; 139:11-12; 147:5; Proverbs 15:3; Isaiah 40:14; 46:10; Acts 15:18; Hebrews 4:13; 1 John 3:20).

One of the great things about God being all-knowing is that He can never discover anything in our lives that will cause Him to change His mind about us being in His family. When we become Christians, God is fully aware of every sin we have ever committed and will ever commit in the future. God knows everything about us and accepts us anyway, and that should give every child of God a profound sense of security.

God Is All-Powerful

Process theology challenges the biblical teaching that God is all-powerful. In this school of thought, some things take place in creation that He has no control over. He seeks to work interdependently with the creation, not by coercing human beings to carry out His wishes but by trying to convince them to bring about the goals He has set for them. He does not have the power to make them do things.

Scripture, by contrast, portrays God as being all-powerful (Jeremiah 32:17). He has the power to do all that He desires and wills. Some 56 times Scripture declares that God is *almighty* (for example, Revelation 19:6). God is abundant in strength (Psalm 147:5) and has incomparably great power (2 Chronicles 20:6; Ephesians 1:19-21). No one can hold back His hand (Daniel 4:35). No one can reverse Him (Isaiah 43:13), and no one can thwart Him (Isaiah 14:27). Nothing is impossible with Him (Matthew 19:26; Mark 10:27; Luke 1:37), and nothing is too difficult for Him (Genesis 18:14; Jeremiah 32:17,27). The Almighty reigns (Revelation 19:6).

There are many ramifications regarding God's unlimited power. He not only has the power to fulfill all the promises He has made to us in Scripture but also the power to see all believers securely into heaven without a single one falling away. Moreover, the same awesome power that raised Jesus from the dead will one day raise us from the dead. We may rest serenely in the knowledge that all is in the hands of our all-powerful God.

God Is Sovereign

I sometimes encounter people in churches who speak of God as if He's a big Grandpa in the sky. He's always there if you need Him and is happy to listen to you talk (in prayer), but He's not in total control of things here on earth. Contrary to such an idea, Scripture portrays God as being absolutely sovereign. He rules the universe, controls all things, and is Lord over all (see Ephesians 1). Nothing can happen in this universe that is beyond His control. All forms of existence are within the scope of His absolute dominion. Psalm 50:1 makes reference to God as the Mighty One who "speaks and summons the earth from the rising of the sun to the place where it sets." Psalm 66:7 affirms that "he rules forever by his power." We are assured in Psalm 93:1 that "the LORD reigns" and "is armed with strength."

God asserts, "My purpose will stand, and I will do all that I please" (Isaiah 46:10). God assures us, "Surely, as I have planned, so it will be, and as I have purposed, so it will stand" (Isaiah 14:24). Proverbs 16:9 tells us, "In his heart a man plans his course, but the LORD determines his steps." Proverbs 19:21 says, "Many are the plans in a man's heart, but it is the LORD's purpose that prevails."

Every believing soul can enjoy the supreme peace of knowing that God is sovereignly overseeing all that comes into our lives. Regardless of what we may encounter, and even though we may fail to understand why certain things happen in life, the knowledge that our sovereign God is in control is like a firm anchor in the midst of life's storms.

God Is Holy

God's holiness means not just that He is entirely separate from all evil but also that He is absolutely righteous (Leviticus 19:2). He is pure in every way. The Scriptures lay great stress on this attribute of God:

"Who is like you—majestic in holiness?" (Exodus 15:11).

"There is no one holy like the LORD" (1 Samuel 2:2).

"The LORD our God is holy" (Psalm 99:9).

"Holy and awesome is his name" (Psalm 111:9).

"Holy, holy, holy is the LORD Almighty" (Isaiah 6:3).

"You alone are holy" (Revelation 15:4).

If we want to fellowship with our holy God, we have to take personal holiness seriously. Walking daily with God in fellowship necessarily involves living in a way that is pleasing to Him.

God Is Just

That God is just means that He carries out His righteous standards justly and with equity. God's dealings with people never include partiality or unfairness (Genesis 18:25; Psalm 11:7; Zephaniah 3:5; John 17:25; Romans 3:26; Hebrews 6:10).

The fact that God is just is both a comfort and a warning. It is a comfort for those who have been wronged in life. They can rest assured that God will right all wrongs in the end. It is a warning for those who think they have been getting away with evil. Justice will prevail in the end!

God Is a Trinity

The doctrine of the Trinity recognizes only one God and that in the unity of the Godhead are three coequal and coeternal persons—the

Father, the Son, and the Holy Spirit. This doctrine is based on three lines of evidence in Scripture: (1) evidence that there is only one true God, (2) evidence that three persons are God, and (3) evidence of three-in-oneness within the Godhead.

Before we examine these three lines of evidence, we need to clarify what we *do not* mean by the word *Trinity*. As we attempt to understand God's triune nature, we must avoid two errors. First, the Godhead is not composed of three separate and distinct individuals such as Peter, James, and Paul, each with their own unique characteristics or attributes. Such a concept would lead to what is known as *tritheism*—the belief in three Gods rather than three persons within the one Godhead. Second, we must not conclude that the Godhead is one person only and that the triune aspect of His being is no more than three modes of manifestation—a view known as *modalism*. The fallacy of these errors will become clearer as we examine the biblical evidence for the Trinity.

I should note at the outset that some people who claim to be Christian today deny the historic doctrine of the Trinity because they think it violates reason. Trinitarians respond that to understand everything about God—including the doctrine of the Trinity—we'd have to have the very mind of God. Only a mind as great as God's could understand everything about Him (Isaiah 55:8-9; Romans 11:33; 1 Corinthians 13:12).

The doctrine of the Trinity may be beyond reason, but it is not against reason. The doctrine does not entail three Gods in one God, or three persons in one person. Such claims would be nonsensical. However, nothing is contradictory in affirming three persons in one God as Scripture does (Matthew 28:19; 2 Corinthians 13:14). Let's look at the facts:

The One True God

In the course of God's self-disclosure to humankind, He revealed His nature in progressive stages. First, God revealed His essential unity and uniqueness—that is, He revealed that He is one and that He is the only true God.

This was a necessary starting point for God's self-revelation. Throughout history Israel was surrounded by pagan nations that worshipped many gods. Through the prophets, God communicated and affirmed to Israel the reality of only one true God (Deuteronomy 6:4; 32:39; 2 Samuel 7:12-16,22; Psalm 86:10; Isaiah 44:6). The New Testament also emphasizes God's oneness (John 5:44; 17:3; Romans 3:29-30; 16:27; 1 Corinthians 8:4; Galatians 3:20; Ephesians 4:6; 1 Thessalonians 1:9; 1 Timothy 1:17; 2:5; James 2:19; 1 John 5:20-21; Jude 25).

Three Persons Who Are Called God

As history unfolded, God progressively revealed more and more about Himself. Eventually mankind learned that within the one God are three distinct persons—the Father, the Son, and the Holy Spirit. Because God's triune nature is as much a part of His self-revelation to man as His oneness is, a proper concept of God must make room for three persons in the one Godhead. God is by nature triune. Each person of the Trinity is thus essential to a correct and full definition of God.

Scripture calls each of the three persons God: the Father (1 Peter 1:2), the Son (Hebrews 1:8), and the Holy Spirit (Acts 5:3-4). Moreover, each of the three persons possess the attributes of deity.

- All three are everywhere-present (Psalm 139:7; Jeremiah 23:24; Matthew 28:20).
- All three are all-knowing (Matthew 9:4; Romans 11:33; 1 Corinthians 2:10).
- All three are all-powerful (Matthew 28:18; Romans 15:19; 1 Peter 1:5).
- All three are holy (John 16:7-14; Acts 3:14; Revelation 15:4).
- All three are eternal (Psalm 90:2; Hebrews 9:14; Revelation 1:8,17).

Still further, each of the three were involved in doing the works of deity. For example, all three were involved in the creation of the world: the Father (Genesis 2:7; Psalm 102:25), the Son (John 1:3; Colossians 1:16; Hebrews 1:2), and the Holy Spirit (Genesis 1:2; Job 33:4; Psalm 104:30).

Evidence for Three-in-Oneness

Finally, we find scriptural indications for three-in-oneness in the Godhead. Just prior to His return to heaven, Jesus told the disciples: "Go and make disciples of all nations, baptizing them in the name of the Father and of the Son and of the Holy Spirit" (Matthew 28:19). The word *name* in this verse is singular in the Greek, referring to one God, but the verse names three distinct persons within the Godhead—the Father, the Son, and the Holy Spirit. Theologian Robert Reymond draws our attention to the importance of this verse for the doctrine of the Trinity:

> Jesus does not say, (1) "into the names [plural] of the Father and of the Son and of the Holy Spirit," or what is its virtual equivalent, (2) "into the name of the Father, and into the name of the Son, and into the name of the Holy Spirit," as if we had to deal with three separate Beings. Nor does He say, (3) "into the name of the Father, Son, and Holy Spirit," (omitting the three recurring articles), as if "the Father, Son, and Holy Ghost" might be taken as merely three designations of a single person. What He does say is this: (4) "into the name [singular] of *the* Father, and of *the* Son, and of *the* Holy Spirit," first asserting the unity of the three by combining them all within the bounds of the single Name, and then throwing into emphasis the distinctness of each by introducing them in turn with the repeated article.[6]

Modern Challenges to the Doctrine of God

In our modern pluralistic society, we should not be surprised that some people—including some who claim to be Christians—voice challenges to the traditional biblical concept of God. I will briefly address three common challenges.

Is Belief in a Heavenly Father Sexist?

Some people today claim that the traditional biblical view of God is sexist because God is portrayed as an exalted male figure (a heavenly Father). These prefer to worship a heavenly Father-Mother, or in some cases, a mother-goddess.

In answering the charge of sexism, let us begin by recognizing that God equally values both men and women, for both were created in

THE BIBLICAL DOCTRINE OF THE TRINITY

There is one God
Deuteronomy 6:4

The Father is called God
1 Peter 1:2

Jesus is called God
Hebrews 1:8

The Biblical Basis for the Trinity

The Holy Spirit is called God
Acts 5:3-4

The Father, Son, and Holy Spirit are distinct from each other
John 3:16-17; 15:26

Therefore, there is one God eternally comprised of three persons
Matthew 28:19

the image of God (Genesis 1:26). Christian men and women are positionally equal before God (Galatians 3:28). Further, the four Gospels indicate that Jesus defended and exalted women in a very anti-woman Jewish culture (see John 4). So Christianity is not sexist; rather, Jesus, the head of the church, vigorously fought the sexism of His day.

The Bible refers to God as Father (and never Mother), but it sometimes uses feminine terms to describe some of His actions. For example, Jesus likened God to a loving and saddened mother hen crying over the waywardness of her children (Matthew 23:37-39). God is also said to have given birth to Israel (Deuteronomy 32:18).

Of course, God is not a gender being as humans are. He is not of the male sex. The primary emphasis in God being called Father is that He is personal. Unlike the dead and impersonal idols of paganism, the true God is a personal being with whom we can relate. In fact, we can even call Him *Abba* (an Aramaic word that loosely means "daddy"). That's how intimate a relationship we can have with Him.

Does the Existence of Evil Prove God Is Not All-Powerful?

Some churchgoers claim that the existence of evil in our world proves that God is not all-powerful. These individuals—influenced by Rabbi Kushner's book *When Bad Things Happen to Good People*—believe that God is all-good, but He is not powerful enough to bring about His good desires.

I have already addressed the fact that God is all-powerful. Let us now consider why our all-powerful God allows evil to exist in our world.

Scripture indicates that the original creation was "very good" (Genesis 1:31). The universe contained no sin, no evil, and no death. Yet today, the world is permeated with sin, evil, and death. What brought it about? Scripture indicates that the turn downward came the moment Adam and Eve used their God-given free wills and chose to disobey God (3:1-7).

Some people wonder why God didn't create man in such a way that he would never sin, thus avoiding evil altogether. But such a scenario would mean that man would no longer have the capacity to make free choices, including the choice to freely love. People would be robots that act only in programmed ways like one of those chatty dolls—pull a string on its back, and it says, "I love you." But love cannot be programmed; it must be freely expressed. God wanted Adam and all humanity to show love by freely choosing obedience.

So God's plan had the potential for evil when He bestowed upon man the freedom of choice, but the actual origin of evil was man, who directed his will away from God and toward his own selfish desires. Ever since Adam and Eve made evil actual on that first occasion in the Garden of Eden, a sin nature has been passed on to every man and woman (Romans 5:12; 1 Corinthians 15:22), and because of that sin nature, we today continue to use our free wills to make evil actual (Mark 7:20-23).

Christian philosophers believe this may not be the best possible world as it now exists, but it is the best way *to* the best possible world (a world of Christians in heaven who have freely chosen to follow Christ). Let us not forget that God is not finished yet. Too often people fall into the trap of thinking that because God has not dealt with evil completely yet, He is not dealing with it at all. He *will* one day do away with evil (on judgment day).

Therefore the existence of evil in the world is compatible with the existence of an all-powerful God. We can summarize the facts this way: (1) If God is all-good, He *will* defeat evil. (2) If God is all-powerful, He *can* defeat evil. (3) Evil is not yet defeated. (4) Therefore, God can and will one day defeat evil.

Would a Loving God Send People to Hell?

I often hear people say, "A loving God would not send people to hell. I don't believe He will do it."

In answering this viewpoint, let us be clear that God does not want to send anyone to hell. God truly is characterized by love (1 John 4:8,16), and He loves every human being (John 3:16). He is "not wanting anyone to perish, but everyone to come to repentance" (2 Peter 3:9).

All throughout Scripture, God *pleads* with people to turn from their sins and turn to Him for salvation.

The fact that God wants people to be saved is precisely why He sent Jesus to pay the penalty for our sins at the cross (John 3:16-17). Sadly, however, not all people are willing to admit that they sin, and they refuse to accept the payment of Jesus' death on their behalf. God therefore allows them to experience the results of their own choice—an eternity in hell (see Luke 16:19-31).

C.S. Lewis once said that in the end there are two groups of people. One group of people says to God, "Thy will be done." These people have placed their faith in Jesus Christ and will live forever with God in heaven. The second group of people are those to whom God says, sadly, "Thy will be done!" These people reject Jesus Christ and will thus spend eternity apart from Him. God does not force anyone to be saved against his or her will.

I have taken comfort in the recognition that God renders perfect justice in regard to the eternal destinies of people. Based on peoples' actions, God assigns levels of reward for those who, having trusted in Christ for salvation, spend eternity in heaven (Psalm 62:12; Jeremiah 17:10; Matthew 16:27; 1 Corinthians 4:5; Ephesians 6:7-8). God also assigns levels of punishment for those who, having rejected Christ, spend eternity in hell (Matthew 10:15; 16:27; Luke 12:47-48; Revelation 20:12-13; 22:12). Perfect justice will prevail in the end.

The late Rich Mullins wrote a wonderful song titled "Our God Is an Awesome God." Our brief survey of Scripture in this chapter has shown why we all have good reason to proclaim that, indeed, our God *is* an awesome God. He is truly worthy to be praised. Do you know Him yet?

Discussion Questions

1. How far along are you in getting to know God?

2. How can the attributes of God strengthen your faith and prayer life?

3. How should we picture God as we pray to Him?

4. How should the attributes of God affect the way we live our lives?

5. How does God's sovereignty relate to some of the difficult circumstances you presently face?

6. Are you concerned because you cannot fully comprehend the triune God? Why or why not?

What a Wonder Is Jesus

Jesus asked one of His disciples, "Who do you say I am?" This is one of the most important questions in all history. Who is Jesus Christ? Christianity stands or falls on the identity and work of this one person.

Everywhere I go, people seem to have different conceptions of Jesus—more often than not, wrong conceptions. This is especially true on today's secular college campuses. Some say Jesus was a mythological figure. Others say that certain claims about Jesus, such as the virgin birth, are rooted in mythology. Still others say He was just a good moral teacher. Sadly, such ideas have penetrated some of today's large liberal Christian denominations. Such liberal Christians would do well to reconsider biblical truth.

Jesus Was No Myth

The view that Jesus was just a mythical figure—or that certain claims about Jesus are based on mythology—violates the historical facts. For one thing, the biblical accounts are all based on eyewitness testimony (Luke 1:1-4). John writes, "That which was from the beginning, which we have heard, which we have seen with our eyes, which we have looked at and our hands have touched—this we proclaim concerning the Word of life" (1 John 1:1). In 2 Peter 1:16 we read, "We did not follow cleverly invented stories when we told you about the power and coming of our Lord Jesus Christ, but we were eyewitnesses of his majesty." Further, the existence and life of Christ have been verified by non-Christian witnesses, including Jewish historian Flavius Josephus (*Antiquities* XX 9:1), Roman historian Cornelius Tacitus (*Annals* XV.44), and Roman historian Suetonius (*Life of Claudius* 25:4).

A fashionable claim among liberal Christians is that such ideas as the virgin birth, Jesus' turning water into wine, His walking on water, and even His resurrection were all derived from Greek mythology and paganism. But the truth is that such claims distort the facts. Regarding the virgin birth, for example, Greek mythology pictures male gods having sex with human women who then give birth to hybrid beings. This bears no resemblance to the virgin birth of Jesus Christ. Jesus is eternal deity. When the Holy Spirit overshadowed Mary (Luke 1:35), it was specifically to produce a human nature within her womb for the eternal Son of God to step into, after which He was born as the God-Man (100 percent God and 100 percent man) nine months later.

Many alleged similarities between Christianity and Greek mythology are either greatly exaggerated or fabricated. For example, some liberal scholars describe pagan rituals in language they borrowed from Christianity, thereby making them falsely appear to be parallel doctrines. Further, the chronology for claims of mythology in the New Testament is all wrong. Most relevant pagan literature dates to around 300 years after the time of Christ. Scholar Ronald Nash, widely considered an expert on ancient mythology and paganism, says, "We must reject the assumption that just because a [pagan] cult had a certain belief or practice in the third or fourth century after Christ, it therefore had the same belief or practice in the first century."[1] Moreover, as New Testament scholar Bruce Metzger notes, "It must not be uncritically assumed that the Mysteries [pagan mythological religions] always influenced Christianity, for it is not only possible but probable that in certain cases, the influence moved in the opposite direction."[2] We should not be surprised that leaders of pagan cults who were being successfully challenged by Christianity should counter the challenge. What better way to do this than by offering a pagan substitute?

Jesus Was Not Just a Good Moral Teacher

Another fashionable claim in our day is that Jesus was just a good moral teacher who came to give us an example of the right way to live. The problem with this viewpoint is that no mere example or moral teacher would ever claim that the destiny of the world lay in His hands or that people would spend eternity in heaven or hell depending on whether they believed in Him (John 6:26-40). This would be lunacy.

No one has summarized this better than C.S. Lewis:

> A man who was merely a man and said the sort of things Jesus said would not be a great moral teacher. He would either be a lunatic—on the level with the man who says he is a poached egg—or else he would be the Devil of Hell. You must make your choice. Either this man was, and is, the Son of God: or else a madman or something worse.[3]

For Jesus to convince people that He was God (John 8:58) and the Savior of the world (Luke 19:10) when He really wasn't would be the ultimate *im*morality. So to say that Jesus was just a good moral teacher and nothing more makes virtually no sense.

The primary reason Jesus (as eternal God) was born into the world (as a man) was not to be some kind of moral influence but rather to die for the sins of humankind. He affirmed that He came into the world for the very purpose of dying (John 12:27). Moreover, His death was a sacrificial offering for the sins of humanity (He said His blood "is poured out for many for the forgiveness of sins" in Matthew 26:26-28). He took His sacrificial mission with utmost seriousness, for He knew that without Him, humanity would certainly perish (Matthew 16:25; John 3:16) and spend eternity apart from God in a place of great suffering (Matthew 10:28; 11:23-24; 23:33; 25:41; Luke 16:22-28).

Jesus Is Absolute Deity

The Bible is a Jesus book. One thing we learn from this Jesus book is that Jesus is absolute deity. Contrary to the bogus claims about Jesus being a myth or a good teacher only, the biblical writers were resolutely clear that Jesus is God.

We find powerful support for this fact in a comparison of the Old and New Testaments. For example, a study of the Old Testament indicates that only God saves. In Isaiah 43:11 God asserts, "I, even I, am the LORD, and apart from me there is no savior." This is an extremely important verse, for it indicates that (1) a claim to be Savior is, in itself, a claim to deity, and (2) the Lord God is the one and only Savior. Against this backdrop, the New Testament highlights Christ's divine nature by presenting Him as "our great God and Savior" (Titus 2:13).

Likewise, God asserted in Isaiah 44:24 (NASB), "I, the LORD, am the maker of all things, stretching out the heavens by Myself, and spreading out the earth all alone." And yet Christ is the Creator of all things (John 1:3; Colossians 1:16; Hebrews 1:2). Surely Christ is God Almighty.

The New Testament quotes Old Testament passages about God and directly applies them to Jesus. For instance, Isaiah 40:3 says, "In the desert prepare the way for the LORD; make straight in the wilderness a highway for our God." Mark's Gospel tells us that Isaiah's prophecy was fulfilled in the ministry of John the Baptist preparing the way for Jesus (Mark 1:2-4). Mark understood that Jesus is God.

In Isaiah 6:1-5, the prophet recounts his vision of God "seated on a throne, high and exalted." He said, "Holy, holy, holy is the LORD Almighty; the whole earth is full of his glory." Isaiah also quotes God as saying: "I am the LORD; that is my name! I will not give my glory to another" (42:8). Later, the apostle John—under the inspiration of the Holy Spirit—wrote that Isaiah "saw Jesus' glory" (John 12:41). He equates God's glory and Jesus' glory.

Christ's deity shines brightly when He performs many of the actions that God performed in the Old Testament. For example, Psalm 119 tells us about a dozen times that God is the one who gives and preserves life. In the New Testament, however, Jesus claims this power for Himself: "Just as the Father raises the dead and gives them life, even so the Son gives life to whom he is pleased to give it" (John 5:21).

The Old Testament compares the voice of God to "the roar of rushing waters" (Ezekiel 43:2). Likewise, we read this of the glorified Jesus in heaven: "His feet were like bronze glowing in a furnace, and his voice was like the sound of rushing waters" (Revelation 1:15). What is true of God is just as true of Jesus.

Further, in Zechariah 12:10, God (Yahweh) speaks prophetically: "They will look on me, the one they have pierced." Though Yahweh is speaking, this is obviously a reference to Christ's future crucifixion. We know that "the one they have pierced" is Jesus, for He is described this same way by the apostle John in Revelation 1:7.

Jesus implicitly ascribed the divine name Yahweh to Himself during a confrontation He had with a group of hostile Jews. Someone in the group had said to Him, "Abraham died and so did the prophets, yet you say that if anyone keeps your word, he will never taste death. Are you greater than our father Abraham?" Jesus responded, "Your father Abraham rejoiced at the thought of seeing my day; he saw it and was glad." The Jews mockingly replied, "You are not yet fifty years old, and you have seen Abraham!" To which Jesus replied, "I tell you the truth, before Abraham was born, I am" (John 8:52-58).

The Jews immediately picked up stones with the intention of killing Jesus, for they recognized He was identifying Himself as Yahweh (God).[4] The Jews were acting on the prescribed penalty for blasphemy in Old Testament Law: death by stoning (Leviticus 24:16).

The name *Yahweh*, which occurs more than 5300 times in the Old Testament, is connected with the Hebrew verb "to be." We first learn of this name in Exodus 3, where Moses asked God by what name He should be called. God replied to him, "I AM WHO I AM...Thus you shall say to the sons of Israel, 'I AM has sent me to you'" (verse 14 NASB).

I AM may seem like an odd name to the modern ear. But Moses understood in some measure what God was saying to him. The name clearly conveys the idea of eternal self-existence. Yahweh never came into being at a point in time, for He has always existed. He was never born; He will never die. He does not grow older, for He is beyond the realm of time. To know Yahweh is to know the eternal one.

All of this adds significance to Jesus' encounter with the Jews. Knowing how much they venerated Abraham, Jesus in John 8:58 deliberately contrasted Abraham's origin with His own eternal, uncreated nature. "It was not simply that he was older than Abraham, although his statement says that much too, but that his existence is of a different kind than Abraham's—that Abraham's existence was created and finite, beginning at a point in time, while Christ's existence never began, is uncreated and infinite, and therefore eternal."[5] In Jesus, therefore, "we see the timeless God, who was the God of Abraham and of Isaac and of Jacob, who was before time and who will be after time, who always *is*."[6]

Jesus' Divine Names

The Bible consistently ascribes divine names to Jesus, clearly indicating His deity.

Jesus is Kurios. We have previously seen that Jesus is equated with Yahweh of the Old Testament. The Greek New Testament equivalent of the Old Testament name *Yahweh* is *Kurios.* Like *Yahweh, Kurios* means "Lord" and usually carries the idea of a sovereign being who exercises absolute authority. To an early Christian accustomed to reading the Old Testament, the word *Lord,* when used of Jesus, would point to His identification with the God of the Old Testament.[7] Theologian William G.T. Shedd comments that "any Jew who publicly confessed that Jesus of Nazareth was 'Lord,' would be understood to ascribe the divine nature and attributes to Him."[8] The statement that "Jesus is Lord" *(Kurios)* is a clear affirmation that Jesus is Yahweh (Romans 10:9; 1 Corinthians 12:3).

The apostle Paul demonstrates the close relationship between *Yahweh* and *Kurios* in Philippians 2. He tells us that Christ was given "the name that is above every name, that at the name of Jesus every knee should bow, in heaven and on earth and under the earth, and every tongue confess that Jesus Christ is Lord [*Kurios*]" (verses 9-11). Paul, an Old Testament scholar *par excellence,* is alluding to Isaiah 45:22-23: "I am God, and there is no other. By myself I have sworn, my mouth has uttered in all integrity a word that will not be revoked: Before me every knee will bow; by me every tongue will swear." Paul was drawing on his vast knowledge of the Old Testament to make the point that Jesus Christ is Yahweh, the Lord (Kurios) of all humankind.

Jesus is Elohim. Elohim, a name used of God about 2570 times in the Old Testament, literally means "strong one," and its plural ending (*im* in Hebrew) indicates fullness of power. Elohim is portrayed in the Old Testament as the powerful and sovereign governor of the universe, ruling over the affairs of humankind.

Jesus is recognized as both Yahweh *and* Elohim in Isaiah 40:3: "In the desert prepare the way for the LORD [Yahweh]; make straight in the wilderness a highway for our God [Elohim]." This verse was written in reference to the future ministry of Christ (see John 1:23) and represents one of the strongest affirmations of Christ's deity in the Old Testament. In referring to "our God," Isaiah was affirming that Jesus Christ was the God of both the Old and New Testaments. Isaiah 9:6 also confirms this, saying of Christ, "And he will be called Wonderful Counselor, Mighty God [Elohim], Everlasting Father, Prince of Peace."

Jesus is Theos. The Greek New Testament word for God, *Theos,* is the corresponding parallel to the Old Testament *Elohim.*[9] "Doubting Thomas" addressed Christ as God (Theos) in John 20. Jesus had been brutally crucified on the cross, but He also gloriously rose from the dead. Thomas was not with the disciples when the risen Christ first appeared to them. While the disciples told Thomas about Christ's appearance to them, Thomas refused to believe. He needed not only to see Christ's wounds but also to actually touch them before he could believe Christ had risen from the dead (John 20:25).

When the risen Jesus appeared the following week, he had a special word for Thomas, inviting him to see and to touch—thereby revealing that He knew what Thomas had said to the others the previous week. The evidence of eye and ear was sufficient, and Thomas felt no further need to satisfy himself with probing fingers (John 20:26-27).

Thomas may have been slower to believe in Christ's resurrection, but when he did so, he touchingly expressed his faith with this affirmation: "My Lord and my God [Theos]" (John 20:28). Certainly this represents a climax in John's Gospel. Christ had earlier given many indications of His deity. He ascribed names of deity to Himself (John 8:58), He claimed holiness (John 8:46), He was all-knowing (John 11:11-14), He raised people from the dead (John 5:28-30), and He claimed to be the Judge of all men (John 5:22,27). At long last, Thomas recognized Christ's deity. He realized that Christ indeed was God.

Jesus continues to be called *Theos* throughout the rest of the New Testament. Recall, for example, that a jailer asked Paul and Silas how to be saved. They responded: "Believe in the Lord Jesus, and you will be saved—you and your household" (Acts 16:31). After the jailer believed and became saved, we are told that the jailer "was filled with joy because he had come to believe in God [Theos]—he and his whole family" (verse 34). Believing in Christ and believing in God are seen as identical acts.

Hebrews 1:8 records the Father's testimony regarding Christ's identity: "Your throne, O God [Theos], will last for ever and ever, and righteousness will be the scepter of your kingdom." This is a quote from Psalm 45:6-7, where "God" is seen addressing "God" [using the Hebrew word *Elohim*]. Though the concept of the Trinity is inscrutable to finite minds, this and other passages show us that the Father and the Son are coequal and coeternal. (And, of course, the same is true of the Holy Spirit.)

The fact that the names *Theos* and *Elohim* are ascribed to Jesus gives added significance to the words recorded for us in Matthew's Gospel: "'The virgin will be with child and will give birth to a son, and they will call him *Immanuel*'—which means, '*God with us*'" (Matthew 1:23). Truly, Jesus Christ was "God with us" in the fullest possible sense. He is the everlasting God who stepped out of eternity and into time to redeem humanity.

Jesus' Divine Attributes

We know that Jesus is God not only because of His divine names but also because of His divine attributes.

Jesus is eternal. John 1:1 flatly affirms, "In the beginning was the Word, and the Word was with God, and the Word was God." The word *was* in this verse is an imperfect tense, indicating continuous, ongoing existence. When God created the time-space universe, Christ already existed. Jesus did not come into being at a specific point in eternity past, but when all else began to be, He already was. Regardless of how far back we go in eternity past, we will never find a time when He was not.

Jesus is self-existent. As the Creator of all things (John 1:3; Colossians 1:16; Hebrews 1:2), Christ Himself must be *un*created. Colossians

JESUS IS GOD

Has divine attributes	Eternal – John 1:1 Everywhere-present – Matthew 18:20 All-knowing – Matthew 17:27 All-powerful – John 1:3
Old Testament parallels prove His deity	Creator — *God – Isaiah 44:24* / *Jesus – John 1:3* Savior — *God – Isaiah 43:11* / *Jesus – Titus 2:13-14*
Has names of God	Yahweh – Exodus 3:14; John 8:58 Elohim – Isaiah 9:6
Does works of God	Created universe – Colossians 1:16 Many miracles – Acts 2:22
Is worshipped as God	By angels – Hebrews 1:6 By humans – John 20:28

Jesus is God

1:17 tells us that Christ is "before all things, and in him all things hold together." Obviously, if Christ is "before all things," He does not depend on anyone or anything outside Himself for His own existence. John 5:26 emphasizes this theme, saying the Son has life in Himself (see also John 1:4).

Jesus is everywhere-present. To say that Christ (as God) is everywhere-present does not mean that His divine nature is diffused throughout space as if part of Him is here and part of Him is there. Rather, it means that Christ is everywhere-present with His whole divine being at all times.

How does this relate to His human body in the incarnation? The fact that Christ (as God) is everywhere-present does not contradict the concept that He also has locality as a human. "While living on earth, He also was omnipresent [everywhere-present] in His deity. At the present time, Christ is at the right hand of the Father (Mark 16:19; 1 Peter 3:22) although at the same time omnipresent."[10]

The New Testament demonstrates Christ's omnipresence in several ways. For example, Christ promised His disciples that "where two or three come together in my name, there am I with them" (Matthew 18:20). Obviously, people all over the planet gather in Christ's name. The only way He could be present with them all is if He is truly omnipresent.

As well, after giving the disciples the Great Commission (to bring the gospel to all nations), Jesus assured them: "Surely I am with you always, to the very end of the age" (Matthew 28:20). With disciples taking the gospel all over the world, the only way Christ could be with them all at the same time would be if He was everywhere-present (Ephesians 1:23; 4:10; Colossians 3:11).

Jesus is all-knowing. All those who came into close contact with Jesus seemed to sense that He was all-knowing. The apostle John said that Jesus "did not need man's testimony about man, for he knew what was in a man" (John 2:25). Jesus' disciples said, "Now we can see that you know all things and that you do not even need to have anyone ask you questions" (16:30). After the resurrection, when Jesus asked Peter for the third time if Peter loved him, Peter responded, "Lord, you know all things; you know that I love you" (21:17). Jesus knew where the fish were in the water (Luke 5:4,6; John 21:6-11), and He knew just which fish contained the coin (Matthew 17:27). He knew the future (John 11:11; 18:4), He knew specific details that would be encountered (Matthew 21:2-4), and He knew from a distance that Lazarus had died (John 11:14). He also knows the Father as the Father knows Him (Matthew 11:27; John 7:29; 8:55; 10:15; 17:25).

Jesus is all-powerful. The New Testament demonstrates in many ways that Christ is all-powerful. For example, Christ created the entire universe (John 1:3; Colossians 1:16; Hebrews 1:2). He sustains the universe by His own power (Colossians 1:17; Hebrews 1:3). During His earthly ministry, He exercised power over nature (Luke 8:25), over physical diseases (Mark 1:29-31), over demonic spirits (Mark 1:32-34), and over death (John 11:1-44). He also raised Himself from the dead (John 2:19).

Jesus is sovereign. Christ also possesses sovereignty that can only belong to God. Peter speaks of Christ presently at the right hand of God the Father, "with angels, authorities and powers in submission to him" (1 Peter 3:22). When Jesus comes again in glory, He will be adorned with a majestic robe, and on the thigh-section of the robe will be the words "KING OF KINGS AND LORD OF LORDS" (Revelation 19:16)—a title indicating absolute sovereignty. Philippians 2:9-10 tells us that someday every knee in heaven and on earth and under the earth will bow in humble submission before Christ the Lord. And eventually all people will be judged before the King of kings (John 5:27; 1 Corinthians 3:10-15; 2 Corinthians 5:10-13; Revelation 20:11-15).

Theologian Robert Reymond points us to further evidences of Christ's sovereignty:

> In claiming the authority to reveal the Father to whomever He chose (Matt. 11:27) and to give life to whomever He chose (John 5:21), in claiming both the prerogative and the power to call all men someday from their graves (5:28-29) and the authority to judge all men (John 5:22, 27), in claiming the authority to lay down His life and the authority to take it up again (John 10:18), in declaring he would return someday "in power and great glory" (Matt. 24:30), and in claiming that all authority in heaven and on earth had been given to Him by the Father (Matt. 28:18), Jesus was claiming, implicitly and explicitly, an absolute sovereignty and power over the universe. If any other man made such claims, we would rightly regard him as insane; but Jesus, because He is the divine Son, deserves men's adoration and praise.[11]

Jesus is sinless. Scripture consistently portrays a sinless Jesus. When Judas betrayed Jesus, he admitted that he had "betrayed innocent blood" (Matthew 27:4). There is "nothing false" about Jesus (John 7:18), and He always did what pleased the Father (John 8:29). Jesus challenged the Jewish leaders: "Can any of you prove me guilty of sin?" (John 8:46). The apostle Paul referred to Jesus as "him who had no sin" (2 Corinthians 5:21). Jesus "loved righteousness and hated wickedness" (Hebrews 1:9). He "was without sin" (Hebrews 4:15) and was "holy, blameless, [and] pure" (Hebrews 7:26). "He committed no sin, and no deceit was found in his mouth" (1 Peter 2:22). Indeed, "in him is no sin" (1 John 3:5).

Jesus' Signs

We see Jesus' deity not only in His divine names and attributes but also in His miracles. The New Testament often refers to Jesus' miracles as *signs*. Signs always *signify* something—in this case, that Jesus is the divine Messiah.

According to the New Testament, Jesus changed water into wine (John 2:7-8); healed the official's son (John 4:50), healed the Capernaum demoniac (Mark 1:25; Luke 4:35), healed Peter's mother-in-law (Matthew 8:15; Mark 1:31; Luke 4:39), caused the disciples to catch a great number of fish (Luke 5:5-6), healed a leper (Matthew 8:3; Mark 1:41), healed a paralytic (Matthew 9:2; Mark 2:5; Luke 5:20), healed a withered hand (Matthew 12:13; Mark 3:5; Luke 6:10), healed a centurion's servant (Matthew 8:13; Luke 7:10), and raised a widow's dead son (Luke 7:14).

He also calmed a stormy sea (Matthew 8:26; Mark 4:39; Luke 8:24), healed the Gadarene demoniac (Matthew 8:32; Mark 5:8; Luke 8:33), healed a woman with internal bleeding (Matthew 9:22; Mark 5:29; Luke 8:44), raised Jairus's daughter (Matthew 9:25; Mark 5:41; Luke 8:54), healed two blind men (Matthew 9:29), healed a dumb demoniac (Matthew 9:33), healed an invalid (John 5:8), fed 5000 men and their families (Matthew 14:19; Mark 6:41; Luke 9:16; John 6:11), walked on the sea (Matthew 14:25; Mark 6:48; John 6:19), healed a demoniac girl (Matthew 15:28; Mark 7:29), healed a deaf man with a speech impediment (Mark 7:34-35), fed 4000 men and their families (Matthew 15:36; Mark 8:6), and healed a blind man (Mark 8:25).

Still further, He healed a demoniac boy (Matthew 17:18; Mark 9:25; Luke 9:42), caused Peter to catch a fish with a coin in its mouth (Matthew 17:27), healed a blind and dumb demoniac (Matthew 12:22; Luke 11:14), healed a woman with an 18-year infirmity (Luke 13:10-17), healed a man with dropsy (Luke 14:4), healed ten lepers (Luke 17:11-19), raised Lazarus from the dead (John 11:43-44), and restored (healed) a severed ear (Luke 22:50-51).

No wonder Peter would later preach to the Jews that Jesus was attested by "miracles, wonders and signs, which God did among you through him" (Acts 2:22).

Jesus Worshipped as God

Jesus was worshipped on many occasions in the New Testament. He accepted worship from Thomas (John 20:28), the angels (Hebrews 1:6), some wise men (Matthew 2:11), a leper (Matthew 8:2), a ruler (Matthew 9:18), a blind man (John 9:38), an anonymous woman (Matthew 15:25), Mary Magdalene (Matthew 28:9), and the disciples (Matthew 28:17). The fact that Jesus willingly received worship on various occasions says a lot about His true identity, for Scripture consistently testifies that only God can be worshipped. Exodus 34:14 tells us, "Do not worship any other god, for the LORD, whose name is Jealous, is a jealous God" (see also Deuteronomy 6:13; Matthew 4:10). The fact that Jesus was worshipped on numerous occasions shows that He is in fact God.

Jesus the Son of God

Perhaps no name or title of Christ has been so misunderstood in our culture as "Son of God." Many people have taken the term to mean that Christ came into existence at a point in time and that He is in some way inferior to the Father. These believe that since Christ is the Son of God, He cannot possibly be God in the same sense as the Father.

Such an understanding is based on a faulty conception of what *Son of* meant among the ancients. Though the term can refer to "offspring of," it carries a more important meaning: "of the order of." The Old Testament often uses the phrase this way. For example, "sons of the prophets" meant "of the order of prophets" (1 Kings 20:35). "Sons of the singers" meant "of the order of singers" (Nehemiah 12:28 NASB). Likewise, the phrase "Son of God" means "of the order of God" and represents a claim to undiminished deity.

Ancient Eastern people used the phrase *Son of* to indicate likeness or sameness of nature and equality of being. When Jesus claimed to be the Son of God, His Jewish contemporaries fully understood that He was making an unqualified claim to be God. Indeed, the Jews insisted, "We have a law, and according to that law he [Christ] must die, because he claimed to be the Son of God" (John 19:7; see also 5:18). Recognizing that Jesus was identifying Himself as God, the Jews wanted to kill Him for committing blasphemy.

Scripture indicates that Christ's sonship is an *eternal* sonship. To say that Jesus *became* the Son of God is one thing; to say that He was *always* the Son of God is another thing altogether. We must recognize that if the Son was ever not the Son, then—to be consistent—the Father was once not the Father. If the first person's designation as Father is an eternal title, then the second person's designation as Son must be as well.

Christ's eternal sonship is clear in passages that show Him as the Son of God prior to His birth in Bethlehem. For instance, Hebrews 1:2 says God created the universe *through* His Son—implying that Christ was the Son of God prior to the creation. Moreover, Christ as the Son existed "before all things" (Colossians 1:17). As well, Jesus, speaking as the Son of God, asserted His eternal preexistence before Abraham (John 8:54-58).

Jesus the Son of Man

If Jesus was the Son of God, why did He say He was the Son of Man (Matthew 20:18; 24:30)? This is no contradiction, for Jesus was both the Son of God *and* the Son of Man. Jesus was not denying He was God when He referred to Himself as the Son of Man. The Bible refers to Christ as the Son of Man in contexts where His deity is quite evident. For example, the Bible indicates that only God can forgive sins (Isaiah 43:25), but Jesus as the Son of Man exercised this prerogative (Mark 2:7-10). Likewise, at the second coming, Christ will return to earth as the Son of Man in clouds of glory to reign on earth (Matthew 26:63-64). The term *Son of Man* is clearly a messianic title. Jesus, as the Son of Man, is the divine Messiah.

Jesus the Divine Messiah

The word *Messiah* comes from the Hebrew term *masiah*, which means "the anointed one." The Greek parallel to this term is *Christ (christos)*. John shows us that the two terms are equated. When Andrew says to Peter, "We have found the Messiah," John adds this note: "that is, the Christ" (John 1:41).

The New Testament is clear that Jesus is the promised divine Messiah. Recall that when the angel announced the birth of Jesus to the shepherds in the field, he identified Jesus this way: "Today in the town of David a Savior has been born to you; he is Christ the Lord" (Luke 2:11). Later, Simeon, who was filled with the Holy Spirit, recognized the baby Jesus as Christ, in fulfillment of God's promise to him that "he would not die before he had seen the Lord's Christ" (Luke 2:26).

Hundreds of messianic prophecies in the Old Testament point to a single Messiah or Christ—Jesus Christ. For example, Isaiah predicted the Messiah's virgin birth (Isaiah 7:14), His deity and kingdom (9:1-7), His reign of righteousness (11:2-5), His vicarious suffering and death on the cross (52:13-53:12), and much more. These and hundreds of other Old Testament messianic prophecies were written hundreds of years before they occurred. They could never have been foreseen, and they depended upon factors outside human control for their fulfillment. All of these prophecies perfectly fit the person and life of Jesus Christ, so Jesus had to be the Messiah.

Certainly others recognized that Jesus was the Christ or the prophesied Messiah. Peter recognized Jesus as the Christ (Matthew 16:16), as did Martha (John 11:25-27). Jesus warned that others would come falsely claiming to be the Christ (Matthew 24:4-5,23-24).

After Jesus was arrested, He stood before Caiaphas the high priest, who demanded, "Tell us if you are the Christ, the Son of God." Jesus answered forthrightly, "Yes, it is as you say" (Matthew 26:63-64). For giving that answer, He paid with His life. But as promised, the divine Messiah rose from the dead (John 2:19-21).

Some skeptics today have asked, if Jesus is truly the divine Messiah, as Christians claim, why didn't He come right out and say from the start, "I am the Messiah"? One very important consideration can help us understand Jesus' *modus operandi.* In the first century, many popular misunderstandings were circulating about the Messiah. The Jews expected the Messiah to appear and immediately deliver them from Roman domination (John 6:15). The people were expecting a political Messiah/deliverer. If Jesus revealed early in His ministry that He was the Messiah, He would have excited the Jews' preconceived imaginations about what this Messiah was supposed to do. The Romans would subsequently mark Him as a rebel leader.

To avoid an erroneous popular response to His words and deeds, Jesus—especially early in His ministry—was cautious about how much He revealed about Himself. He did not want anyone prematurely speaking of His actual identity until He had had sufficient opportunity to make the character of His mission clear to the masses. As time passed, Christ's identity became increasingly clear to those who encountered Him.

Jesus had another reason to be cautious about revealing His identity too quickly. By the time Jesus came on the scene, people had only seen

Old Testament glimpses of the doctrine of the Trinity such as Isaiah 48:16. Revelation in the Bible is *progressive,* and the Old Testament's primary emphasis about the doctrine of God was His oneness. For Jesus to come right out and say, "I am the divine Messiah," or "I am God," would have caused incredible confusion. People would not have understood His claim or that He was the second person of the Trinity. Jesus slowly revealed all that needed to be revealed about Himself and His relationship with the Father and the Holy Spirit. To do otherwise would have caused a huge distraction for people and would have been counterproductive to His ministry.

The Words of Jesus the Messiah

Jesus always presented His teachings with ultimate and final authority. He never wavered in this. Jesus unflinchingly placed His teachings above Moses' and the prophets'—and in a Jewish culture at that!

Jesus always spoke in His own authority. He never said, "This is what the Lord says," as did the prophets; He always said, "Truly, truly, I say to you." He never retracted anything He said, never guessed or spoke with uncertainty, never made revisions, never contradicted Himself, and never apologized for what He said. He even asserted that "heaven and earth will pass away, but my words will never pass away" (Mark 13:31), elevating His words directly to the realm of heaven.

Jesus' teachings had a profound effect on people. His listeners always seemed to realize that these were not the words of an ordinary man. When Jesus taught in Capernaum on the Sabbath, the people "were amazed at his teaching, because his message had authority" (Luke 4:32). After the Sermon on the Mount, "the crowds were amazed at his teaching, because he taught as one who had authority, and not as their teachers of the law" (Matthew 7:28-29). When some Jewish leaders asked the temple guards why they hadn't arrested Jesus when He spoke, they responded, "No one ever spoke the way this man does" (John 7:46).

One cannot read the Gospels long before recognizing that Jesus knew He and His message were inseparable. The reason Jesus' teachings had ultimate authority was because He is God. The words of Jesus were the very words of God! Indeed, what mere human teacher would dare speak words like this to his peers?

- "If anyone is thirsty, let him come to me and drink. Whoever believes in me, as the Scripture has said, streams of living water will flow from within him" (John 7:37-38).

- "Peace I leave with you; My peace I give to you; not as the world gives do I give to you" (John 14:27 NASB).

- "I am the bread of life; he who comes to Me will not hunger, and he who believes in Me will never thirst" (John 6:35 NASB).

- "Come to Me, all who are weary and heavy-laden, and I will give you rest" (Matthew 11:28 NASB).

- "I came that they may have life, and have it abundantly" (John 10:10 NASB).

To give His words the stamp of divine authority, Jesus often performed a miracle immediately following a teaching. For example, after telling the paralytic that his sins were forgiven, Jesus healed him to prove He had the divine authority to forgive sins (Mark 2:1-12). After telling Martha that He was the resurrection and the life, He raised her brother, Lazarus, from the dead—thereby proving the veracity and authority of His words. After rebuking the disciples in the boat for having too little faith, He stilled a raging storm to show them they had good reason to place their faith in Him (Matthew 8:23-27).

I hope you now understand why I titled this chapter, "What a Wonder Is Jesus." Jesus is no myth and no mere moral teacher. Rather, He is absolute deity, worthy of our unending praise and worship for all eternity!

Discussion Questions

1. Can you think of any ways that your concept of Jesus has been distorted by modern scholars and cultural religion?

2. In what ways does Christianity stand or fall on the identity and work of Jesus Christ?

3. How does a correct understanding of Jesus' identity enhance your faith? Do you feel confident in entrusting Jesus with your life for all eternity?

4. If someone were to ask you to prove the deity of Jesus Christ, how would you do so?

5

God's Magnificent Creation

As a young shepherd, David must have spent many nights under the open sky as he led his sheep across vast fields of green. As he looked up to the starry heavens at night, waves of emotion must have swept through him as he contemplated how the Lord—his divine Shepherd—had created all of it. On one such night, David penned Psalm 19. Consider his words:

> The heavens declare the glory of God;
> > the skies proclaim the work of his hands.
> Day after day they pour forth speech;
> > night after night they display knowledge.
> There is no speech or language
> > where their voice is not heard.
> Their voice goes out into all the earth,
> > their words to the ends of the world (Psalm 19:1-4).

David considered the magnificence of interstellar space a universal testimony to the Creator's glory. This glory is visible to people all over the world. We too catch a glimpse of the Creator's greatness by observing the magnificent universe He has made.

The Majesty of the Interstellar Universe

About four thousand stars are visible to the human eye without a telescope. The Creation's *true* vastness is becoming more evident, however, as astronomers have used giant new telescopes to estimate that the universe contains about 10^{25} stars (that is, 10 million billion billion). Scientists also estimate that this is about the number of grains of sand in the world. And who but God knows how many stars exist beyond the reach of our finite telescopes? We have no reason to assume that our telescopes have penetrated to the boundaries of the universe.[1]

Even though the stars are innumerable from a human perspective, God knows precisely how many exist and has even assigned a name to each one of them (Psalm 147:4; Isaiah 40:26). In the same way Adam named animals according to their characteristics (Genesis 2:19-20), so God in His infinite wisdom named each star according to its particular characteristics. Late scholar Henry Morris suggests that "this can only mean that, despite the immensity of their number, each has been created for a particular purpose, with distinctive characteristics and attributes of its own, to be discovered or revealed in God's good time."[2]

Earth: A Center of Divine Activity

Though the interstellar universe is so vast, God sovereignly chose our tiny planet as a center of divine activity. Relatively speaking, the earth is but an astronomical atom among the whirling constellations, only a tiny speck of dust among the ocean of stars and planets in the universe. To the naturalistic astronomer, the earth is but one of many planets in our small solar system, all of which are in orbit around the sun. But the earth is nevertheless the center of God's work of salvation in the universe. "On *it* the Highest presents Himself in solemn covenants and Divine appearances; on *it* the Son of God became man; on *it* stood the cross of the Redeemer of the world; and on *it*—though indeed on the new earth, yet still on the earth—will be at last the throne of God and the Lamb (Revelation 21:1-2; 22:3)."[3]

The centrality of the earth is evident in the creation account, for God created the earth *before* He created the rest of the planets and stars. Bible scholar John Whitcomb makes this comment:

> Why did God create the sun, moon, and stars on the fourth day rather than the first day? One possible explanation is that in this way God has emphasized the supreme importance of the earth among all astronomical bodies in the universe. In spite of its comparative smallness of size, even among the nine planets, to say nothing of the stars themselves, it is nonetheless absolutely unique in God's eternal purposes.[4]

The Universe Is Intelligently Designed for Life on Earth

Our universe is literally fine-tuned to promote human life on planet earth. Numerous highly improbable factors have to be precisely in place in a balanced fashion for life to survive on earth. Without any one of these factors, life would not be possible. As one scholar put it, almost everything about the basic structure of the universe is "balanced on a razor's edge for life to occur."[5] Indeed, "one could think of the initial conditions of the universe and the fundamental parameters of physics as a dart board that fills the whole galaxy, and the conditions necessary for life to exist as a small one-foot wide target: unless the dart hits the target, life would be impossible."[6] Well, life has emerged on earth because the dart in fact "hit the target."

Scientists tell us, for example, that if the strength of gravitational attraction were different, life on earth would not be possible. If our moon were significantly larger, the gravitational pull of the moon would be greater, and this would cause tidal waves that would engulf the land. Likewise, more than one moon would cause great tidal instability. If earth were significantly closer to the sun, the heat would increase and make life on earth impossible. Earth has just enough oxygen for creatures to be able to breathe. In short, everything about our earth and the universe seems tailor-made for the existence of human life (and other life forms).

Are these and a host of other similar factors the result of a random cosmic coincidence, or was an intelligent designer involved? Like many others, I believe the universe was indeed intelligently designed—and the intelligent designer was none other than Jesus Christ (John 1:3; Colossians 1:16).

Creationists Phillip Johnson and Hugh Ross thus speak of a God who left His fingerprints all over the creation.[7] William Dembski speaks of a God who has left His footprints throughout the creation.[8] The more scientists study the universe, the more evidence they find for these fingerprints and footprints.

The Creation of Human Beings

When God created man on this fine-tuned earth, He made him from the dust of the ground and breathed the breath of life into him (Genesis 1:26-27; 2:7,22-23). How awesome a moment that must have been! At one moment no man existed; the next moment, there he stood. God then created a woman from the first man's rib.

The Hebrew word for *Adam* literally means "humanity" and is an appropriate term for the first representative of the human race. The Hebrew word for *Eve* means "giver of life"; through her body the rest of humanity was born.

The words translated *man* and *woman* in Genesis 2:21-22 are based on a play on words in the Hebrew. *Man* in Hebrew is *ish,* and *woman* is *ishshah.* The names indicate that woman has the same nature as man *(ish)* but also is different in some way *(shah).* The woman is a perfect companion of the opposite gender for man.

We learn from Scripture that human beings are creatures, created a little lower than the angels (Psalm 8:3-6; Hebrews 2:7-8) by God's own hands (Job 10:8-12; Isaiah 64:8). They are wonderfully complex (Psalm 139:14) and designed specifically to live on the earth (Isaiah 45:12). Ultimately, all human beings alive today are descended from one man and woman (Acts 17:26).

Humans Are Created in God's Image

Human beings were created in the image of God (Genesis 1:26-27). Some churchgoers have wrongly concluded from this verse that since humans are created in God's image, they too must be divine. They too must be gods. This, however, is a gross misunderstanding of Genesis and the rest of the Bible.

Consider the facts: If people were divine, one would expect them to display qualities similar to God's. This seems only logical. However, a comparison of humankind's attributes with God's (as described in Scripture) provides more than ample testimony for the truth of Paul's statement in Romans 3:23 that human beings "fall short of the *glory of God.*"

- God is all-knowing (Matthew 11:21), but man is limited in knowledge (Job 38:4).
- God is all-powerful (Revelation 19:6), but man is weak (Hebrews 4:15).
- God is everywhere-present (Psalm 139:7-12), but man is confined to a single space at a time (John 1:50).
- God is holy (1 John 1:5), but even man's "righteous" deeds are as filthy rags before God (Isaiah 64:6).
- God is eternal (Psalm 90:2), but man was created at a point in time (Genesis 1:1,21-27).
- God is truth (John 14:6), but man's heart is deceitful above all else (Jeremiah 17:9).

- God is characterized by justice (Acts 17:31), but man is lawless (Romans 3:23; 1 John 3:4).

- God is love (Ephesians 2:4-5), but man is plagued with numerous vices like jealousy and strife (1 Corinthians 3:3).

If man is a god, one could never tell it by his attributes!

The fact that human beings are created in the image of God simply means that they are a finite reflection of God's...

- rational nature (Colossians 3:10)

- moral nature (Ephesians 4:24)

- relational nature (Genesis 1:26)

- dominion over creation (Genesis 1:27-28)

In the same way that the moon reflects the brilliant light of the sun, so finite man (as created in God's image) reflects God in these aspects. Man is the noblest part of God's creation.

Human Beings Have Both a Material and an Immaterial Nature

Though many people today believe humans are strictly material (physical) beings, the Bible shows they have both a material *and* an immaterial nature—that is, a body *and* a spirit and/or soul (Matthew 10:28; Revelation 6:9-10). Scholars debate, however, whether people are composed of two aspects (body and soul/spirit) or three (body, soul, and spirit).

The dichotomist view is that people are composed of two parts— material (body) and immaterial (soul/spirit). In this view, *soul* and *spirit* are essentially interchangeable. People's entire immaterial part is called "soul" in 1 Peter 2:11 and "spirit" in James 2:26.

The trichotomist view is that the soul and spirit are separate entities. People thus have three realities—body, soul, and spirit. Trichotomists generally say the body involves world-consciousness, the soul involves self-consciousness, and the spirit involves God-consciousness. Hebrews 4:12 and 1 Thessalonians 5:23 tend to support this view.

Perhaps a few distinctions would be helpful. If we are talking about mere *substance,* then we must conclude that man has only a material and an immaterial aspect. However, if we are talking about *function,* then we may say that man's immaterial aspect includes a number of functions—including that of soul and spirit. Other components of man's immaterial nature include the heart (Matthew 22:37; Hebrews 4:12), the conscience (Hebrews 10:22; 1 Peter 2:19), and the mind (Romans 12:2).

All Races of Humanity are Equal

Some people—even some churchgoing people—vainly try to find justification for racist views from the Bible. But the truth is that God created all races of man. All human beings are completely equal—equal in terms of their creation (Genesis 1:27-28), the sin problem (Romans 3:23), God's love for them (John 3:16), and God's provision of salvation for them (Matthew 28:19). The apostle Paul affirmed, "From one man he made every nation of men, that they should inhabit the whole earth; and he determined the times set for them and the exact places where they should live" (Acts 17:26). Revelation 5:9 (NASB) tells us that God's redeemed will be from "every tribe and tongue and people and nation." The Bible leaves no place for racial discrimination, for all human beings are equal in God's sight.

As for differences in skin color, scientists tell us this is related to small genetic changes that occurred as humanity grew from generation to generation. Further, the Bible *nowhere* says that skin color is a sign of superiority or inferiority. Contrary to this, the Shulammite woman is characterized as being "dark" and "lovely" (Song of Songs 1:5).

Men and Women in the Bible

How we need a balanced perspective of what the Bible teaches about male-female relations! On the one hand, the Bible indicates that men and women are equal in worth before God, and both are created in His image. On the other hand, God has set order in the family unit by placing the man as the head of the household. This is certainly not politically correct, and it flies in the face of cultural religion. But the Bible is clear on this issue.

God formed man from the soil and entrusted its cultivation to him (Genesis 2:15; 3:17). God created woman, on the other hand, from a rib taken from man's side, and He called her to be man's helper. Their different modes of creation seem to be closely related to their respective tasks in life.

When God gave instructions about moral responsibility, He gave them to Adam alone. After the fall, God first summoned Adam, not Eve, even though she was the one who had led him into sin (Genesis 3:9). Adam, the head of the family, was responsible for what had happened. Indeed, Romans 5:12 ascribes the guilt to Adam alone.

Sadly, I have personally observed that some men have abused the teaching of Adam's headship so that women have suffered various forms of discrimination. Contrary to such discrimination, Jesus openly displayed a very high view of women in an anti-woman first-century Jewish society.

Ancient Jews considered women "in all things inferior to the man" (Jewish historian Flavius Josephus, in his *Against Apion* [622], said this). This was a common Jewish blessing: "Blessed be the Lord, who did not make me a heathen; blessed be He who did not make me a woman; blessed be He who did not make me an uneducated person."

Jewish rabbis in the first century were encouraged not to teach or even to speak with women. Jewish wisdom literature tells us that "he that talks much with womankind brings evil upon himself and neglects the study of the Law and at the last will inherit Gehenna [hell]" (*M. Aboth 1.5*). Ancient Jewish teachers believed women could lead men astray: "From garments cometh a moth and from a woman the iniquities of a man" (Ecclesiasticus 42:13). Indeed, extra-biblical Hebrew literature presented men as intrinsically better than women, for "better is the iniquity of a man than a woman doing a good turn" (Ecclesiasticus 42:14).

Because of this low status of women, they enjoyed few legal rights in Jewish society. Women were not even allowed to give evidence in a court of law. Moreover, according to the rabbinic school that followed Rabbi Hillel, a man could legally divorce his wife for burning his dinner.

In this Jewish context, Jesus protected women and elevated them in a male-chauvinist society. In a Jewish culture that discouraged women from studying the law, Jesus taught women right alongside men as equals (Matthew 14:21; 15:38). And when He taught, He often used women's activities to illustrate the character of the kingdom of God, such as baking bread (Luke 13:20-21), grinding corn (Luke 17:35), and sweeping the house to find a lost coin (Luke 15:8-10). Some Jewish rabbis taught that a man should not speak to a woman in a public place, but Jesus not only spoke to a woman (who, incidentally, was a Samaritan) but also drank from her cup in a public place (John 4:1-30). The first person He appeared to after rising from the dead was Mary, not one of the male disciples (Luke 24:1-12).

Galatians 3:28 tells us that there is neither male nor female in Jesus Christ. First Peter 3:7 says men and women are fellow heirs of grace. Ephesians 5:21 speaks of mutual submission between man and wife. In John 7:53–8:11 Jesus wouldn't permit the double standard of the woman being taken in adultery and letting the man go free. In Luke 10:39 Jesus let a woman sit at His feet, which was a place reserved for the male disciples. Verses such as these show that in God's eyes, men and women are spiritually equal.

Nevertheless, as noted earlier, Scripture also speaks of male leadership in the family and in the church (1 Corinthians 11:3; 14:34; Ephesians 5:22-23; 1 Timothy 2:11). We should not take this to mean, however, that women are prohibited from active participation in various forms of leadership. Miriam played an important role in the Exodus account (see Exodus 15:20). Deborah was a judge (Judges

4:4-14). Lydia was apparently influential in the Philippian church (Acts 16:14,40). Phoebe may have been a deaconess in Cenchrea (Romans 16:1). Even though the Bible speaks of the husband being the head of the family (1 Corinthians 11:3), and teaches that only males are to be pastors of the church (1 Timothy 2:11-12), women can participate with God's blessing in various leadership roles. Notice that Aquila *and* Priscilla trained the great Apollos (Acts 18:26).

We must have a balanced understanding of scriptural teaching about men and women. Then we will avoid extremes and abuses.

Human Beings Did Not Evolve

Many people today—some Christians included—choose not to believe that God created the universe (including humankind) but rather believe that evolutionary theory best explains the issue of origins. This theory, however, is plagued by a number of critical problems:

1. Scientists largely agree that the universe had a beginning. They may disagree as to *how* that beginning happened, but they largely agree a beginning did occur. A beginning implies the existence of a Beginner—a Creator. As Scripture says, "Every house is built by someone, but God is the builder of everything" (Hebrews 3:4).

2. The universe around us points to a Designer. As we saw earlier, everything appears to be fine-tuned by the hands of an intelligent Designer. The earth's size, composition, distance from the sun, rotational period, and many other characteristics are all just right for life. The chances of even one planet existing with all of these factors converging by accident are practically nonexistent.

3. As we examine the fossil records, we not only find no evidence supporting evolution but find evidence against it. If evolution were true, we would expect to see fossils of progressively complex evolutionary forms, indicating transitions that took place. But no such evidence exists. No transitional (species evolving to a different species) links have been discovered in the fossil records.

4. The theory of evolution assumes a long series of positive and

upward mutations. In almost all known cases (over 99 percent), however, mutations are not beneficial but are harmful to living beings, and they often cause death. Deformities typically lessen the survival potential of an animal rather than strengthening it. Even if a few good mutations did take place, the incredible number of damaging mutations would utterly overwhelm the good ones.

5. The first and second laws of thermodynamics are foundational to science, and no observations of nature have contradicted them. The first law says that matter and energy are neither created nor destroyed; they just change forms. The second law says that in an isolated system (like our universe), the natural course of things is to degenerate. The universe is running down (*devolving*), not evolving upward.

6. Evolutionists often make false claims. Some have claimed that scientific evidence proves that evolution is true. These individuals generally appeal to the fact that mutations within species do happen (*microevolution*). This is entirely different from *macroevolution,* which involves one species evolving into an entirely different species through mutations. Scientists have never observed macroevolution. You cannot breed two dogs and get a cat!

Considering all the evidence, people need more faith to believe in evolutionary theory than creationism. Credible, substantive evidence supports the biblical account of creation.

Humans Do Not Become Angels at Death

A popular myth in cultural religion is that human beings become angels at the moment of death. Countless movies and television shows have portrayed this idea. One poll I came across indicates that about 15 percent of all Americans believe humans become angels when they die. But Scripture indicates that Christ Himself created *all* the angels (Colossians 1:16).

We see the distinction between humans and angels in several biblical passages. For example, Psalm 8:5 indicates that man was made lower than the angels but will be made higher in the afterlife (in heaven).

In Hebrews 12:22-23 the "thousands upon thousands of angels" are clearly distinguished from the "spirits of righteous men made perfect." First Corinthians 6:3 tells us a time is coming (in the afterlife) when believers will judge angels. As well, 1 Corinthians 13:1 distinguishes between the languages of human beings and angels. Clearly, the Bible portrays humans and angels as different classes of beings.

Of course, angels and humans do have some similarities. For example, both angels and humans are created beings, both are finite and limited, both depend on God for their continued existence and well-being, and both are responsible and accountable to God for their actions (John 16:11; 1 Corinthians 6:3; Hebrews 9:27). So angels and humans have some similarities, but in terms of nature, they are in different classes altogether.

Bowing Before the Creator

David pondered,

> When I consider your heavens,
>   the work of your fingers,
> the moon and the stars,
>   which you have set in place,
> what is man that you are mindful of him,
>   the son of man that you care for him? (Psalm 8:3-4).

As David beheld the greatness of God's creation, he sensed his own smallness and insignificance. In short, David was humbled. Every thoughtful person should be humbled when pondering the Creator's greatness—more specifically, Christ the Creator (John 1:3; Colossians 1:16).

Scripture is resoundingly clear about the attitude God desires human beings to have toward Him. We are to recognize that we are creatures who are responsible to Him, our Creator. As the psalmist says,

> Know that the LORD is God.
>   It is he who made us, and we are his;

we are his people, the sheep of his pasture (Psalm 100:3).

This recognition of creaturehood should lead us, as it did David of old, to humility and a worshipful attitude toward God. Again the psalmist tells us:

Come, let us bow down in worship,
    let us kneel before the LORD our Maker;
for he is our God
    and we are the people of his pasture,
    the flock under his care (Psalm 95:6-7).

In the beginning of this chapter, I touched on the magnificence of the interstellar universe that Christ Himself created. As glorious as the interstellar universe is, however, it is dim in comparison to the glory of the divine abode. Erich Sauer's words are worthy of meditation:

The light in which He dwells is superior to all things visible; it is something other than the radiance of all suns and stars. It is not to be beheld by earthly eyes; it is "unapproachable" (1 Timothy 6:16), far removed from all things this side (2 Corinthians 12:4). Only the angels in heaven can behold it (Matthew 18:10); only the spirits of the perfected in the eternal light (Matthew 5:8; 1 John 3:2; Revelation 22:4); only the pure and holy, even as He Himself is pure (1 John 3:2-3).[9]

One day, we shall dwell with Christ face-to-face in His unveiled, glorious presence. Even now, Christ is preparing an eternal, glorious dwelling place for us (John 14:1-3). If the present created universe is any indication of what Christ can do, this eternal dwelling place must be sublimely supreme.

Discussion Questions

1. How much do you appreciate the excellence of God's creation?

2. What does the immense magnitude and design of the creation indicate to you about God? Be specific.

3. What does knowing that you are created in the image of God mean to you?

Not the Way It's Supposed to Be: Human Sin

Many people in our day think sin is an outdated concept.

When you think about it, though, this denial doesn't seem reasonable. Suppose a medical doctor were to say that disease is an outdated concept. If he ignored the widespread evidence for disease—with people suffering all kinds of deadly illnesses—you would think he was a madman, right?

Such a doctor would do you very little good. After all, if you got sick, he wouldn't be able to help you because he wouldn't accurately diagnose your problem.

In the same way, many people today ignore the evidence of sin everywhere around us. But anyone who reads the morning newspaper will find overwhelming evidence to confirm that human beings have made a mess of this world.

Of course, if people do not recognize a sin problem, they will never seek the cure for their spiritual ills—Jesus Christ, the Savior. A weak view of sin always produces a weak view of salvation. A weak view of sin blinds us to our need for a Savior.

Some people seem to think we may have a sin problem, but it's nothing we can't overcome. But is that accurate? I hardly think so.

Suppose that each of us commits an average of three "little" sins per day. That adds up to 21 sins a week, 90 sins a month, 1095 sins a year, or 76,650 sins by the time we're 70. That's a pretty serious sin problem. And who among us would dare claim that we are guilty of only three "little" sins a day?

Let us be clear on this: The only way to have an accurate cure is to have an accurate diagnosis. God diagnoses man with a serious sin problem—and the cure is believing in Jesus Christ for salvation.

The Beginning of Sin: Satan's Rebellion

Sin in the universe began not with man but with a great angelic personage known as Lucifer. Scripture reveals that God created Lucifer as an incredibly beautiful and powerful angel. Lucifer became so impressed with his beauty and power that he wanted to take God's place.

First Timothy 3:6 tells us that Lucifer's sin was pride. In Isaiah 14:13-14 we read that Lucifer, in his pride, wanted to exercise the authority and control in this universe that rightfully belongs to God alone. His sin was a direct challenge to God's power and authority. It was especially wicked for four reasons:

- The universe had no previous example of sin. Lucifer was the first to fall.

- God originally created Lucifer in a state of beauty and perfection. Lucifer had everything going for him. But he corrupted himself.

- Lucifer had incredibly great intelligence. He was certainly aware that he would suffer consequences for rebelling against God.

• Lucifer enjoyed perfect fellowship with God. Despite living in such a perfect environment, Lucifer rebelled against the one who brought him into existence.

Lucifer's sin, of course, had widespread and devastating effects—on creation (Genesis 3:17; Romans 8:20-22), on other angels (Revelation 12:7), and on people everywhere (Ephesians 2:2). It positioned him as the diabolical ruler of this world (John 16:11). And it negatively affected all the nations of the world, for he works to deceive them (Revelation 20:3).

As a result of this heinous sin against God, Lucifer was banished from living in heaven (Isaiah 14:12). He became corrupt, and his name changed from *Lucifer* ("morning star") to *Satan* ("adversary"). His power became completely perverted (Isaiah 14:12-17). His purpose in life is now to stand against God and all who are related to God. Ultimately, God will throw him into the lake of fire, where he will suffer forever (Matthew 25:41).

Adam and Eve's Sin

Soon after their creation, Adam and Eve sinned against God and catapulted the entire human race into sin. The serpent (Satan), who had previously fallen into prideful sin, sneaked up to Eve, and in a fatal conversation, he led her astray. He tempted her to eat the forbidden fruit, and she gave in to the temptation. Sin was then conceived in humanity (Genesis 3:1-7).

When Adam and Eve sinned, they broke their relationship and fellowship with God, acquired a nature of sin and rebellion against God, and infected all their descendants with that sinful nature (Romans 5:12). This nature is the source of all our individual acts of sin and is the major reason we are not acceptable for a relationship with a holy God.

Many people today—even some who claim to be Christians—deny the doctrine of original sin. In so doing, however, they are denying the clear teaching of Scripture. Romans 5:19 emphasizes the idea that *all* human beings are born in sin: "Through the disobedience of the one man the many were made sinners." In keeping with this, 1 Corinthians 15:21-22 tells us that "death came through a man" and "in Adam all die."

In Psalm 51:5 King David said, "Surely I was sinful at birth, sinful from the time my mother conceived me." According to this verse, we are born into the world in a state of sin. Parents transmit the sin nature to their children at conception. This is why Ephesians 2:3 says we are *"by nature objects of wrath."*

The universality of sin bears witness to the reality of original sin. In Ecclesiastes 7:20 we read, "There is not a righteous man on earth who does what is right and never sins." Isaiah 64:6 says, "All of us have become like one who is unclean, and all our righteous acts are like filthy rags; we all shrivel up like a leaf, and like the wind our sins sweep us away." John writes in 1 John 1:8, "If we claim to be without sin, we deceive ourselves and the truth is not in us." *All* of humanity is fallen in sin as a result of the initial sin of our first parents, and it has affected us all in a dreadful, awful way.

Theologians often refer to humankind's state of sin as *total depravity.* This term does not mean human beings are as bad as they can be, or that they commit all the sins that are possible, or that they are incapable of doing kind and benevolent things to others. Rather, it means humans are contaminated in every part of their being by sin, and they can do nothing to earn merit before a just and holy God. Humans are too entrenched in sin to impress God with their "good works." C.H. Spurgeon once said, "He who doubts human depravity had better study himself."[1]

Adam's own initial sin, then, caused him to fall, and in the fall he became an entirely different being from a moral standpoint. Every child of Adam is born with the Adamic nature and is always prone to sin. This nature remains an active force in every Christian's life. It cannot be removed or eradicated in this life (Romans 8:3-4; Galatians 5:16-17).

When Adam and Eve sinned, they were immediately alienated from God and even went so far as to try to hide themselves from Him (Genesis 3:8). In their panic, they frantically tried to do the impossible: to withdraw and avoid having to face God altogether.

You and I are the same way. We often sense that we have let God down, and in our attitude and actions we tend to try to hide from Him in shame. This sense of separation from God and the accompanying shame are among the worst results of man's sin problem.

We are born into this world with our back to God. As a result of the fall, we naturally do over and over again what Adam and Eve attempted to do in Genesis 3: We sin and then try to hide from God so that we don't have to face our guilt. What futility!

Missing the Target

A key meaning of *sin* in the Bible is "to miss the target." Sin is the failure to live up to God's standards. All of us miss the target. No one person is capable of fulfilling all of God's laws at all times (Romans 3:23). All of us fall short of God's infinitely perfect standards. Nobody can measure up to His perfection.

In the presence of God's holiness—His "light"—the stain of sin is painfully obvious. Remember what happened to the prophet Isaiah? He was a relatively righteous man. But when Isaiah beheld God in His infinite holiness, the prophet's own sin came into clear focus, and he could only say, "Woe to me!…I am ruined! For I am a man of unclean lips, and I live among a people of unclean lips" (Isaiah 6:5).

When we measure ourselves against other people, we may come out looking okay. In fact, measuring ourselves against other people might lead us to believe that we are fairly righteous. But we cannot use other people as our moral measuring stick. God is the standard. And as we measure ourselves against God in His infinite holiness and righteousness, our sin shows up in all of its ugliness.

Billy Graham told this story to illustrate the way human sin shows up best in the light of God's holiness.

Several years ago I was to be interviewed at my home for a well-known television show and, knowing that it would appear on nationwide television, my wife took great pains to see that everything looked nice. She had vacuumed and dusted and tidied up the whole house and had gone over the living room with a fine-tooth comb since that was where the interview would be filmed.

When the film crew arrived with all the lights and cameras, she felt that everything in that living room was spic and span. We were in place along with the interviewer when suddenly the television lights were turned on and we saw cobwebs and dust where we had never seen them before. In the words of my wife: "That room was festooned with dust and cobwebs which simply did not show up under ordinary light."

The point is, of course, that no matter how well we clean up our lives and think we have them all in order, when we see ourselves in the light of God's Word, in the light of God's holiness, all the cobwebs and all the dust do show up.[2]

The Depth of Human Sin

Jesus taught a great deal about human sin. In fact, He paints a rather bleak picture of the human predicament.

Jesus taught that since the fall, all men and women are evil (Matthew 12:34) and are capable of great wickedness (Mark 7:20-23). Moreover, He said that man is utterly lost (Luke 19:10), that he is a sinner (Luke 15:10), that he is in need of repentance before a holy God (Mark 1:15), and that he needs to be born again (John 3:3,5,7).

Jesus often spoke of sin in metaphors that illustrate the havoc sin can wreak in a person's life. He described sin as blindness (Matthew 23:16-26), sickness (Matthew 9:12), slavery (John 8:34), and darkness (John 12:35-46).

Jesus also taught that both inner thoughts and external acts render a person guilty (Matthew 5:28). He taught that from within the human heart come evil thoughts, sexual immorality, theft, murder, adultery, greed, malice, deceit, envy, slander, arrogance, and folly (Mark 7:21-23). He also affirmed that God is fully aware of every person's sins, both external acts and inner thoughts; nothing escapes His notice (John 4:17-19).

Because human sin is such a dire problem, we need a powerful cure or remedy. No spiritual Band-Aid will be sufficient for man's ailment. As we'll soon see, that remedy is Jesus Christ.

Mortal Sin and Venial Sin

Some people, particularly Roman Catholics, distinguish between mortal sins (deadly sins) and venial sins (lesser sins). The problem with such a view is that if a person grows up thinking that most of his sins have been venial sins, he may think he's essentially a good person. He may not see his dire need of a Savior.

The Bible makes no such distinction between mortal sins and venial sins. Some sins are in fact worse than others (Proverbs 6:16-19), but never does Scripture say that only certain kinds of sin lead to spiritual death. *All* sin leads to spiritual death, not just one category of sins (Romans 3:23).

We might say, then, that every single sin a person commits is a mortal sin because it brings about spiritual death and separates us from God. As we will see, even the smallest sin makes us legally guilty before God and warrants the death penalty (Romans 6:23).

The Penalty for Sin: Death

When Adam and Eve sinned, they passed immediately into a state of spiritual death—that is, they were spiritually separated from God. God banished them from the Garden of Eden and posted a sword-bearing angel to guard it.

But the penalty for sin includes both spiritual and physical death (Romans 6:23; 7:13). Death, in the biblical sense, literally refers to separation. *Spiritual* death, then, is spiritual separation from God. *Physical* death is separation of the soul from the body. Physical death is the inevitable result of spiritual death. The fall into sin introduced the process of age and decay, leading ultimately to death—the separation of the soul from the body.

Adam and Eve's expulsion from the Garden of Eden was a geographical expression of humankind's spiritual separation from God—our unfitness to stand before Him and enjoy the intimacy of His presence (Genesis 3:23). Because of our sin, God's presence becomes a place of dread. The fiery sword of the guarding angel—which barred the way back to Eden—demonstrates the terrible truth that in his sin, man is separated from God (Romans 1:18).

So Scripture connects sin directly to death (Romans 5:12). One causes the other. Death came into the universe because of sin.

This means that the popular maxim "Death is a natural part of life" is a cultural lie. The truth is, death—and separation from God—is not natural. It is an unnatural intruder. God intended for people to live and have fellowship with Him. Death is therefore foreign and hostile to human life. Death arose because of our rebellion against God. It is a form of God's judgment.

But in a way, God shows His grace even in physical death. For physical death, as a judgment against sin, prevents us from living forever in a state of sin. When Adam and Eve sinned in the Garden of Eden (Genesis 2:17; 3:6), God assigned an angel to guard the tree of life. This was to protect Adam and Eve from eating from the tree of life while they were yet in a body of sin. How horrible eternity would be in such a state!

Today man still sins, still defies authority, and still acts independently of God. A great gulf exists between sinful man and God (Isaiah 59:2). Twentieth-century men and women are no different from Adam and Eve. We may have created some sophisticated technology, built a few skyscrapers, and written millions of books. But a chasm remains between sinful man and a holy God.

Today we still struggle with a sense of separation from God. Each of us is born into this world in a state of spiritual death; therefore, each of us is born in a state of separation from God. Our sins blot out God's face from us more completely than the clouds do the sun. Until our sins are forgiven, we are exiles, far from our true home. We have no communion with God.

Our perfect God cannot relate with imperfect people. In 1 John 1:5 we read, "This is the message we have heard from him and declare to you: God is light; in him there is no darkness at all." God, who is light, cannot fellowship with the darkness of human sin. Man's sin put a barrier—a wide chasm—between him and God.

A Glimmer of Hope

Immediately after the fall, God pronounced judgment against Adam, Eve, and Satan (the serpent). As dark and depressing as this situation was, however, God also introduced a glimmer of hope into the scenario when He spoke to the serpent of the coming Redeemer: "I will put enmity between you and the woman, and between your offspring and hers; he will crush your head, and you will strike his heel" (Genesis 3:15).

The "offspring" of the woman is a reference to Jesus' future birth as a human being. His work on the cross would deal a fatal blow to Satan and his dark kingdom. Jesus would come as the Savior to bring salvation to all people who believe in Him. This is the good news of the gospel. I'll talk about this Savior in detail in the next chapter.

Discussion Questions

1. Have modern Christians lost sight of the seriousness of sin? Explain your answer.

2. Does the severity of sin help you appreciate God's grace? How so?

3. The more you grow as a Christian, and the older you get, do you sense that you are becoming increasingly righteous, or do you sense your unworthiness as never before?

4. Does God want you to deal with any areas of perpetual sin in your life?

Jesus the Savior
Became a Man

Some books I read suggest that Jesus was a good man whose goal was to show us how to live. The doctrine of the incarnation completely obliterates such an idea.

In the incarnation, the incomprehensible happened. The glorious and eternal Son of God forsook the splendor of heaven and became as genuinely human as we ourselves are. Surrendering His glorious state, He voluntarily entered into human relationships in the world of time and space. Jesus became a man, was crucified on the cross, rose from the dead as the glorified God-man, and ascended back into His original glory. All of this He did for our sakes.

When we consider that Christ as eternal God took on a human nature, we are deluged with a flood of fascinating questions. How could Christ be both fully human *and* fully divine at the same time? What is the relationship between the human and divine natures in Christ? Do the two natures merge to form a third compound nature, or do they remain forever distinct? Did Christ have conflicting desires—some human and some divine? Did Christ give up any of His divine attributes during His incarnate state? Was Christ *still* human following His death and resurrection? In this chapter, I will focus attention on these and other interesting issues related to Christ in His incarnate state.

The Humanity of Christ

To deny either the undiminished deity *or* the perfect humanity of Christ in the incarnation is to put oneself outside the pale of orthodoxy. First John 4:2-3 makes this clear: "This is how you can recognize the Spirit of God: Every spirit that acknowledges that Jesus Christ has come in the flesh is from God, but every spirit that does not acknowledge Jesus is not from God. This is the spirit of the antichrist, which you have heard is coming and even now is already in the world."

Innumerable passages in the New Testament confirm Christ's full humanity in the incarnation. Hebrews 2:14 tells us, for example, that since His children "have flesh and blood, he too shared in their humanity so that by his death he might destroy him who holds the power of death—that is, the devil." First Timothy 3:16 affirms that Jesus "appeared in a body, was vindicated by the Spirit, was seen by angels, was preached among the nations, was believed on in the world, was taken up in glory." Romans 8:3 says that God sent Jesus "in the likeness of sinful man to be a sin offering."

Normal Fetal Growth and Birth

While remaining fully God within the womb, as a human being Jesus experienced a normal fetal state, had an umbilical cord through which His human body received sustenance from His mother Mary, developed for nine months in the womb, and experienced a natural human birth. As Bible scholar Robert Gromacki put it, "Apart from the virgin conception and overshadowing ministry of the Holy Spirit, Mary's pregnancy was no different than that of any other human mother."[1]

Jesus' *conception* in Mary's womb was supernatural, not His *birth* (see Isaiah 7:14; Luke 1:35; 2:6-7). The miraculous conception that resulted from the overshadowing ministry of the Holy Spirit (Luke 1:35) allowed the preexistent, eternal Son to take on a human nature through Mary.

Normal Human Development

Even though Jesus never for a moment surrendered any aspect of His deity, He experienced normal human development through infancy, childhood, adolescence, and into adulthood. According to Luke 2:40, Jesus "grew," "became strong," and was "filled with wisdom." These are things that could never be said of Jesus' divine nature.

Likewise, Luke 2:52 tells us that "Jesus grew in wisdom and stature." Again, Jesus' growth in wisdom and stature is something that can only be said of His humanity. Many scholars have noted that Jesus' expert use of the Old Testament Scriptures during His three-year ministry was due to His "growth in wisdom" as He studied the Old Testament while growing up.[2]

Christ's development as a human being was normal in every respect, with two major exceptions: (1) Christ always did the will of God, and (2) He never sinned. As Hebrews 4:15 tells us, in Christ "we do not have a high priest who is unable to sympathize with our weaknesses, but we have one who has been tempted in every way, just as we are—yet was without sin." Indeed, Christ is "holy, blameless, pure" (Hebrews 7:26).

We see Jesus' full humanity in His human characteristics. Besides growing as a normal child (Luke 2:40,52), Jesus had a physical body of flesh and bones (Luke 24:39), experienced weariness (John 4:6), hunger (Luke 4:2), sorrow (Matthew 26:37), and weeping (John 11:35), and He needed sleep (Luke 8:23).

Condescension and Exaltation

How does Christ's deity relate to His humanity? Paul deals with this question in Philippians 2:6-9. Speaking of the incarnation, he says that Christ, "being in very nature God, did not consider equality with God something to be grasped, but made himself nothing, taking the very nature of a servant, being made in human likeness."

Paul's affirmation that Christ was "in very nature God" is extremely significant. Christ in His essential being is and always has been eternal God—just as much as the Father and the Holy Spirit. Theologian Charles Ryrie notes that the word *nature* in the Greek connotes "that which is intrinsic and essential to the thing."[3] Our Lord in His preincarnate state possessed essential deity.

The word *being* (in the phrase, "being in very nature God") is a present-tense participle and carries the idea of continued existence as God. Here the thought is that Christ always has been in the form of God with the implication that He still is.[4] Thus this verse indicates that Jesus Christ, in eternity past, continually and forever existed in the form of God, outwardly manifesting His divine attributes. This is the one who was born from the womb of Mary as a human being, all the while retaining His full deity.

If Christ retained His essential deity during the incarnation, then in what way did He make Himself "nothing" when He became a man (Philippians 2:7)? Three basic issues are involved: the veiling of Christ's preincarnate glory, a voluntary nonuse of some of His divine attributes on some occasions, and the condescension involved in taking on the likeness of human beings.

Christ's Veiled Glory

Scripture indicates that Christ had to give up the outer appearance of God in order to take upon Himself a human form. Of course, Christ never actually surrendered His divine glory. Recall that on the Mount of Transfiguration (prior to His crucifixion), Jesus allowed His intrinsic glory to shine out for a brief time, illuminating the whole mountainside (Matthew 17:1-13). Nevertheless, Jesus had to *veil* His preincarnate glory in order to dwell among humans.

Had Christ *not* veiled His preincarnate glory, humankind would

Jesus the Savior Became a Man

not have been able to behold Him. When the apostle John, more than 50 years after Christ's resurrection, beheld Christ in His glory, he said, "I fell at his feet as though dead" (Revelation 1:17). When Isaiah beheld the glory of Christ in his vision in the temple, he said, "Woe to me...I am ruined" (Isaiah 6:5; John 12:41).

Christ's Divine Attributes

A second issue involved in Christ making Himself "nothing" in the incarnation has to do with His nonuse of some of His divine attributes on some occasions in order for Him to accomplish His objectives. Christ could never actually *surrender* any of His attributes, for then He would cease to be God. But He did voluntarily cease using some of them on some occasions during His time on earth (approximately 4 BC to AD 29) in order to live among people and their limitations.

Though Christ sometimes chose not to use His divine attributes, at other times He *did* use them. For example, on different occasions during His three-year ministry, Jesus demonstrated that He was all-knowing (John 2:24; 16:30), everywhere-present (John 1:48), and all-powerful (John 11). Whatever limitations Christ may have imposed on Himself when He "made himself nothing" (Philippians 2:7), He did not subtract a single divine attribute from Himself or in any sense make Himself less than God.

So we must ask, *why* did Jesus choose on occasion not to use some of His divine attributes? The answer has to do with His purpose of living among people and their limitations. He never used His divine attributes on His own behalf, though certainly His attributes were gloriously displayed in the many miracles He performed for others.

To be more specific, Jesus as God could have just willed Himself from Bethany to Jerusalem, and He would have been instantly there. But instead He traveled by foot like every other human and experienced fatigue in the process. Jesus restricted the benefits of His divine attributes as they pertained to His walk on earth and of

His own accord chose not to use His powers to lift Himself above ordinary human limitations.

Christ's Condescension

When Christ made Himself "nothing" in the incarnation, He took on the likeness (literally "form" or "appearance") of humans and the form ("essence" or "nature") of a bondservant.[5] Christ was thus truly human. Jesus was subject to temptation, distress, weakness, pain, sorrow, and limitation. But the word *likeness* suggests not only similarity but also difference. As theologian Robert Lightner explains, "though His humanity was genuine, He was different from all other humans in that He was sinless."[6] Nevertheless, when Christ took on the likeness of humans, this involved a great condescension on His part.

Theologians have been careful to point out that in the incarnation, Christ gained human attributes without giving up divine attributes. Paul affirms that in the incarnation, Christ was "taking the very nature of a servant, being made in human likeness," and "being found in appearance as a man" (Philippians 2:7-8). J.I. Packer says Jesus was no less God in the incarnation than before, but He had begun to be man: "He was not now God *minus* some elements of His deity, but God *plus* all that He had made His own by taking manhood to Himself. He who *made* man was now learning what it felt like to *be* man."[7] In other words, the incarnation did not subtract His deity but added His humanity.

Christ's Human and Divine Natures

Christ in the incarnation had two natures—a divine nature and a human nature. *Nature* when used of Christ's divinity refers to all that belongs to deity, including all the attributes of deity. *Nature* when used of Christ's humanity refers to all that belongs to humanity, including all the attributes of humanity.

Though the incarnate Christ had both a human and a divine nature, He was only one person—as indicated by His consistent use of *I, me,*

THE INCARNATE CHRIST

Jesus in the Incarnation was 100 percent God and 100 percent man.

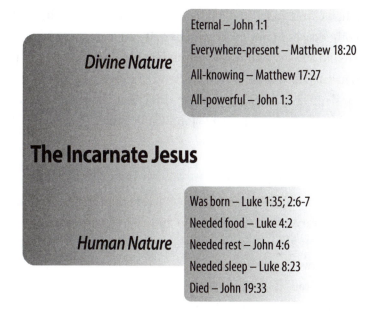

Divine Nature

Eternal – John 1:1

Everywhere-present – Matthew 18:20

All-knowing – Matthew 17:27

All-powerful – John 1:3

The Incarnate Jesus

Was born – Luke 1:35; 2:6-7

Needed food – Luke 4:2

Human Nature   Needed rest – John 4:6

Needed sleep – Luke 8:23

Died – John 19:33

and *mine* in reference to Himself. Jesus never used the words *us, we,* or *ours* in reference to His human-divine person. Nor did the divine nature of Christ ever carry on a verbal conversation with His human nature.

An Inscrutable Mystery

This is one of the most complex aspects of the relationship of Christ's two natures: The attributes of one nature are never attributed to the other, but the attributes of both natures are properly attributed to His one person. Thus Christ at the same moment in time had what seem to be contradictory qualities. He was finite and yet infinite, weak and yet all-powerful, increasing in knowledge and yet all-knowing, limited to being in one place at one time and yet everywhere-present. In the incarnation, the person of Christ partakes of the attributes of both natures so that whatever is true of either nature—human or divine—is true of the one person.

Though Christ sometimes operated in the sphere of His humanity and in other cases in the sphere of His deity, we can attribute everything He did and everything He was to His one person. Christ in His human nature knew hunger (Luke 4:2), weariness (John 4:6), and the need for sleep (Luke 8:23) at the same time that He was all-knowing (John 2:24), everywhere-present (John 1:48), and all-powerful (John 11). He experienced all of this as *one person.*

The Eternal Human-Divine Union

When Christ became a man in the incarnation, He did not enter into a temporary union of the human and divine natures that ended at His death. Rather, Scripture is clear that Christ's human nature continues forever.

Christ was raised immortal in the very same human body in which He died (Luke 24:37-39; Acts 2:31; 1 John 4:2; 2 John 7). When Christ ascended into heaven, He ascended in the same physical human body, as witnessed by several of His disciples (Acts 1:11). When Christ returns, He will return as the "Son of Man"—a messianic title that points to His humanity (Matthew 26:64). At the same time, even though Jesus has fully retained His humanity and will return as the glorified God-man, the glory that He now has in heaven is no less than the resplendent glory that has been His as God for all eternity past (see John 17:5).

The Relation of the Human and Divine Natures

How could two different natures—one infinite and one finite—exist within one person? Would not one nature dominate the other? Would not each nature have to surrender some of its qualities in order for each to coexist beside the other? Could Jesus be truly God and truly man simultaneously?

The early church was understandably confused about the two incompatible natures joining in one person without one or the other losing some of its essential characteristics. The discussion that resulted from this confusion, however, led to the orthodox statement that the two natures are united without mixture and without loss of any essential attributes, and that the two natures maintain their separate identities without transfer of any property or attribute of one nature to the other.[8] As theologian Robert Lightner put it,

> In the union of the human and divine in Christ each of the natures retained its own attributes. Deity did not permeate humanity, nor did humanity become absorbed into deity. The two natures retain their complete identity even though they have been joined together in a personal union…Embracing perfect humanity made him no less God, and retaining his undiminished deity did not make him less human.[9]

When the human and divine natures joined in one person in the incarnation, they never mixed to form a third compound nature. The human nature always remained human, and the divine nature always remained divine. To divest the divine nature of God of a single attribute would destroy His deity, and to divest man of a single human attribute would result in the destruction of a true humanity. The two natures of Christ cannot lose or transfer a single attribute. They remain distinct.

Jesus' Consciousness of the Two Natures

In the recent novel *Christ the Lord: Out of Egypt,* Anne Rice suggests that Jesus came into a slow awareness of His true identity as God. Contrary to such an idea, Jesus during His incarnate state was always aware of His deity. His divine self-consciousness was as fully operative when He was a babe in Mary's arms in Bethlehem as it was in His most mature experience as an adult.

But what about a human self-consciousness? In his book *Jesus Christ Our Lord,* John F. Walvoord notes that there is evidence that...

> the human nature developed and with it a human self-consciousness came into play... It seems possible to conclude that He had both a divine and a human self-consciousness, that these were never in conflict, and that Christ sometimes thought, spoke, and acted from the divine self-consciousness and at other times from the human.[10]

We may legitimately conclude, then, that Jesus in the incarnation was one person with two different kinds of consciousness—a divine consciousness and a human consciousness. In His divine consciousness He could say, "I and the Father are one" (John 10:30), "Before Abraham was born, I am" (John 8:58), and "I am the way and the truth and the life" (John 14:6). In His human consciousness Jesus could make such statements as "I thirst" (John 19:28 KJV).

Two Spheres of Activity—Human and Divine

The Gospel accounts are clear that Christ operated at different times under the major influence of one or the other of His two natures. Indeed, Christ had to operate in the human sphere to accomplish His earthly purpose according to the eternal plan of salvation. At the same time, He operated in the divine sphere to the extent that it was possible in the period of His humiliation.

Both of Christ's natures come into play in many events recorded in the Gospels. For example, Christ's initial approach to the fig tree to pick and eat a fig to relieve His hunger reflected the natural limitation of the human mind (Matthew 21:19). (That is, in His humanity He did not know from a distance that no fruit was on that particular tree.) But then He immediately revealed that He was all-powerful by causing the tree to wither.

On another occasion, Jesus in His omniscience (the quality of being all-knowing) knew that His friend Lazarus had died, and He set off for Bethany (John 11:11). When Jesus arrived in Bethany, He asked (in His humanness, without exercising omniscience) where Lazarus had been laid (verse 34). Theologian Robert Reymond notes that as the God-man, Jesus is "simultaneously omniscient as God (in company with the other persons of the Godhead) and ignorant of some things as man (in company with the other persons of the human race)."[11]

Could the Incarnate Christ Have Sinned?

Some people have claimed that since Christ became a human being, He could have fallen into sin. They bolster their argument by pointing to the New Testament record of Jesus being tempted (Matthew 4:1-11). Others say that the very idea of Jesus being tempted proves He is not fully God.

The fact that Jesus was tempted, however, is not a proof against His full deity. In the incarnation, Jesus took on an additional nature—a human nature. In His humanity He was subject to temptation, distress, weakness, pain, sorrow, and limitation. But because he was also fully God, the temptation stood no chance of success. As the God-man, Christ could not have sinned:

- In His divine nature, He is all-knowing, with full awareness of all the consequences of sin.

- In His divine nature, He is all-powerful in His ability to resist sin.

- Hebrews 4:15 tells us that He was tempted yet was without sin.

- Christ had no sin nature like all other human beings and was perfectly holy from birth (Luke 1:35).

- Just as the written Word of God (the Bible) has a human element and a divine element and is completely without error, so the living Word of God (Christ) is fully divine and fully human and is completely without (and unable to) sin.

This does not mean Christ's temptations were unreal. Christ was genuinely tempted, but the temptations stood no chance of luring Christ to sin. A canoe may genuinely attack a U.S. battleship, but it stands no chance of success.

I believe the reason why Christ went through the temptation experience with the devil (Matthew 4:1-11) was not to see whether He *could* be made to sin, but to prove that He *could not* be made to sin. In fact, some theologians have suggested that Christ was the aggressor in this encounter. The devil may have hoped to avoid the encounter altogether. After 40 days in the wilderness, at the height of Christ's weakness from a human standpoint, the devil gave his best shot in tempting Christ. The rest is history. The devil was unsuccessful.

Results of the Human-Divine Union

One could write an entire book on the important results of the human-divine union in the person of Christ. Here I will focus only on two: Christ as Redeemer and High Priest.

Christ Our Redeemer

Humankind's redemption was completely dependent upon the human-divine union in Christ. If Christ the Redeemer had been *only* God, He could not have died, since God by His nature cannot die. Only as a man could Christ represent humanity and die. As God, however, Christ's death had infinite value, sufficient to provide redemption for the sins of all humankind. Clearly, then, Christ had to be both God and man to secure man's salvation (1 Timothy 2:5).

This is related to the Old Testament concept of the kinsman-redeemer. In Old Testament times, a kinsman-redeemer was related by blood to someone he was seeking to redeem from bondage. If someone was sold into slavery, for example, a blood relative—the next of kin—could act as that person's kinsman-redeemer and buy him out of slavery (Leviticus 25:47-48).

Jesus is the Kinsman-Redeemer for sin-enslaved humanity. For Jesus to become a Kinsman-Redeemer, however, He had to become related by blood to the human race. This indicates the necessity of the incarnation. Jesus became a man in order to redeem man (Hebrews 2:14-16). And because Jesus was also fully God, His sacrificial death had infinite value (9:11-28).

Christ Our High Priest

Christ's human-divine union also enabled Him to become our eternal High Priest. Through the incarnation, Christ became a man and therefore could act as a human priest. As God, Christ's priesthood could be everlasting and perfect in every way.

Because the divine Christ became a man in the incarnation, He as our Priest is able to intercede in prayer for us. Jesus was truly one of us, experiencing all of the temptations and trials of human existence, so He is fully able to understand and empathize with us in our struggles as human beings. Hebrews 4:15-16 tells us that "we do not have a high priest who is unable to sympathize with our weaknesses, but we have one who has been tempted in every way, just as we are—yet was without sin. Let us then approach the throne of grace with confidence, so that we may receive mercy and find grace to help us in our time of need."

If Christ was not human, or only incompletely human, He would not have been able to make the kind of intercession a priest must make on behalf of those whom He represents. Because Christ is fully human *and* fully God, "he is able to save completely those who come to God through him, because he always lives to intercede for them" (Hebrews 7:25).

Even now, Christ—the glorified God-man in His heavenly abode—is interceding on our behalf on an individual, personal basis. He knows each of us intimately, including all our weaknesses, temptations, and human failings. How reassuring to know that Christ, who is completely familiar with the human experience, prays for us specifically according to our need. Praise be to our eternal God, Savior, Redeemer, and High Priest, Jesus Christ.

Some of the biggest misconceptions about Jesus come from not understanding what took place in the incarnation. By contrast, those who have thoroughly studied the incarnation typically have the greatest appreciation and reverence for Jesus—especially relating to how He, as the God-man, died on our behalf at the cross. What a wonder is our Jesus!

1. How does an understanding of Jesus' humanity help you pray confidently, especially about tough issues that all humans face?

2. How does a clear understanding of Jesus' humanity help you deal with your temptations?

3. Has this chapter helped you better understand the Jesus of the Gospels? How so?

4. The God-man, Jesus, is your Redeemer and High Priest. What does that mean to you personally?

Bought with a Price: Human Salvation

When man sinned, God faced a problem: How could God remain holy and just and at the same time forgive the sinner and allow him into His presence? God's ineffable purity cannot tolerate sin. His eyes are too pure to behold evil. How could God deal justly with the sinner and at the same time exercise His compassion and save man from doom?

God's *justice* burned in wrath against man for outraging His holiness, and God's *love* equally yearned to find a way to forgive him and bring him back into fellowship with Himself. But how could God express His love, His righteousness, and His justice toward man all at the same time?

God settled this problem in eternity past. Even before the creation of the world, God decreed the solution. He decreed a plan of salvation.

The Eternal Plan of Salvation

Because God is all-knowing, He knows the future just as clearly as He knows the past. This means that before man was even created, God already knew man would fall into sin in the Garden of Eden. And because God knew that would happen, He had a plan of salvation before He even created man. *What an awesome God we have!*

Before the world began—indeed, in eternity past—God had already settled the issue of how He would bring about salvation for people. Scripture tells us that even before God created the world, He had decided that Jesus, the Lamb of God, would die on the cross for the sins of man (Revelation 13:8).

God decided to carry out this eternal plan of salvation on earth, an insignificant planet when compared to the whole of God's magnificent universe. Although earth is a mere atom in comparison with the colossal stars of universal space, in terms of God's redemptive plan, it is the center of the universe. On earth the Most High God entered into covenants with human beings in Old Testament times; on earth the Son of God became a man; and on earth stood the cross of the Redeemer.

Because the plan of salvation was formulated in eternity past and is being worked out in human history, we must come to regard human history from the standpoint of eternity. We must recognize a uniform plan, guided by God, which in the course of human history has been unfolding and will one day find its culmination when Christ comes again (the second coming).

Each of the three persons of the Trinity plays a significant role in man's salvation.

The Father's Role

A careful reading of Scripture shows that the Father's role was to devise the plan of salvation (Ephesians 1:4). He sovereignly decreed it in eternity past. The Father works in an orderly way and has not left the salvation of humankind to haphazard and uncertain experimentation.

He has a definite plan of salvation. This plan includes the means to provide salvation (Jesus' death on the cross), the objective (the forgiveness of sins), and the beneficiaries (those who believe in Jesus).

Jesus' Role

The Son's task in the eternal plan of God included...

- playing a key role in the creation of the universe (John 1:3; Colossians 1:16; Hebrews 1:2)
- making preincarnate appearances to the patriarchs in Old Testament times (Genesis 16:7; 22:11)
- coming to earth as God's ultimate revelation (John 1:18; Hebrews 1:1-2)
- dying on the cross as a substitutionary sacrifice for man's sins (John 3:16)
- rising from the dead (1 Peter 1:3; 3:21)
- mediating between the Father and humankind (1 Timothy 2:5)

The eternal plan also called for the second coming of the Son in glory to consummate human redemption (Revelation 19-22).

In his sermon at Pentecost, Peter specifically spoke of Christ's suffering and crucifixion as part of God's eternal plan of salvation: "This man was handed over to you by God's set purpose and foreknowledge; and you, with the help of wicked men, put him to death by nailing him to the cross" (Acts 2:23). Some time later, Peter and John acknowledged that those who had crucified Christ were doing what the Father had determined in the eternal plan of salvation (Acts 4:28). Still later, Peter said that people are redeemed by "the precious blood of Christ, a lamb without blemish or defect. He was chosen before the creation of the world" (1 Peter 1:19-20). Theologian Benjamin Warfield thus concludes that Jesus "was not the prey of chance or the victim of the hatred of men, to the marring of His work or perhaps even the defeat of His mission, but was following step by step, straight to its goal, the predestined pathway marked out for Him in the counsels of eternity."[1]

As Jesus was dying on the cross as a substitutionary sacrifice for the sins of humankind, He uttered the words, "It is finished" (John 19:30). This declaration from the Savior's lips is fraught with meaning. Surely the Lord was doing more than announcing the end of His physical life. That fact was obvious. What those who carried out the brutal business at Calvary didn't know was that somehow, despite the sin they were committing, God through Christ had completed the final sacrifice for sin.

The phrase *it is finished* is better translated from the Greek, "it *stands* finished." On the cross, the Son of God was announcing that God's eternal plan of salvation had been enacted in time and space. And the sacrificial aspect of that plan had been completed.

We see that Christ's role in the outworking of the eternal plan of salvation was absolutely central. As German theologian Erich Sauer put it, "Jesus Christ is the innermost center of the whole divine counsel of salvation. Everything which came to pass before Him took place with a view to His coming; everything in the history of the kingdom of God which is later than His coming is wrought in His name."[2]

The Holy Spirit's Role

The Holy Spirit also has an important role in the plan of salvation. Here are just a few of the notable ministries of the Holy Spirit:

- The Holy Spirit undertook the ministry of inspiring Scripture (2 Peter 1:21). He superintended the human authors of Scripture so that they wrote exactly what God wanted written. This way we could learn all about God's plan of salvation.

- The Holy Spirit "regenerates" (or gives new life—*spiritual* life) to believers (Titus 3:5 NASB). The moment you believe in Jesus, the Holy Spirit gives you this new life.

- The Holy Spirit seals believers for the day of redemption

(Ephesians 4:30). This means that believers are secure in their salvation. A seal indicates possession and security. God possesses believers as His children, and He will see them securely into heaven.

• The Holy Spirit enables believers to overcome sin and gives them the power to live righteously (Galatians 5:22-23).

Popular Misconceptions About the Gospel

The *gospel* refers to the good news of salvation in Jesus Christ. Perhaps the single best definition of the gospel is found in 1 Corinthians 15:3-4: "For what I received I passed on to you as of first importance:

THE ROLES OF THE FATHER, SON, AND HOLY SPIRIT IN SALVATION

Each person of the Trinity has a role in our salvation:

The Father
Devised plan of salvation
Ephesians 1:4

The Triune God and Salvation

The Son
Redeemer and Savior who died for our sins
John 3:16

The Holy Spirit
Regenerates believers and seals them for the day of redemption
Titus 3:5; Ephesians 4:30

that Christ died for our sins according to the Scriptures, that he was buried, that he was raised on the third day according to the Scriptures." The gospel, according to this passage, has four components: (1) Man is a sinner, (2) Christ is the Savior, (3) Christ died as man's substitute, and (4) Christ rose from the dead. This is the gospel Paul and the other apostles preached; it is the gospel we too must preach.

Popular cultural misconceptions about the gospel abound. Here are three examples:

1. Some have taught that we must plead for mercy before we can be saved. However, this idea is found nowhere in Scripture. Salvation comes by faith in Christ (John 3:16; Acts 16:31). God provides pardon for anyone who believes; no one has to plead for it.

2. Some have taught that we must follow Christ's example and seek to live as He lived in order to be a Christian. *The Imitation of Christ* by Thomas à Kempis has been understood by many to teach that we become Christians by living as Christ did and obeying His teachings, seeking to behave as He behaved. From a scriptural perspective, however, we simply do not have it in us to live as Christ lived. We are fallen human beings (Romans 3:23). Only the Holy Spirit working in us can imitate Christ in our lives (Galatians 5:16-23).

3. Some have inadvertently communicated that prayer is a necessary component in becoming saved. In other words, one must pray the "prayer of repentance." The scriptural perspective is that even though prayer may be a vehicle for the expression of a person's faith, the faith brings about salvation, not the prayer that communicates that faith. In fact, a person can bypass prayer altogether by simply exercising faith in his or her heart, thereby becoming saved at that moment.

How Believers Receive Salvation

Salvation is a gift of grace that believers receive by faith alone, not by doing good works. Because false religions and cults often challenge this view of salvation, firmly grasping this truth of Christianity is critically important for us.

Salvation Is a Gift of Grace

Grace is often hard for us to understand. After all, our society rates people by their performance. Good grades in school depend on how well we perform on our schoolwork. Climbing up the corporate ladder depends on how well we perform at our job. Nothing of real worth is free in our society. But God's gift of salvation is a grace-gift. The word *grace* means "undeserved favor." Because salvation is a gift, it can't be earned. It's free! We can't attain it by a good performance. Scripture is clear on this:

- Ephesians 2:8-9 says, "By grace you have been saved through faith—and this not from yourselves, it is the gift of God—not by works, so that no one can boast."

- Titus 3:5 (NASB) tells us that God "saved us, not on the basis of deeds which we have done in righteousness, but according to His mercy."

- Romans 3:20 (NASB) says that "by the works of the Law no flesh will be justified [or declared righteous] in His sight."

- In Galatians 2:16 the apostle Paul tells us that we are "justified by faith in Christ and not by observing the law."

Grace and meritorious works are mutually exclusive. Romans 11:6 says this about God's salvation: "If by grace, then is it no longer by works; if it were, grace would no longer be grace."

Gifts cannot be earned—only wages and awards can be earned. As Romans 4:4-5 tells us, "When a man works, his wages are not credited to him as a gift, but as an obligation. However, to the man who does not work but trusts God who justifies the wicked, his faith is credited as righteousness." Because salvation is a gift, it cannot be earned.

Believers Receive Salvation Through Faith

God has not made the gospel complicated. In fact, according to the New Testament, a relationship with Jesus begins simply by placing faith in Him. This may sound too good to be true, yet it is the clear teaching of Scripture. Some people try to add good works as a condition for salvation, but this goes against Scripture. The Bible portrays salvation as a gift that we receive by faith alone.

A key verse you will want to make note of is Acts 16:31. In this verse we find the apostle Paul and his companion Silas in jail. The jailer asked Paul and Silas how he could become saved. They responded quite forthrightly, "Believe in the Lord Jesus, and you will be saved." The jailer then believed and became saved at that moment.

So that you don't miss the force of this passage, note that one moment the jailer was not saved. The next moment he was. The factor that brought him salvation was exercising simple faith in Jesus.

Close to 200 times, the New Testament teaches that salvation is by faith alone—with no works in sight. Here are a few examples:

- In John 5:24 Jesus says, "I tell you the truth, whoever hears my word and believes him who sent me has eternal life and will not be condemned; he has crossed over from death to life."

- In John 11:25 Jesus says, "I am the resurrection and the life. He who believes in me will live, even though he dies."

- In John 12:46 Jesus says, "I have come into the world as a light, so that no one who believes in me should stay in darkness."

If salvation were not by faith alone, then Jesus' message in these statements from the Gospel of John would be deceptive. If salvation is obtained by both faith and good works, then Jesus would have been deceptive to say so many times that the only condition for salvation is faith.

Scripture teaches that we are saved *by* faith but *for* good works. That is, works are not the condition of our salvation but are a consequence of it. We are saved not by works but by the kind of faith that ends up producing good works.

Nothing is complicated about faith. Actually, faith is central to all of life. For example, when we go to a doctor, we are often unfamiliar with the doctor's training and degree. Yet by faith we trust his diagnosis of our ailment. Then, by faith we go to a pharmacy, have a prescription filled, and take a medicine with a strange name based on our belief that the doctor knows what he's doing.

Placing faith in Jesus Christ involves taking Christ at His word. Faith involves believing that Christ is who He says He is. It also involves believing that Christ can do what He claims He can do—He can forgive me and come into my life. Faith is an act of commitment in which I open the door of my heart to Him.

Is Repentance a Condition for Salvation?

To be sure, a child of God is repentant, but the term must be carefully defined. The biblical word translated *repent* literally means "a change of mind toward something or someone."

Repentance as it relates to Jesus Christ, for example, means to change our mind about Him—who He is and what He's done to provide forgiveness and deliverance from our sins. Repentance in this sense refers to changing our mind about the particular sin of rejecting Christ.

In the book of Acts, Peter preaches to Jews who had rejected Jesus as the Messiah. So when he admonishes them to repent and believe in Jesus (Acts 2:38; 3:19), they were actually being admonished to change their minds about Jesus and believe in Him as the Messiah/Savior so their sins could be forgiven.

People everywhere are called to do the same. Instead of rejecting

Christ, we are to change our minds about Him and believe in Him as the Messiah/Savior.

Is Obedience to the Law a Condition for Salvation?

If salvation is a gift received by faith in Christ, why did God give us the law (or commandments—such as the Ten Commandments)? That's an important question.

God gave us the law for several reasons. As we have already seen, however, God did *not* give us the law as a means of attaining salvation. Remember, Romans 3:20 says that "no one will be declared righteous in his sight by observing the law."

So why did God give us the law? First, to show us what sin is. The law set up God's holy standards of conduct. The law also shows us the consequences if we don't measure up to those high standards. God did this purposefully, for as we grow to see that we don't measure up to the holy standards of the law, we're all forced to admit that we have a sin problem.

Second, though this may sound very strange to you, another purpose of the law is to provoke sin all the more in people. Scripture tells us that the law was given to us so that "trespass might increase" (Romans 5:20). (This is somewhat like a child immediately deciding to do the very thing his mom just told him not to do. Mom's "law" provoked sin.) You see, God wants us to become so overwhelmed with the sin problem that we cannot deny its reality and severity. He wants us all to see how much we need the Savior, Jesus Christ. The law, by provoking sin to increase, effectively points us to the dire need for a Savior. And, as the apostle Paul said, "where sin increased, grace increased all the more."

Still another very important function of the law is that it is like a tutor that leads us to Christ (Galatians 3:24-25). Among the ancient Romans, a tutor led a child to school. Likewise, the law is our tutor, leading us straight to Jesus Christ, the Savior. The law does this by showing us our sin and then pointing to the marvelous grace of Christ.

Once we have trusted in Him as our Savior, the law has done its job and no longer holds sway over us. For believers, "Christ is the end of the law so that there may be righteousness for everyone who believes" (Romans 10:4). For those in Christ, the law no longer holds sway.

Instead of focusing our attention on the law, you and I as Christians are to focus on Christ and seek to walk in moment-by-moment dependence on the Holy Spirit. As we do this, God Himself progressively brings our lives into conformity with the holiness that is reflected in the law. If we instead focus our primary concern on external obedience to God's law, then we're focusing on the results of the Christian life instead of on the source of it—Jesus Christ. So keep your eyes on Jesus!

Is Baptism a Condition for Salvation?

Many sincere people have wondered whether baptism is a requirement for salvation. I do not believe it is. Please don't misunderstand; without a doubt baptism is important, and it should be among the first acts of obedience to God following our conversion to Christ. But baptism is not a requirement for salvation.

Several observations from Scripture led me to this conclusion. First, when Jesus was crucified, two thieves were crucified along with Him. One of them placed his faith in Christ while he was hanging on his cross. Jesus immediately said to him, "I tell you the truth, today you will be with me in paradise" (Luke 23:43). The thief had no opportunity to jump down from the cross and get baptized, but he was still saved.

Second, in Acts 10 we find Cornelius—a devout Gentile—placing faith in Christ and becoming saved. Yet the account in Acts 10 makes it clear that Cornelius was saved prior to being baptized in water. At the moment Cornelius believed in Christ, the gift of the Holy Spirit was poured out on him (Acts 10:45). The fact that the Holy Spirit came upon Cornelius prior to being baptized shows that he was saved before his baptism.

Third, in 1 Corinthians 1:17 the apostle Paul said, "Christ did not send me to baptize, but to preach the gospel." Here a distinction is made between the gospel and being baptized. We are told elsewhere that the gospel brings salvation (1 Corinthians 15:2). Because baptism is not a part of the gospel, it is not necessary for salvation. Nevertheless, we should still get baptized because God has instructed us to.

We must keep in mind the purpose of baptism. In the New Testament, baptism is portrayed as a symbol of our death and resurrection with Jesus Christ. Going down into the water symbolizes our death with Christ, and rising up out of the water symbolizes our resurrection and new life with Christ. So baptism is a symbolic way to make public our identification with Jesus.

In a way, baptism is like a wedding ring: They both symbolize transactions. A wedding ring symbolizes marriage; baptism symbolizes salvation in Jesus Christ. The mere wearing of a wedding ring does not make a person married any more than being baptized makes a person saved.

The Blessings of Salvation

Suppose your best friend came by one day with a special gift for you. How would you respond? Would you immediately pull out your wallet to pay for the gift? Of course not. To do so would be a great insult.

A gift must be accepted for what it is—something freely given and unmerited. If you have to pay for a gift or do something to deserve or earn it, it is not really a gift. True gifts are freely given and freely received. To attempt to give or receive a gift in any other manner makes it not a gift.

The same is true with our salvation in Jesus Christ. God offers us salvation as a gift. He does not attach strings to it because to do so would make it something other than a gift. Any attempt on our part (regardless of how small) to pay for our salvation by doing something is an insult to God.

No one in heaven will ever be able to say, "Look at me! I made it! With a little help from God, I made it!" Salvation is *all* by God. Not even the smallest part of it is the result of anything we do or don't do (Ephesians 2:8-9).

Far more blessings go along with our salvation in Christ than we can mention in a single chapter. But in the little that we cover here, I think you'll agree that the blessings of salvation are astounding.

We Are Born Again

Being born again literally means to be born from above. It refers to God's act of giving eternal life to the person who believes in Christ (Titus 3:5).

Being born again places a person in God's eternal family (1 Peter 1:23). Just as a physical birth places a new baby into a family, so also does a spiritual birth place a person into the family of God.

In John 3 Jesus told Nicodemus about his need to be born again. Nicodemus was a Pharisee (a Jewish leader) who would have been trusting in his physical descent from Abraham and his obedience to the law of Moses for entrance into heaven. The Jews believed that because they were physically related to Abraham, they were in a specially privileged position before God.

Jesus, however, denied such a possibility. The fact is, parents can transmit to their children only the nature that they themselves possess. Every human parent has a sin nature, so these parents transmit this same nature to their children. All people are born in sin. And what is sinful cannot enter the kingdom of God (John 3:5). The only way a person can enter God's forever family is to experience a spiritual rebirth, and that is precisely what Jesus emphasized to Nicodemus.

The moment we place our trust in Jesus, the Holy Spirit infuses our dead human spirits with the eternal life of God, and we're reborn spiritually. What a blessing!

One moment we are spiritually dead, and the next moment we are spiritually alive. At the moment of the new birth, the believer receives a new spiritual nature or capacity that expresses itself in spiritual concerns and interests. Whereas that person was formerly uninterested in the things of God, now (following the new birth) he becomes concerned with the things of God—His Word, His people, His service, His glory, and above all, God Himself.

We Are Declared Righteous

Humankind's dilemma of falling short of God's glory (Romans 3:23) pointed to the need for a solution. Because of man's sin—his utter unrighteousness—he could never come into a relationship with God on his own. Humankind was guilty before a holy God, and this guilt of sin put a barrier between man and God.

One of the wonderful blessings of salvation is that God solved this seemingly insurmountable problem by declaring righteous all those who believe in Jesus. Because of Christ's work on the cross—taking our place and bearing our sins—God acquits believers and pronounces a verdict of not guilty.

Romans 3:24 tells us that God gives His declaration of righteousness to believers "freely by his grace." As noted previously, the word *grace* literally means "unmerited favor." It is because of God's unmerited favor that believers can freely be declared righteous before God.

This doesn't mean God's declaration of righteousness has no objective basis. God didn't just subjectively decide to overlook man's sin or wink at his unrighteousness. Jesus died on the cross for us. He died in our stead. He paid for our sins. Jesus ransomed us from death by His own death on the cross.

God has made a great exchange. As the great reformer Martin Luther said, "Lord Jesus, You are my righteousness, I am Your sin. You have taken upon Yourself what is mine and given me what is Yours. You have become what You were not so that I might become what I was not."[3]

A key blessing that results from being declared righteous is that we now have peace with God (Romans 5:1). The Father sees believers through the lens of Jesus Christ. And because the relationship between the Father and Jesus Christ is filled with peace, so is the relationship between the Father and believers who are in Christ.

If we were to look through a piece of red glass, everything would appear red. If we were to look through a piece of blue glass, everything would appear blue. If we were to look through a piece of yellow glass, everything would appear yellow, and so on.

Likewise, when we believe in Jesus Christ as our Savior, God looks at us through the Lord Jesus Christ. He sees us in all the white holiness of His Son. Our sins are imputed to the account of Christ and Christ's righteousness is imputed to our account. For this reason, the Scriptures say that there is now no condemnation—literally, no punishment—for those who are in Christ Jesus (Romans 8:1).

We Are Reconciled to God

Elizabeth Barrett Browning's parents disapproved so strongly of her marriage to Robert that they disowned her. Almost weekly, Elizabeth wrote love letters to her mother and father, asking for a reconciliation. They never once replied.

After ten years of letter writing, Elizabeth received a huge box in the mail. She opened it. To her dismay and heartbreak, the box contained all of her letters to her parents. Not one of them had ever been opened!

Today those love letters are among the most beautiful in classical English literature. Had her parents opened and read only a few of them, a reconciliation might have been effected.[4]

The Bible is God's letter of reconciliation to us. We should open and read it thoroughly and often.

The New Testament uses two Greek words for *reconciliation*. One word is used when two parties need to be reconciled; the other is used when only one party needs to be reconciled. In 2 Corinthians 5:19 Paul says that "God was reconciling the world to himself in Christ." He uses the single-party word, for man needs to be reconciled to God. God has done nothing wrong and needs no reconciliation toward man.

By believing in Jesus, who paid for our sins at the cross, we are reconciled to God. The alienation and estrangement that formerly existed is gone.

We Are Forgiven

We all have seen and used handheld electronic calculators. What happens if you make an error? You press the Clear button, and the information you entered is eliminated from the calculator. Then you begin again, and you don't have to deal with your earlier mistake. In fact, no record of your mistake exists—it is lost forever!

That's what happens to our sins when God forgives us. The consequences may remain, but the guilt—the legal condemnation for the offense—is gone. This is one of the greatest blessings of salvation. We are truly and completely forgiven.

Meditate on the following verses and let them saturate your mind:

- "Their sins and lawless acts I will remember no more" (Hebrews 10:17).
- "Blessed is he whose transgressions are forgiven, whose sins are covered. Blessed is the man whose sin the LORD does not count against him and in whose spirit is no deceit" (Psalm 32:1-2).
- "You will again have compassion on us; you will tread our sins underfoot and hurl all our iniquities into the depths of the sea" (Micah 7:19).
- "As high as the heavens are above the earth, so great is his love for those who fear him; as far as the east is from the west, so far has he removed our transgressions from us" (Psalm 103:11-12).

Look at that last verse again. North and south point to definite locations—the North and South Poles. But no such points exist for east and west. Regardless of how far you go to the east, you will never arrive where east begins because east is the opposite of west. The two never meet. They never will meet and never could meet because they are opposites. To remove our sins "as far as the east is from the west" is to put them where no one can ever find them. That is the forgiveness God has granted us.

Though we cannot understand how God can do this, He is able to forget our past. God throws our sins into the depths of the sea and puts up a sign on the shore that reads, "No fishing."

Perhaps one of the best illustrations of the way God has forever removed our sins is the apostle Paul's comment on the "certificate of debt" in Colossians 2:14 (NASB). In ancient times, criminal offenders were put in jail, and a certificate of debt was posted on the jail door. This certificate listed all the crimes the offender had committed. Upon release, after serving the prescribed time in jail, the offender was given the certificate of debt, and on it was stamped "Paid in Full."

Christ took the certificates of debt posted on each of our lives and nailed them to the cross. He paid for all our sins at the cross. Jesus' sacrifice paid in full the price for our sins. When Jesus completed the work of salvation on the cross, He uttered the words "It is finished," another translation of the Greek words for "paid in full." We are truly forgiven!

We Are Adopted into God's Family

One of the greatest blessings of salvation is that believers are adopted into God's forever family. We become "sons of God" (Romans 8:14).

God adopts into His family anyone who believes in His Son, Jesus Christ. This is noticeably different from most adoptions, for people generally seek to adopt only the healthiest and best-behaved children. But all people are welcome in God's family (John 1:12-13; Galatians 3:26).

Adoption into God's family creates a relationship of privilege and responsibility. As sons and daughters of God, we are to live in a way that reflects our new family relationship. We are to reflect the family likeness (Matthew 5:48).

Contrary to enslavement to sin, which leads to fear, the believer has received the "Spirit of sonship" (Romans 8:15). The word *sonship* in that verse literally means "placing as a son."

This is significant, for in New Testament times an adopted son enjoyed all the rights and privileges of a natural-born son. Therefore we have no need to be fearful about approaching God. We can boldly approach His throne and say, "Abba, Father" (Romans 8:15). *Abba* is an Aramaic term of affection and intimacy—similar to the English word *daddy*.

Because of this new relationship with God, believers are called "heirs of God" and "co-heirs with Christ" (Romans 8:17). In a typical family, all the children in the family receive a share in their parents' estate. This makes each child an heir, and the children as a group are coheirs. As God's children we are heirs, and collectively we are coheirs with Christ (Galatians 4:7).

If you are a believer, you must never forget your primary identity: You are a member of God's forever family. This should affect your attitude, your behavior—everything in your life. Let your identity as a child of God be a source of strength and encouragement to you.

We Are Secure in Our Salvation

How horrible life would be for my children if they thought I would kick them out of our family if they did something wrong. Their lives would be plagued by fear. They would have no peace. Likewise, life would be horrible for you and me as Christians if we constantly feared being kicked out of God's family for doing something wrong.

Scripture consistently teaches that once a person trusts in Christ and becomes a part of God's forever family, he or she is saved forever

(Romans 8:28-30). Regardless of what that child of God does after the moment of salvation, he or she is saved.

Of course, that does not mean Christians can get away with living in sin. If children of God sin and refuse to repent, God brings discipline—sometimes very severe discipline—into their lives to bring them to repentance (Hebrews 12:4-11). Christians will respond to God's light, or they'll respond to His heat.

What are the scriptural evidences for our security in salvation? Ephesians 4:30 says that we are sealed unto the day of redemption by the Holy Spirit (see also Ephesians 1:13). Roman emperors sealed their letters with wax and then stamped them with their own personal seal. That seal guaranteed the letter would reach its final destination. Anyone who opened the letter before it arrived at its destination would be put to death. The believer in Jesus is like a letter destined for heaven, and the Holy Spirit (God Himself) is our seal, guaranteeing that we will arrive at our final destination.

In addition, Jesus taught that the Father keeps us in His sovereign hands, and no one can take us out of His hands (John 10:28-30). God has us in His firm grip, and that grip will never let us go.

Not only that, but the Lord Jesus Himself regularly intercedes and prays for us (Hebrews 7:25). His work of intercession, as our divine High Priest, is necessary because of our weaknesses, our helplessness, and our immaturity as children of God. He knows our limitations, and He knows the power and strategy of our foe (Satan). He is therefore faithful in making intercession for us. (And His prayers are always answered!)

Is Everyone Saved in the End?

I sometimes encounter Christians today who hold to a doctrine called *universalism*—the idea that, in the end, all people will be saved. Certain verses—John 12:32; Philippians 2:11; and 1 Timothy 2:4—are typically twisted out of context in support of this viewpoint. Such verses, properly interpreted, do not support universalism.

- John 12:32 says that Christ's work on the cross makes possible the salvation of both Jews and Gentiles. Notice, however, that the Lord also warned of judgment of those who reject Christ (verse 48).

- Philippians 2:10-11 says that someday all people will acknowledge that Jesus is Lord, but not necessarily as Savior. (Even those in hell will have to acknowledge Christ's lordship.)

- First Timothy 2:4 expresses God's desire that all be saved, but does not promise that all will be. This divine desire is only realized in those who exercise faith in Christ (Acts 16:31).

Matthew 13:49 records these words of Jesus: "This is how it will be at the end of the age. The angels will come and separate the wicked from the righteous." He mentions two classes—unbelievers and believers, or the wicked and the righteous. Likewise, in Matthew 25:32 Jesus said that following His second coming, "All the nations will be gathered before him, and he will separate the people one from another as a shepherd separates the sheep from the goats." Here believers and unbelievers are differentiated by the terms *sheep* and *goats*. The sheep will enter into God's kingdom (verse 34) and inherit eternal life (verse 46). The goats go into eternal punishment (verse 46). Universalism is therefore a false doctrine.

More Than One Way to Salvation?

Many people today—even some Christians—claim that Jesus is one of many ways to salvation. This line of thinking embraces the idea that all the world religions teach the same basic truths.

Some years ago, Christian philosopher Ravi Zacharias noted that many people believe the various religions are essentially the same and only superficially different. The truth is, he said, that the various religions are essentially different and are only superficially the same.

One cannot read the Bible for long without coming to the realization that the Jesus it depicts is unique in every way, especially in view of the fact that He is absolute deity (see John 1:1; 8:58; 10:30; 20:28). Jesus did not just claim to have a way *to* God, as did the founders of the other world religions. Rather, Jesus claimed *to be* God. Moreover, Jesus and His message were inseparable. The reason Jesus' teachings have absolute authority is that He is God. This is not the case with the leaders of the other world religions. Indeed, the Buddha taught that his ethical teachings were important, not he himself. He emphasized that these teachings were important whether or not he himself even existed. But Jesus said, *"I* tell you the truth…" with the very authority of God.

Jesus claimed that what He said took precedence over all other teaching. He said He is humanity's only means of coming into a relationship with God: "I am the way and the truth and the life. No one comes to the Father except through me" (John 14:6). This claim was confirmed by people who followed Jesus. A bold Peter said in Acts 4:12, "Salvation is found in no one else, for there is no other name under heaven given to men by which we must be saved." The apostle Paul said, "For there is one God and one mediator between God and men, the man Christ Jesus" (1 Timothy 2:5). Moreover, Jesus sternly warned His followers about people who would try to present a different Christ (Matthew 24:4-5). And Jesus proved the veracity of all He said by rising from the dead (Acts 17:31), something that no other religious leader did. Jesus' resurrection proved that He was who He claimed to be—the divine Messiah (Romans 1:4).

How great a salvation we have in Jesus Christ! And how wondrous are the blessings that accompany that salvation! Have you yet trusted in the one way of salvation—Jesus Christ?

Discussion Questions

1. How do you feel knowing that God planned your salvation far before you were even born?

2. Can you summarize some false contemporary views of the gospel? What is the true gospel?

3. Why might people have a relentless propensity to seek to earn salvation by good works?

4. Do you think Christians are eternally secure in their salvation? Why or why not?

5. What are the main problems with universalism?

9

Jesus the Savior Is Risen

Jesus' crucifixion must have been utterly horrific. Scripture indicates that He was beaten and scourged beyond recognition, forced to carry His crossbeam to the place of execution (which He was not able to complete by Himself), and stripped of His clothing. Then the blows of a heavy mallet drove huge spikes through His wrists. Another huge spike tore its way through His feet and into the wood beneath. The cross, with the body attached by spikes, was then heaved up and dropped into a hole in the ground (Matthew 27:35-50).

Jesus would have experienced a variety of physical and emotional symptoms on the cross—blood loss and the accompanying dizziness, extreme pain, growing infection from the wounds caused by the spikes, fever due to the infection, great thirst and hunger as time slowly passed, difficulty breathing as a result of hanging by the arms, deep shame as those below watched the horror, and an ever-present anticipation of the moment of death. Shortly after Jesus died, a Roman soldier thrust a spear into Jesus' side so that blood and water came out (John 19:34). Four Roman executioners pronounced Him dead, and He was taken to be buried.

You Can't Keep a Good Man Down

Dwight Moody, one of the great evangelists of the nineteenth century, reminded us, "You can't find directions in the New Testament on how to conduct a funeral because Jesus broke up every funeral He attended."[1] He brought other people back to life and rose from the dead Himself (John 2:19)!

Friends and enemies of Christianity have long recognized that the resurrection of Christ is the foundation stone of the Christian faith. The apostle Paul wrote to the Corinthians, "If Christ has not been raised, your faith is futile; you are still in your sins" (1 Corinthians 15:17).

Paul realized that the most important truths of Christianity stand or fall on the doctrine of Christ's resurrection. If Christ did not rise from the dead, then Christianity is little more than an interesting museum piece.

Reasons to Believe

Many people today argue that believing just about any other alternative scenario is more reasonable than accepting the resurrection stories of Jesus at face value.[2] Even some who call themselves Christians deny the resurrection. Contrary to such skepticism, believing in the resurrection is reasonable because the historical evidence supports it (Matthew 28:1-15; Mark 16:1-11; Luke 24:1-12; John 20:1-18). Consider the facts:

The circumstances at the tomb reveal a missing body. Following Jesus' crucifixion, His body was buried in accordance with Jewish burial customs. He was wrapped in a linen cloth, and about 100 pounds of aromatic spices—mixed together to form a gummy substance—were applied to the wrappings of cloth around His body.

After His body was placed in a solid rock tomb, an extremely large stone was rolled by means of levers against the entrance. This stone would have weighed in the neighborhood of two tons (4000 pounds). It was not a stone that people could have moved easily.

Roman guards were then stationed at the tomb. These strictly disciplined men were highly motivated to accomplish their mission. Fear of cruel punishment produced flawless attention to duty, especially in the night watches. These Roman guards would have affixed on the tomb the Roman seal, a stamp representing Roman power and authority.

All this makes the situation at the tomb following Christ's resurrection highly significant. The Roman seal was broken, which meant the person responsible would be crucified upside down. Furthermore, the large stone was moved a good distance from the entrance, as if it had been picked up and carried away. The Roman guards had also fled. The penalty in Rome for a guard leaving his position was death. We can therefore assume they must have had a substantial reason for fleeing!

The biblical account has Jesus appearing first to a woman, Mary Magdalene (John 20:1). If the disciples had fabricated the resurrection story, they would not have invented it this way. In first-century Jewish culture, a woman's testimony was unacceptable in any court of law except in a very few circumstances. A fabricator would have been much more likely to portray Peter or the other male disciples at the tomb. Our biblical text, however, tells us that the Lord appeared first to Mary because that was the way it actually happened.

Following this, Mary promptly told the disciples the glorious news. That evening, the disciples gathered in a room with the doors shut for fear of the Jews (John 20:19). This fear was well-founded, for after Jesus had been arrested, Annas the high priest specifically asked Jesus about the disciples (18:19). Jesus had also previously warned the disciples in the upper room, "If they persecuted me, they will persecute you also" (15:20). These facts no doubt lingered in their minds after Jesus was brutally crucified.

Their gloom soon turned to joy. The risen Christ appeared among them and said to them, "Peace be with you" (John 20:19). This phrase was a common Hebrew greeting (1 Samuel 25:6). This occasion, however, added significance to Jesus' words. After their conduct on Good Friday (they all scattered after Jesus' arrest), the disciples may well have expected a rebuke from Jesus. Instead, He displayed compassion by pronouncing peace to them.

Jesus immediately showed the disciples His hands and His side (John 20:20). The risen Lord wanted them to see that He was truly alive. The wounds showed that He did not have another body but the *same* body. He had been dead, but now He is alive forevermore.

The disciples came away from the crucifixion frightened and full of doubt, and yet following Jesus' resurrection appearances to the disciples, their lives were transformed. As Michael Green put it, "How have [these early followers] turned, almost overnight, into the indomitable band of enthusiasts who braved opposition, cynicism, ridicule, hardship, prison, and death on three continents, as they preached everywhere Jesus and the resurrection?"[3]

As Jews, these followers would have been predisposed to believe that no one would rise from the dead before the general resurrection at the end of time. They would not have expected Jesus' physical resurrection. The only thing that could account for their sudden incredible transformation into powerful witnesses for Jesus is the resurrection. This is the only thing that can explain why they were even willing to die for their beliefs. Christian theologian Barry Leventhal put it this way:

> When Yeshua [Jesus] died, all of his followers, in despair and fear, went into hiding. They thought that Yeshua's entire messianic movement was over. Even though they knew that the Hebrew Scriptures had prophesied that the Messiah would not see bodily corruption in the grave and that Yeshua had even predicted his own resurrection on at least three different occasions, they thought his messianic program had collapsed in utter defeat. And yet in a short time, these very same disciples appeared on the historical

scene boldly proclaiming the good news of the gospel, that this Jesus who had been crucified, dead, and buried was now alive from the dead and the Lord of life and the sole determiner of men's eternal destinies.

And what did they get for such an open and bold proclamation? They endured some of the worst abuse and punishment known in their own day. In fact, many of them were tortured and even martyred for their faith in this resurrected Messiah. Men may live for a lie, but to think that thousands will die for that same lie requires a stretch of the imagination.[4]

The apostles defended their belief in Jesus and His resurrection before the Jewish Sanhedrin and the high priest, an intimidating audience to say the least. The high priest said to them, "We gave you strict orders not to teach in this name…Yet you have filled Jerusalem with your teaching and are determined to make us guilty of this man's blood" (Acts 5:28). Peter and the other apostles replied, "We must obey God rather than men! The God of our fathers raised Jesus from the dead—whom you had killed by hanging him on a tree. God exalted him to his own right hand as Prince and Savior that he might give repentance and forgiveness of sins to Israel" (verses 29-31). These witnesses seemed convinced beyond any doubt about the reality of Jesus' resurrection (John 20:24-29; Acts 2:32; 3:15; 4:18-20; 10:39-40; 1 Corinthians 15:3-8).

The many thousands of Jews who became unflinching followers of Jesus abandoned many of their long-held and cherished sacred beliefs and practices. Such abandonment of Jewish doctrine, according to Jewish authorities, could lead to an eternity in hell. The only thing that can explain this radical change among so many Jews is the resurrection of Christ. Christian apologist J.P. Moreland suggests that the resurrection explains…

how a large generation of Jewish people (remember, most of the early Christians were Jewish) would have been willing to risk the damnation of their own souls to hell and reject what had been sociologically embedded in their community for centuries; namely, the Law must be kept for salvation, sacrifices must be kept for salvation, the Sabbath must be kept, nontrinitarian monotheism, and there is only a political Messiah, not a dying and rising one. How does a group of people in a short time span, a society, disenfranchise themselves from that into which they had been culturally indoctrinated for centuries and risk the damnation of their own souls to hell to follow a carpenter from Nazareth? The most reasonable explanation is there was something about that man that caused this change. He was a miracle worker who rose from the dead.[5]

Only the resurrection of Jesus could explain the conversion of hard-core skeptics in New Testament times. The apostle Paul is an example. Saul, as he was known formerly, delighted in breathing out "murderous threats against the Lord's disciples" (Acts 9:1). We are told that he "went to the high priest and asked him for letters to the synagogues in Damascus, so that if he found any there who belonged to the Way, whether men or women, he might take them as prisoners to Jerusalem" (verses 1-2). Clearly, Saul was not open to following Jesus; he hated Jesus' disciples. Yet, as the rest of Acts 9 reveals, Saul had an encounter with the living, resurrected Jesus and not only became His follower but became Jesus' most explosive preacher and promoter to ever appear on the planet. Only a resurrected and living Christ could cause such a radical conversion of a hard-core skeptic like Paul.

Only the resurrection of Jesus could explain the growth and survival of the Christian church. Vast numbers of people—Jews and Gentiles—believed in Jesus and continued to believe in Jesus despite the fact that the Roman sword was against Christianity's throat. Many of these people died for their testimony and commitment to Jesus. The only thing that could explain such widespread commitment is a resurrected Jesus who promised eternal life to those who followed Him.

Jesus made too many appearances over too many days to too many people for the resurrection to be easily dismissed. Acts 1:3 says, "He showed himself to these men and gave many convincing proofs that he was alive. He appeared to them over a period of forty days and spoke about the kingdom of God." Moreover, "He appeared to more than five hundred of the brothers at the same time, most of whom are still living, though some have fallen asleep" (1 Corinthians 15:6). Paul mentions that many of these were "still living" because if Paul had uttered any falsehood, plenty of people could have stepped forward to call Paul a liar. They did not do this, however, because the resurrection appearance of Christ was well attested.

The apostle Paul in 1 Corinthians 15:1-4 includes Christ's resurrection in a public confession that had been handed down for years. First Corinthians was written around AD 55, a mere 20 years after Christ's resurrection. But biblical scholars believe the confession in 1 Corinthians 15:1-4 was formulated within a few years of Jesus' death and resurrection. Christian theologian Gary Habermas writes, "We know that Paul wrote 1 Corinthians between AD 55 and 57. He indicates in 1 Corinthians 15:1-4 that he has already passed on this creed to the church at Corinth, which means it must predate his visit there in AD 51. Therefore the creed was being used within 20 years of the resurrection, which is quite early."[6] Some scholars trace the confession back to within *two years* of the actual resurrection.

Were Jesus' Followers Hallucinating?

Some people have responded to claims of Jesus' resurrection by claiming His followers were hallucinating. However, hallucinations are by nature individual experiences. They generally happen to individuals. First Corinthians 15:6, by contrast, indicates that 500 people saw the resurrected Jesus at a single time. All 500 people could not have seen the same hallucination at the same time. Moreover, Jesus appeared to too many different kinds of people on too many occasions (literally dozens) over too long a time (40 days) for this view to be feasible. Further, people saw the resurrected Jesus doing a number of different things—walking with people, eating with people, speaking with people, and being touched by people. The hallucination theory cannot explain this wide diversity of personal interactions.

If Jesus' resurrection involved hallucinations, the Roman and Jewish authorities could have easily put an end to it all by parading Jesus' dead body around town for all to see. The Roman and Jewish leaders would have loved to have had this option, but this was not an option because the body was missing from the tomb.

One must also wonder how this many people could hallucinate about something that is completely foreign to the Jewish mind-set and Jewish expectations. These Jewish people had been conditioned to believe in a single resurrection at the end of time—a general res-urrection. A resurrection of a single individual prior to this general resurrection was completely foreign to their theology. For countless Jews to experience the same hallucination of a single individual rising from the dead, when they had been conditioned to believe in a general resurrection at the end of time stretches all credulity.

Did Jesus' Followers Have Distorted Memories?

Other people today explain stories of Jesus' resurrection from the dead by calling them distorted memories among His followers. His followers were, after all, subjected to tremendous social pressures, their emotions were undeniably tense, and they were gullible. Perhaps all this led to their distorted memories.

Not a shred of evidence supports such a view. One could easily make this same kind of argument against any event of ancient history. In fact, if we used this methodology of skepticism consistently, we could know very little if anything about ancient history. One scholar suggests that "if one could really refute the specific evidence for putatively historical accounts so summarily...one might as well just close the history department at the university."[7]

Further, one must challenge the claim that people in biblical times were gullible. C.S. Lewis addressed this:

> When St. Joseph discovered that his bride was pregnant, he was "minded to put her away." He knew enough biology for that. Otherwise, of course, he would not have regarded pregnancy as a proof of infidelity. When he accepted the Christian explanation, he regarded it as a miracle precisely because he knew enough of the laws of nature to know that this was a suspension of them.[8]

Moreover, Lewis observed,

> When the disciples saw Christ walking on the water they were frightened: they would not have been frightened unless they had known the laws of nature and known that this was an exception. If a man had no conception of a regular order in nature, then of course he could not notice departures from that order.[9]

Nothing seems abnormal until we first grasp the norm. People in biblical times knew enough of the norm not to be gullible.

Still further, would critics have us believe that multitudes of Jews left Judaism, joined the cause of Christ, and suffered torture and even martyrdom for their faith in Christ, all because of distorted memories? Are we to believe that the 500 who saw the resurrected Jesus at the same time (1 Corinthians 15:6) were all suffering from memory problems? Such a view is beyond credulity.

Was the Body of Jesus Stolen?

Some people have suggested that the dead body of Jesus was stolen, and the disciples simply assumed He had risen from the dead.[10] Such a scenario is highly unlikely. The tomb had a huge stone that weighed two tons blocking it. It had a seal of the Roman government. It was guarded by brawny Roman guards who were trained in the art of defense and killing and who would have risked their lives to fulfill their mission. A tomb robbery would have been quite a feat. Besides, the biblical text indicates that the disciples were scared, discouraged, and disheartened (Mark 16:10). They were in no frame of mind to attack the Roman guards and steal the body.

Certainly neither the Romans nor the Jews would have stolen the body. When Christians began claiming Christ had risen from the dead, they would have loved to be able to parade the dead body around town, but they were unable to do so because they did not have it.

Further, why would Christians steal the body and then, instead of recanting their false claim of resurrection to save their lives, become imprisoned and go to their deaths (often after being tortured) defending the lie of the resurrection? Why engage in such a mad, self-defeating, futile endeavor? If they had stolen the body, why would they go around preaching Christ's resurrection not only to strangers but to their friends and family members—indeed, even to their own children? Why try to pull off such a massive hoax? No one can offer a good explanation for this.

One must also consider the noble character of these men. Christ's disciples had been raised from early childhood to obey the Ten Commandments, including the commandment against bearing false witness (Exodus 20:16 NASB). To say that *all* these men stepped outside of their normal character to commit such an act stretches credulity.

Besides, they had insufficient time to pull off such a stunt. Jesus was buried late on a Friday afternoon, and by dawn on Sunday His body was missing. The window of opportunity for brainstorming such an idea, assembling the necessary people, and accomplishing the theft is too narrow for such an explanation.[11]

Did Jesus Merely "Swoon" on the Cross?

Still other people have speculated that Jesus did not really die on the cross. He was nailed to the cross and suffered from loss of blood and went into shock. But He didn't die. He merely fainted (or *swooned*) from exhaustion. The disciples mistook Him for dead and buried Him alive in a tomb. (They were easily fooled, living in the first century as they did.) Suddenly, the cold tomb woke Jesus from His state of shock. When Jesus emerged from the tomb and the disciples saw Him, they reasoned He must have risen from the dead.

This theory is highly imaginative. In fact, I think it requires more faith to believe this theory than the actual resurrection account. Consider the claims:

- Jesus went through six trials and was beaten beyond description.

- He was so weak that He couldn't even carry the wooden crossbeam.

- Huge spikes were driven through His wrists and feet, causing a substantial loss of blood.

- A Roman soldier thrust a spear into His side so that blood and water came out.

- Four Roman executioners (who had many years of experience) pronounced Jesus dead.

- More than a hundred pounds of gummy spices were applied to Jesus' body, and during this process, no one saw Jesus breathing.

- A large stone weighing two tons was rolled against the tomb, Roman guards were placed there, and a seal was wrapped across the entrance.

- Still, Jesus awoke in the cool tomb, split off the garments, pushed the two-ton stone away, fought off the Roman guards, and appeared to the disciples.

I don't think so!

Was the Resurrection a Conspiracy?

Some years ago, a Jewish scholar by the name of Hugh Schonfield developed a theory and wrote a book on it called *The Passover Plot.*

Schonfield argued that Jesus conspired with Joseph of Arimathea, Lazarus, and an anonymous young man to convince His disciples that He was the Messiah. He allegedly manipulated events to make it appear that He was the fulfillment of numerous prophecies. Regarding the resurrection, Jesus allegedly took some drugs and feigned death but was revived later. Unfortunately, the crucifixion wounds ultimately proved fatal and He died. The plotters then stole and disposed of Jesus' body, and the appearances of Christ were simply a case of mistaken identity.

This theory is full of holes. First, Christ's life and teaching displayed the highest moral character. To say that Jesus was deceitful and sought to fool people into believing He was the Messiah breaches all credulity. Moreover, Jesus fulfilled many prophecies that He couldn't have conspired to fulfill—such as His birth in Bethlehem (Micah 5:2) and being born of a virgin (Isaiah 7:14).

As we have seen, no one could have stolen Jesus' dead body in order to dispose of it. The tomb had a huge stone (weighing two tons) blocking it, had a seal of the Roman government, and was guarded by Roman guards.

We have also seen that the idea that the appearances of Christ were simply a case of mistaken identity is ridiculous. Jesus appeared to too many people (including 500 at a single time—1 Corinthians 15:6) on too many occasions (dozens), over too long a time (40 days) for this to be the case.

Did the Disciples Go to the Wrong Tomb?

Some people explain away Christ's resurrection by saying the women and the disciples went to the wrong tomb—and when they didn't see the dead body of Jesus, they merely assumed He rose from the dead. To believe in this theory, we'd have to conclude that the women went to the wrong tomb, that Peter and John ran to the wrong tomb, that the Jews then went to the wrong tomb, and that the Jewish Sanhedrin and the Romans went to the wrong tomb. We'd also have to say that Joseph of Arimathea, the owner of the tomb, also went to the wrong tomb, as did the angel from heaven. Besides all this, how are the many postresurrection appearances of Christ to be explained—including the appearance to more than 500 people at a single time (1 Corinthians 15:6)? This theory is literally grasping at straws in its attempt to deny the resurrection.

Did Jesus Just Spiritually Rise from the Dead?

Some churchgoing Christians have suggested that perhaps Jesus rose from the dead spiritually but not physically.[12] Scripture, however, is emphatic that Christ's resurrection was physical. The Greek word for *body (soma)*, when used of a human being, always refers to a physical body in the New Testament. There are no exceptions to this. Greek scholar Robert Gundry, in his authoritative book *Soma in Biblical Theology*, published by Cambridge University Press, speaks of "Paul's exceptionless use of *soma* for a physical body."[13] All references to Jesus' resurrection body *(soma)* in the New Testament must be taken to mean a resurrected *physical* body.

Christ Himself said to the disciples, "See My hands and My feet, that it is I Myself; touch Me and see, for a spirit does not have flesh and bones as you see that I have" (Luke 24:39 NASB). Notice three things here: (1) The resurrected Christ indicates in this verse that He is not a spirit, (2) Christ indicates that His resurrection body is made up of flesh and bones, and (3) Christ's physical hands and feet represent physical proof of the materiality of His resurrection from the dead.

Moreover, consider the verbal exchange that took place between Jesus and some Jewish leaders recorded in John 2:19-21: "Jesus answered them, 'Destroy this temple, and I will raise it again in three days.' The Jews replied, 'It has taken forty-six years to build this temple, and you are going to raise it in three days?' But the temple he had spoken of was his body." Jesus here indicated that He would be bodily raised from the dead.

We also note that after His resurrection Christ ate on four different occasions. He did this to prove that He had a real physical body (Luke 24:30,42-43; John 21:12-13; Acts 1:4).

Still further, different people touched and handled Jesus' physical resurrection body. For example, Mary (John 20:17) and some other women touched Him (Matthew 28:9). He also challenged the disciples to physically touch Him so they could rest assured that His body was material (Luke 24:39).

Finally, we note the teaching of the apostle Paul that the body that is "sown" in death is the *very same* body that is raised in life (1 Corinthians 15:35-44). That which goes into the grave is raised to life.

Weighing the Evidence

The factual evidence for Christ's resurrection is truly staggering. Canon Westcott, a brilliant scholar at Cambridge University, said it well: "Taking all the evidence together, it is not too much to say that there is no historic incident better or more variously supported than the resurrection of Christ."[14]

Sir Edward Clarke similarly said, "As a lawyer, I have made a prolonged study of the evidences for the events of the first Easter Day. To me, the evidence is conclusive, and over and over again in the High Court I have secured the verdict on evidence not nearly so compelling."[15]

Professor Thomas Arnold was the author of the famous three-volume *History of Rome* and was appointed to the Chair of Modern History at Oxford University. He was well acquainted with the value of evidence in determining historical facts. After examining all the data on Christ's resurrection, he concluded this: "I know of no one fact in the history of mankind which is proved by better and fuller evidence of every sort, to the understanding of a fair inquiry, than the great sign which God has given us that Christ died and rose again from the dead."[16]

He is risen!

Discussion Questions

1. What do you believe are the most convincing evidences that Jesus has risen from the dead?

2. How would you respond to a person who tries to explain away the resurrection by suggesting that Jesus' followers were hallucinating or merely had distorted memories?

3. What biblical evidence can you cite in support of a physical resurrection of Jesus (as opposed to a mere spiritual resurrection)?

Power from on High:
The Holy Spirit

In John's Gospel we find a touching account of Jesus with His disciples in the upper room (chapters 14–16). Jesus is soon to be crucified, and before His departure, He wanted to give His disciples some final encouragements. One of these encouragements relates to the promise of the Holy Spirit.

In John 14:16 Jesus informed the disciples, "I will ask the Father, and he will give you another Counselor to be with you forever." The word *counselor* is a rich one—carrying the meaning of "comforter, helper, advocate, one who strengthens." This one word conveys the concepts of encouragement, support, assistance, care, and shouldering responsibility for another's welfare.

Two New Testament Greek words can be translated into the English word *another.* The first Greek word means "another of a different kind." The second means "another of the same kind." John 14:16 uses this second word.

Jesus was saying that He would ask the Father to send another

Helper of the same kind as Himself—that is, a personal, ever-present helper. Just as Jesus was a personal comforter who helped the disciples for three years during His earthly ministry, so also would Christ's followers have another personal comforter—the Holy Spirit—who would be with them throughout their lives.

What a wonderful truth this is! We are never alone in our troubles. When life seems too much for us—when we encounter tough times or we're treated unfairly—we can rejoice in the presence of the Holy Spirit, who comforts, helps, and encourages us.

The Comforter Is a Real Person

Are you surprised to hear me say that the Holy Spirit is a person? Many people today—including some Christians—have assumed that

THE HOLY SPIRIT

Scripture reveals that the Holy Spirit is both God and a person—the third person of the Trinity.

The Holy Spirit

Is God
- Is called God – Acts 5:3-4
- Is called Lord – 2 Corinthians 3:17-18
- Is identified with Yaweh – Acts 7:51
- Is called "Spirit of God" – Genesis 1:2
- Has attributes of deity – Psalm 139
- Is spoken of as divine – Mark 3:29

Is a Person

Has attributes of personality	Mind – Romans 8:27 Emotions – Ephesians 4:30 Will – 1 Corinthians 12:11
Works confirm personality	Bears witness – John 15:26 Prays – Romans 8:26 Issues commands – Acts 8:29
Is treated as a person	Is sent – John 14:26 Can be blasphemed – Matthew 12:3 Can be lied to – Acts 5:3

the Holy Spirit is God's power or a divine force that emanates from Him. But Scripture portrays the Holy Spirit as a person. Let's look at the facts:

The Holy Spirit Has All the Attributes of Personality

The three primary attributes of personality are mind, emotions, and will. A power or force does not have these attributes. But the Holy Spirit does.

The Holy Spirit has a mind. We see the Holy Spirit's intellect in 1 Corinthians 2:10 where Paul writes that "the Spirit searches all things" (see also Isaiah 11:2; Ephesians 1:17). The Greek word for *search* means "thoroughly investigate." The very next verse (verse 11) says the Holy Spirit "knows" the thoughts of God. Romans 8:27 (NASB) tells us that just as the Holy Spirit knows the things of God, so God the Father knows "what the mind of the Spirit is." The Holy Spirit has a mind like all other persons.

The Holy Spirit has emotions. In Ephesians 4:30 we find this admonishment: "Do not grieve the Holy Spirit of God." Grief is an emotion and is not something that a power or force can experience. The Holy Spirit feels the emotion of grief when believers sin. In the context of Ephesians, such sins include lying, anger, stealing, laziness, and speaking words that are unkind (verses 25-29).

The Holy Spirit has a will. The Holy Spirit's will is displayed in 1 Corinthians 12:11 (NASB), where we are told that He distributes spiritual gifts "to each one individually just as He wills." The phrase "He wills" translates the Greek word *bouletai,* which refers to "decisions of the will after previous deliberation."[1] The Holy Spirit makes a sovereign choice regarding what spiritual gifts each respective Christian receives. A power or force does not have such a will.

The Holy Spirit's Works Confirm His Personality

The Holy Spirit does many things in Scripture that only a person can do. The Holy Spirit teaches (John 14:26), bears witness (John 15:26), guides (Romans 8:14), commissions people to service (Acts 13:4), issues commands (Acts 8:29), prays for believers (Romans 8:26), and speaks to people (John 15:26; 2 Peter 1:21). Let's consider three of these in a little more detail.

The Holy Spirit bears witness. John 15:26 tells us that the Holy Spirit "will testify about" Christ. Bearing witness is something only a person can do. The disciples bore witness about Christ (John 15:27). John the Baptist bore witness to the truth (John 5:33). Likewise, the Holy Spirit bears witness about Christ.

The Holy Spirit prays for believers. Romans 8:26 (NASB) tells us, "In the same way the Spirit also helps our weakness; for we do not know how to pray as we should, but the Spirit Himself intercedes for us with groanings too deep for words." Just as Jesus (a person) intercedes for believers (Romans 8:34; Hebrews 7:25), so the Holy Spirit (a person) intercedes for believers.

The Holy Spirit issues commands. Acts 8:29 tells us that the Holy Spirit directed Philip to speak to the Ethiopian eunuch. Acts 13:2 tells us that the Holy Spirit commanded that Paul and Barnabas were to be set apart for missionary work. Acts 13:4 (NASB) affirms that these two men were "sent out by the Holy Spirit." A power or force cannot send individuals to certain places. Only a person can do that.

The Holy Spirit Is Treated as a Person

Certain acts can be performed toward the Holy Spirit that would not make sense if He did not possess true personality. For example:

The Holy Spirit is sent. Just as Jesus was sent by the Father (John 6:38), so also was the Holy Spirit sent by the Father (John 14:26; 16:7). (One does not send an impersonal power.)

The Holy Spirit can be blasphemed. One does not normally think of a force (electricity, for example) or a thing (a computer, for example) being blasphemed. One normally thinks of a holy person being blasphemed. Scripture indicates that the Father can be blasphemed (Revelation 13:6; 16:9) as can the Son (Matthew 27:39; Luke 23:39). Likewise, the Holy Spirit can be blasphemed (Matthew 12:32; Mark 3:29-30).

The Holy Spirit can be lied to. Acts 5:3 indicates that Ananias and Sapphira were guilty of lying to the Holy Spirit. A person does not lie to a mere power. (Can you imagine how people might respond if I stood up in church one Sunday morning and confessed to lying to the electricity in my home?)

In view of the above—since the Holy Spirit has all the attributes of personality, does things only a person can do, and is treated as a person—we must conclude that the Holy Spirit, the divine comforter, is truly a person.

Why Doesn't the Holy Spirit Have a Name?

Some people today raise the objection that because the Holy Spirit does not have a personal name, He cannot truly be a person. Spiritual beings, however, are not always named in Scripture. For example, unclean spirits are rarely named in Scripture. More often than not, they are identified by their particular character (that is, "unclean," "wicked," and so forth). In the same way, by contrast, the Holy Spirit is identified by His character—which is holiness. Besides, the Holy Spirit is related to the name of the first and second persons of the Trinity in Matthew 28:19: "Therefore go and make disciples of all nations, baptizing them in the name of the Father and of the Son and of the Holy Spirit."

The Comforter Is Truly God

Not only is the Holy Spirit a person, He is also God. He is just as much God as the Father and Jesus are. He is the third person of the holy Trinity.

How do we know the Holy Spirit is God? For one thing, the Holy Spirit is called *God* in the Bible (Acts 5:3-4). Further, the Holy Spirit is called *Lord* (2 Corinthians 3:17-18), is often identified with Yahweh (Acts 7:51; 28:25-27; 1 Corinthians 2:12; Hebrews 3:7-9; 10:15-17; 2 Peter 1:21), and is spoken of as divine (Matthew 12:32; Mark 3:29; 1 Corinthians 3:16; 6:19; Ephesians 2:22). As well, the Holy Spirit is referred to as the "Spirit of God," thus indicating His full deity (Genesis 1:2; Exodus 31:3; Numbers 24:2; Job 33:4; Ezekiel 11:24; Romans 8:9,14; 1 Corinthians 2:11,14; John 4:2).

Beyond that, the Holy Spirit has all the attributes of God. For example, the Holy Spirit is everywhere-present (Psalm 139:7), all-knowing (1 Corinthians 2:10), all-powerful (Romans 15:19), eternal (Hebrews 9:14), and, of course, holy (John 16:7-14).

Furthermore, the Holy Spirit performs works that only God can do. For example, He was involved in the work of creation (Genesis 1:2; Job 33:4; Psalm 104:30) and inspired Scripture (2 Timothy 3:16; 2 Peter 1:21).

The Comforter Glorifies Christ

Scripture reveals that a primary purpose of the Holy Spirit is to bring glory to Jesus. Indeed, Jesus told the disciples in the upper room that the Holy Spirit would "bring glory to me by taking from what is mine and making it known to you" (John 16:14).

The goal of the Spirit is not to make Himself prominent but to magnify and exalt the person of Jesus. He seeks to interpret and apply Jesus' teaching to His followers so that Jesus becomes central to their thinking and real in their lives. Nothing makes the Holy Spirit happier than for people to fall absolutely in love with Jesus and follow Him in all their ways.

We might say that the work of the Holy Spirit among believers is *Christocentric*—meaning that Christ is the very center of the Spirit's work among believers. Everything He does is related in some way to glorifying Christ.

Marvelous Ministries of the Holy Spirit

The Scriptures tell us that the Holy Spirit is involved in a number of wonderful ministries among believers. Let's look at some of these ministries.

The Holy Spirit Seals Believers

The apostle Paul informs us that at the moment we believe in Jesus, we are "sealed for the day of redemption" (Ephesians 4:30). Indeed, we are "marked in him with a seal, the promised Holy Spirit" (1:13).

I noted previously in the book that in ancient Rome, scrolls or documents sent from one location to another were sealed with wax that was imprinted with a Roman stamp. The authority of the Roman government protected that document against unauthorized opening. The seal could not be broken until the document reached its final destination.

In the same way, you and I as believers are sealed by the Holy Spirit for the day of redemption. We are sealed by God Himself. And that seal cannot be broken. This seal guarantees that you and I will be "delivered" into eternal life—on the "day of redemption." The Holy Spirit, as our seal, represents possession and security.

Notice in Ephesians 1:13 that the seal is also called a "mark" on the Christian. This mark stays with us, guaranteeing that we will enter heaven.

I live in Texas. Each spring the cattle ranchers round up all their one-year-old calves for branding. The brand is placed directly on the calf's flank. This is the rancher's mark of ownership. Once the brand is applied, no one can dispute that the calf belongs to him.

In the same way, God has placed His mark of ownership on us by the mark of the Holy Spirit. No one can remove us from His ownership anytime before the day of redemption.

The Holy Spirit Guides Believers

Guidance is another vital ministry of the Holy Spirit. John 16:13 tells us that He guides us into all truth and reveals the things of Christ to us.

We are not left to find our way alone. We are not abandoned to wander around in the darkness, trying to find the light. We are not left to ourselves in our journey toward the promised land of heaven. The Holy Spirit is ever with us, guiding us along the way.

The following poem beautifully depicts this ministry of the Holy Spirit:

> Holy Spirit, faithful guide,
> > Ever near the Christian's side;
> Gently lead us by the hand,
> > Pilgrims in a desert land;
> Weary souls for e'er rejoice,
> > While they hear that sweetest voice,
> Whisp'ring softly, wanderer come!
> > Follow Me, I'll guide thee home.[2]

The Filling of the Holy Spirit

Every Christian is commanded to be filled with the Holy Spirit (Ephesians 5:18). And we are to continually keep on being filled by the Spirit. We know this because the word *filled* is a present-tense verb. That indicates continuing action. Day by day, moment by moment, you and I are to be filled with the Spirit. But what does this mean?

The context provides us with the answer. The verse literally says, "Do not get drunk on wine, which leads to debauchery. Instead, be filled with the Spirit" (Ephesians 5:18). Both drunk and spiritual persons are controlled persons—that is, they're under the influence of either liquor or the Spirit, and as a result they do things that are unnatural to them. In both cases they abandon themselves to an influence.

So, to be filled with the Holy Spirit means that we will be controlled or governed no longer by self but by the Holy Spirit. This filling is not a matter of acquiring more of the Spirit but rather of the Spirit of God acquiring all of the individual.

A believer becomes filled with the Spirit when he or she is fully yielded to the indwelling Holy Spirit. This yieldedness results in a spiritual condition in which the Holy Spirit controls and empowers the individual moment by moment. The person who is full of the Holy

Spirit behaves in a way that's consistent with that filling. The person acts in a way that's pleasing to God.

Walking in the Spirit

Ever since Adam and Eve's fall into sin, all people have been born into the world with a sin nature. This sin nature becomes manifest through numerous kinds of sin—covetousness, jealousy, dissension, bickering, and much more. In our own strength, we do not have the power to resist the evil inclinations of our sin nature. But we can have victory over the sin nature by walking in dependence on the Holy Spirit. Galatians 5:16 tells us, "Live [or walk] by the Spirit, and you will not gratify the desires of the sinful nature."

In that verse, the word *live* (or *walk*) is also a present-tense verb, indicating continuing action. We are to persistently and continually walk in dependence on the Spirit. As we do this, we will live in a way that pleases God.

The Fruit of the Spirit

As we depend on the Spirit, we not only enjoy victory over sin but also find the fruit of the Spirit cropping up in our lives. Galatians 5:22-23 tells us that "the fruit of the Spirit is love, joy, peace, patience, kindness, goodness, faithfulness, gentleness and self-control."

Many theologians have noted that as we look at the qualities listed in Galatians 5:22-23, we find an accurate profile of Jesus Christ Himself. As we walk in the Spirit, He reproduces Jesus' character in us. In this way, we progressively take on the family likeness (as members of God's forever family).

I once read a story about a slothful man who had moved into a new house. The house quickly began to show the effects of his slipshod lifestyle. The yard became littered with trash. The lawn withered for lack of care. The house was a wreck and was never cleaned.

Later, a young family bought the house and moved in. They painted the house, cleaned the yard, and replanted the lawn. The results were dramatic. What happened? The appearance of the house improved because of the new occupants.

The same is true with a person who becomes a Christian and walks in dependence on the Spirit. That person's life changes dramatically because of a perfect, new resident within—the Holy Spirit. And as we walk in dependence on the Spirit, His fruit begins to grow in our lives.

Don't Grieve the Spirit

Closely related to walking in the spirit is the instruction that we "not grieve the Holy Spirit of God" (Ephesians 4:30). In the original Greek text, this verse reads, "*Stop* grieving the Holy Spirit."

Are you consistently falling into a particular sin? If so, Scripture exhorts you to stop grieving the Holy Spirit and walk in dependence upon Him. If you do that, you will enjoy victory over the sin.

When a believer grieves the Spirit of God, the fellowship, guidance, instruction, and power of the Spirit are hindered. The Holy Spirit—though He still indwells the believer—is not free to accomplish His work. To grieve the Holy Spirit is to say goodbye to the fruit of the Spirit—such as love, joy, and peace. If these qualities are missing in your life, then consider the possibility that you may be doing something that grieves the Spirit.

The Holy Spirit Bestows Spiritual Gifts

Yet another ministry of the Holy Spirit is that He gives believers spiritual gifts (1 Corinthians 12:11). What are some of these gifts? The apostle Paul explains:

> We have different gifts, according to the grace given us. If a man's gift is prophesying, let him use it in proportion to his faith. If it is serving, let him serve; if it is teaching, let him teach; if it is encouraging, let him encourage; if it is contributing to the needs of others, let him give generously; if it is leadership, let him govern diligently; if it is

showing mercy, let him do it cheerfully (Romans 12:6-8; see also 1 Corinthians 12:8-10).

We each have different spiritual gifts. But our gifts are to be used for the mutual benefit of the church, which is the body of Christ. I believe that my spiritual gift is the gift of teaching. I exercise this gift by writing books, speaking in churches and Bible schools, and much more. I discovered my gift as I became active in ministry in my church.

If you are unsure of what your spiritual gift is, the best advice I can give you is to get involved in the work of ministry at your local church. Your spiritual gift will surface as you serve in ministry.

Go ahead—contact someone on your church's pastoral staff and volunteer for a ministry. God will use you in ministry, and you will discover what your unique spiritual gift is!

Avoiding Extremes

Many churchgoers today have taken some extreme positions on certain aspects of the Holy Spirit's work and ministry. These include so-called holy laughter, being "slain in the spirit," and the idea that speaking in tongues is necessary for salvation. Let us take a brief look at these.

Holy Laughter

In some churches, you might walk into the service and find that everyone is laughing hilariously—with some even rolling on the floor in uncontrollable, hysterical laughter. This is claimed to be a mighty manifestation of the Holy Spirit. Examining the phenomenon in the light of Scripture, however, causes me to reject it for five reasons:

First, the Bible admonishes us to test all things against Scripture (1 Thessalonians 5:21; Acts 17:11). I don't know of a single verse in the Bible that says that when the Holy Spirit comes upon a person, he breaks out into uncontrollable laughter. There are good passages on joy in the Bible (like Psalm 126), but holy laughter advocates who cite such passages to support this phenomenon are reading something into the text that simply is not there.

Second, one fruit of the Holy Spirit is self-control (Galatians 5:23). In the holy laughter phenomenon, people laugh *un*controllably, even when there is nothing funny to laugh about.

Third, a major leader of the holy laughter movement said people were laughing at his meeting even when he was preaching on hell. But Scripture tells us that God takes no joy at the perishing of the wicked (Ezekiel 18:23,32). It would thus be absurd to say that God was inspiring such laughter in this context.

Fourth, in 1 Corinthians 14:33 the apostle Paul speaks of the need for order in the church: "Everything should be done in a fitting and orderly way" (1 Corinthians 14:40). In outbreaks of holy laughter, all order is lost in the church.

Fifth, the ministry of our Lord Jesus (who had the Holy Spirit without measure), does not include a single recorded instance of people breaking out into uncontrolled laughter. Neither was there any laughter when the apostle Paul or the apostle Peter ministered in the book of Acts.

"Slain in the Spirit"

Sometimes on television, we witness a televangelist touching someone on the forehead, and the person is knocked cold, allegedly by the power of the Holy Spirit. The person is said to be "slain in the Spirit." Is this a biblical practice?

Not only is the phrase "slain in the Spirit" not found in the Bible, the experience is not in the Bible either. Scripture does record people falling to their knees as they witness the incredible glory of God. This is what happened to Isaiah (Isaiah 6:1-5). But the idea of being touched by a minister who is so "anointed" by the Spirit that a mere touch of his hand knocks someone out cold is not a biblical phenomenon. I challenge anyone to find an example of this happening with a prophet of God in the Old Testament or an apostle of God in the

New Testament. If the experience is not in the Bible, then we would be wise not to make it a part of our belief system.

How do we explain such an experience? It may be a psychological or emotional phenomenon. Someone may so strongly expect to be knocked cold by the Spirit (thought to be present in the anointed preacher) that when the preacher touches him or her, down he or she goes. Sociologists have noted that this type of experience is actually common to many religions.

Interestingly, I have seen quite a few televangelists on TV who touch someone's forehead, and the person does not get "slain." Perhaps such an individual has not been sufficiently conditioned (in his or her belief in the phenomenon) to actually pass out when touched.

The powers of darkness may also be involved in this experience (2 Thessalonians 2:9). One must not forget that some people affiliated with Eastern religions, and who participate in the martial arts, claim to be able to knock someone cold by a mere touch, and they believe the "chi force" or "Prana energy" accomplishes this.

I recognize that many who believe in this phenomenon like to cite certain passages in its support, such as Genesis 15:12-21; Numbers 24:4; 1 Samuel 19:20; and Matthew 17:6. But in every case they are reading their own meaning into the text instead of drawing the meaning out of the text. This is called *eisegesis*. These passages, in context, offer virtually no support for the idea of being slain in the spirit. (Go ahead and read the verses for yourself. You'll see what I mean.)

Speaking in Tongues: A Condition of Salvation?

Some people have claimed that a person cannot be saved unless he or she has given evidence of being baptized in the Holy Spirit—and this evidence is speaking in tongues. Is this a biblical view?

We can derive a number of Scriptural facts about speaking in tongues from Scripture:

- The Holy Spirit is the one who bestows spiritual gifts on

believers (1 Corinthians 12:11). Not every Christian has every gift.

- Speaking in tongues is not an evidence of the baptism of the Holy Spirit. Not all the Corinthians spoke in tongues (1 Corinthians 14:5), but they had all been baptized (12:13).

- The fruit of the Holy Spirit (Galatians 5:22-23) does not include speaking in tongues. Therefore, Christlikeness does not require speaking in tongues.

- Most of the New Testament writers are silent on tongues. Only three books (Acts, 1 Corinthians, and Mark) mention it. (Note: Mark 16:17 is not in the two best Greek manuscripts.) Significantly, many of the other New Testament books speak a great deal about the Holy Spirit but fail to mention speaking in tongues a single time.

- We are to seek more important gifts than tongues (1 Corinthians 12:28,31).

- Faith in Christ alone is what saves a person (Acts 16:31).

One of my seminary professors told me about the "pendulum effect." Some people overreact to an extreme teaching by swinging to the opposite extreme. Some people respond to extreme teachings about the Holy Spirit by swinging to the opposite extreme of virtual noninvolvement with the Holy Spirit. Don't fall into this trap. You can't have a healthy spiritual life without the Holy Spirit's involvement.

My challenge, then, is this: Walk in daily dependence on the Holy Spirit. Your life will never be the same.

Discussion Questions

1. Have you ever thought of the Holy Spirit as more of a power or force than a person? How has your perspective changed?

2. Do you feel that the doctrinal extremes of some televangelists—emphasizing such things as holy laughter and the necessity of speaking in tongues—have soured your view on the Holy Spirit? Do you need to make any adjustments regarding your attitude toward the Holy Spirit?

3. Do you think you can live the Christian life without a proper relationship to the Holy Spirit?

4. What ministries of the Holy Spirit do you most appreciate?

The Church—God's Forever Family

Scripture refers to both the universal church and the local church. The universal church is a global company of people who have one Lord and who share together in one gift of salvation in the Lord Jesus Christ (Titus 1:4; Jude 3). It is "the ever-enlarging body of born-again believers who comprise the universal body of Christ over whom He reigns as Lord."[1]

Although the members of the church may differ in age, sex, race, wealth, social status, and ability, they are all joined together as one people (Galatians 3:28). All of them share in one Spirit and worship one Lord (Ephesians 4:3-6).

The word *church* is translated from the Greek word *ekklesia.* This Greek word comes from two smaller words. The first is *ek,* which means "out from among." The second is *klesia,* which means "to call." Combining the two words, *ekklesia* means "to call out from among." The church represents people whom God calls out from among the world. And these people come from all walks of life. All are welcome in Christ's church.

The way you become a member of this universal body is to simply place your faith in Jesus Christ. This body is comprised only of believers in Christ. If you're a believer, you're in!

Some Christians believe the church began in Old Testament times. However, this view conflicts with Scripture. Matthew 16:18 cites Jesus as saying that "I will build my church" (future tense). This indicates that at the moment He spoke these words, the church was not yet existent. This is consistent with the Old Testament, which doesn't include any references to the church. In the New Testament, the church is portrayed as distinct from Israel in such passages as 1 Corinthians 10:32 and Hebrews 12:22-24. We would therefore be wrong to equate the church with believing Israelites in Old Testament times.

Scripture indicates that the universal church was born on the Day of Pentecost (see Acts 2; compare with 1:5; 11:15; 1 Corinthians 12:13). We are told in Ephesians 1:19-20 that the church is built on the foundation of Christ's resurrection, meaning that the church could not have existed in Old Testament times. Paul calls the universal church a "new man" in Ephesians 2:15.

Though only one universal church exists, many local churches are scattered throughout the world. For example, we read of a local church in Corinth (1 Corinthians 1:2) and another in Thessalonica (1 Thessalonians 1:1). Churches soon cropped up around the globe through the missionary efforts of the early Christians.

Distinguishing the Universal Church from the Local Church

	UNIVERSAL CHURCH	LOCAL CHURCH
MEMBERSHIP	Embraces all believers from Pentecost to the rapture	Embraces believers in a specific locale who meet for fellowship and worship
LIVING OR DEAD	Includes living and dead believers	Includes living believers only

	UNIVERSAL CHURCH	LOCAL CHURCH
DENOMINATIONAL RELATIONSHIP	Includes all true believers, regardless of denominational affiliation	Normally affiliated with a specific denomination
JOINING	A person becomes a member by faith in Christ.	A person becomes a member by profession of faith in Christ, plus any requirements unique to the denomination (such as baptism).

A brief chapter on the church belongs in this book, for the church involves two very important relationships—relationships with other Christians and a corporate relationship with the Lord. One relationship affects the other. If we don't attend church and worship with other Christians, our relationship with the Lord will suffer. If we don't have a good relationship with the Lord, we may treat other Christians poorly. We do well to take both relationships seriously.

Christ Is the Head of the Body

In Matthew 16:18 Jesus affirmed to Peter, "I will build my church." This is a foundational truth. The church is not built by a pastor or priest or body of elders or governing hierarchy. It is not owned by a denomination.

Christ Himself builds the church. The church is His and His alone. And Christ doesn't have to clear His decisions regarding the church with any council or church hierarchy. It's His!

Christ not only owns the church but is also the head of it. Ephesians 5:23 tells us that Christ is the head of the church (the "body of Christ") just as the husband is the head of the wife. A husband is to provide for his wife, preserve her, protect her, and cherish her. Christ does the same for the church. He provides for, preserves, protects, and cherishes the church as His own.

The fact that Christ is the head of the church is what brings unity to it. The various parts of the human body move when the brain sends the signal to do so. In fact, the entire body depends on the brain in one way or another. As the brain gives simultaneous signals to different parts of the body, the body functions in unity and is able to go through all kinds of complex motions. Disconnect the brain from the body—such as happens in certain spinal injuries—and body movement is cut off.

In the body of Christ, every member depends on and should be in submission to Christ, the head of the body. When each member is connected to Christ, the result is a smooth functioning organism. When members disconnect, or choose not to submit to Christ, dissension arises. In fact, dissension in the church is often a sign that one or more parts of the body have forgotten that Christ is the head.

A Place of Equipping and Discipleship

I like to think of the church as God's body-building program. Ephesians 4:12 says that a primary role of the church is to equip and disciple church members (that is, build the body) in regard to Bible study, worship, ministry, and much more. If the church fails to equip members in these ways, each of the members suffers.

Chuck Colson, in an interview, stressed the importance of churches equipping their members:

> If you read Ephesians 4, the job of the pastor is to equip the saints so that when the saints come together in their congregations—for worship, for the study of the Word, for the celebration of the sacraments, for discipline and accountability—they are being discipled by that pastor and equipped for works of service in the world. And by being equipped they can be the light and the salt that influences the world. This is the whole purpose of the church. The task of the church is to be a place of equipping.

Colson then illustrated the importance of equipping with a story from his past:

I compare it to my experience in the Marines. I was a lieutenant in the Marines during the Korean War. And that was a very dangerous time. Fifty percent of the Marine lieutenants being commissioned then were coming back in pine boxes. And so, when I went to basic training, let me tell you, I became "equipped" for 18 hours a day—going over that obstacle course, disassembling my rifle, assembling it blindfolded, engaging in night maneuvers, going under barbed wire, learning to survive live artillery shells, and memorizing the *Marine Handbook*. Why? Because I was going into combat, and I was going to have 50 lives in my hands.

"Should we be any less serious about the equipping and discipling of the church?" Colson asks. "No! We're in spiritual combat—cosmic combat for the heart and soul of humankind. We ought to treat it just as seriously as I treated preparing to be a Marine lieutenant in the Korean War."[2]

A Place of Salt and Light

Jesus said, "You are the salt of the earth" (Matthew 5:13). Salt is an effective preservative. We are to have a preserving effect on the world by influencing it for Christ.

Jesus also said, "You are the light of the world. A city on a hill cannot be hidden" (Matthew 5:14). Jesus did not call us to be "secret agent" Christians. We are not to cloak our lights. Someone once said, "No one is a light unto himself, not even the sun." Because the darkness of our world is hovering over humanity as never before, the light of each individual Christian is more necessary than ever. As evangelist Billy Graham said, "The Christian should stand out like a sparkling diamond."[3] Sparkling Christians are those who take personal evangelism seriously.

A Place of Fellowship

I grew up in a large family of eight kids. That was quite an experience! No one was ever lonely in the Rhodes house because someone was always around.

Likewise, Christian fellowship and sharing should be the family activity of God's people in the local church (Hebrews 10:25). This gathering together with fellowship and sharing gives believers strength. The church, then, is for our benefit. God does not want us to be Lone Ranger Christians.

John Wesley, the founder of Methodism, said, "There is nothing more unchristian than a solitary Christian."[4]

C.S. Lewis commented, "The New Testament does not envisage solitary religion; some kind of regular assembly for worship and instruction is everywhere taken for granted in the Epistles. So we must be regular practicing members of the church."[5]

I once read a story about a certain church member who had been attending services regularly but suddenly stopped going to church. After some weeks, the minister decided to visit the absent member.

On a chilly evening, the minister found the man at home alone, sitting before a blazing fire. Guessing the reason for his pastor's visit, the man welcomed him in, led him to a big chair by the fireplace, and waited.

The minister made himself comfortable and said nothing. In grave silence, he contemplated the play of the flames around the burning logs. After some minutes, he took the fire tongs, carefully picked up a brightly burning ember, and placed it to one side of the hearth. Then he sat back in his chair, still silent.

The host watched all this in quiet fascination. The lone ember's flame diminished to a soft glow. Soon the fire was no more, and the ember was cold and dead.

Neither man had spoken a word since the initial greetings. But as the minister rose to leave, the host said, "Thank you so much for your visit—and especially for your fiery sermon. I'll be at church next Sunday."[6]

Billy Graham summarized the point of that story succinctly when he said, "Churchgoers are like coals in a fire. When they cling together, they keep the flame aglow; when they separate, they die out."[7]

A Place of Involvement

Every church member should get involved in serving the Lord Jesus and ministering to the needs of other Christians (1 Corinthians 12:4-6). The church is not to be a place where the professional clergy does everything. This is not what God intended.

Every Person Is Important

Too many Christians today tend to stay on the sidelines and watch the clergy do the work of the ministry. Dr. F.B. Meyer, responding to this situation, addresses the need for each person's involvement in the local church:

> It is urgently needful that the Christian people of our charge should come to understand that they are not a company of invalids, to be wheeled about, or fed by hand, nursed, and comforted, the minister being the Head Physician and Nurse; but a garrison in an enemy's country, every soldier of which should have some post or duty, at which he should be prepared to make any sacrifice rather than quitting.[8]

We Need Each Other

One reason for each person to get involved is that we need each other. God has given every member of the church unique gifts and talents, and each person can render service in ways that no one else can. That's the way God designed it. Each part of the body of Christ is important (1 Corinthians 12:1-20).

The body of Christ is a lot like the human body, which has many kinds of cells. The nerve cells, blood cells, muscle cells, and many others each have a distinct function in the body. The body operates smoothly, not because the cells decide for themselves what they want to do but because each one does what it was *designed* to do.

Certainly the body would not operate properly if each cell chose to go its own way. A rebellion of the cells in your stomach is called stomach cancer. A revolt of your brain cells is called a brain tumor. Whenever the cells in your body don't operate properly, the body is sick.

Many of the problems in the church today result from individual members forgetting that the church is a body with each member contributing according to the unique gifts and talents he or she has. We need each other!

Alpine climbers rope themselves together on steep slopes. That way, if one climber slips, he won't fall to his death. He'll be held by the others until he can regain his footing.

God designed the church to function in the same way. When one believer slips and falls, the others can hold him up until he regains his footing. Believers in the church are to make every effort to minister to individual members (Hebrews 10:24) and care for the needy in their midst (2 Corinthians 8–9).

A Place of Worship

The church is a place of worship. In worship we reverence God, adore Him, praise Him, venerate Him, and pay homage to Him, not just externally (by rituals and singing songs) but in our hearts as well (Isaiah 29:13; see also 1 Samuel 15:22-23). The Hebrew word for worship, *shaha,* means "to bow down" or "to prostrate oneself" (see Genesis 22:5; 42:6). Likewise, the New Testament word for worship, *proskuneo,* means "to prostrate oneself" (see Matthew 2:2,8,11). Biblical worship, then, emphasizes the act of prostration or falling on your knees. A person who kneels before God does so because he or she feels that God is worthy of such honor and adoration.

In Old English, *worship* was rendered *worthship,* denoting the worthiness of the God we worship. Such worship is the proper response of a creature to the divine Creator (Psalm 95:6). Worship can be congregational (1 Corinthians 11–14) or individual (see Romans 12:1). Worship does not stop on earth but continues in heaven when believers enter into glory (see Revelation 4–5).

Too often genuine worship—the kind that involves vibrant praise and truly worshipful singing—is missing in the church. However, the combination of praise and song should be a regular part of every church service.

> My heart leaps for joy
>   and I will give thanks to him in song.
> I will praise God's name in song
>   and glorify him with thanksgiving.
> Let us come before him with thanksgiving
>   and extol him with music and song.
> Praise the Lord.
> Sing to the Lord a new song,
>   his praise in the assembly of the saints.
> (Psalm 28:7; 69:30; 95:2; 149:1)

Likewise, Ephesians 5:19-20 says, "Speak to one another with psalms, hymns and spiritual songs. Sing and make music in your heart to the Lord, always giving thanks to God the Father for everything, in the name of our Lord Jesus Christ." Colossians 3:16 instructs, "Let the word of Christ dwell in you richly as you teach and admonish one another with all wisdom, and as you sing psalms, hymns and spiritual songs with gratitude in your hearts to God."

Of course, because Jesus is the heart and soul of Christianity, much of our worship should be directed at Him. Christ was worshipped as God many times during His three-year earthly ministry—and He always regarded such worship as appropriate. Jesus received worship from Thomas (John 20:28), the angels (Hebrews 1:6), wise men (Matthew 2:11), a leper (Matthew 8:2), a ruler (Matthew 9:18), a blind man

(John 9:38), Mary Magdalene (Matthew 28:9), the disciples (Matthew 28:17), and others. So let the worship of Christ be a central part of our church services!

A Ministry of Comfort

Sally could not restrain her tears as she poured out her heart to Pastor Dave at my church. After a series of medical tests, Sally's doctor had called to inform her that the baby she was expecting would be born with Down syndrome. Pastor Dave shared Sally's grief at the news. He vowed to help Sally and her husband, Jim, in any way he could.

The following day Pastor Dave decided to send Sally and Jim a postcard with a word of encouragement. On the card, Dave assured them of how much God loved them and their soon-to-be-born Down syndrome baby.

The postcard was delivered to a wrong address several miles from Sally and Jim's house. Sue—who lived at the house the card was mistakenly delivered to—decided to take the postcard to Sally personally.

When Sally opened the door, Sue said, "This card from your pastor was delivered to my house by mistake. I wanted to come by and deliver the card personally because I too have a child with Down syndrome, and I want to help you through this if you'll let me. God has shown me so much blessing that I would like to share with you."

Here's a case in which I believe the God of all comfort sent one of His angels to reroute the mail. God wanted to bring Sally and Jim comfort in their grief.

Sue is the person I want to focus on here, however. Sue was able to minister to Sally and Jim precisely because she had been through the same experience. And she was able to share with this grieving couple the insights she had learned through her experience. She was exercising the ministry of comfort.

In 2 Corinthians 1:3-4 the apostle Paul makes reference to "the God of all comfort, who comforts us in all our troubles, so that we can comfort those in any trouble with the comfort we ourselves have received from God." God used Sue as a channel of comfort and blessing through whom His own comfort flowed. This ministry of comfort should characterize every church.

Church Attendance Isn't Optional

Despite all these blessings of church attendance, I still encounter people who assure me they are Christians but say they feel no need to regularly attend church. Scripture, however, does not present church attendance as a mere option. Hebrews 10:25 (NASB) specifically instructs us not to forsake "our own assembling together." Scripture shows us that we are to live the Christian life within the context of the family of God and not in isolation (Ephesians 3:14-15; Acts 2). Moreover, by attending church, we become equipped for the work of ministry (Ephesians 4:12-16). As we have seen, the Bible knows nothing of a Lone Ranger Christian (see Ephesians 2:19; 1 Thessalonians 5:10-11; and 1 Peter 3:8).

Is Tithing Required?

One of the ways Christians participate in the ministry of the church is by giving to it financially. Some churches require a 10 percent tithe. But is this biblical?

The Hebrew word for *tithe* literally means "a tenth." In Old Testament times, God commanded tithing because "the earth is the LORD's, and all it contains, the world, and those who dwell in it" (Psalm 24:1 NASB). The people of God tithed to acknowledge that God owned all things and was sovereign over them. Their tithe proclaimed that all the good things we have in life ultimately come from Him. God commanded His people to tithe from the land and its produce (Leviticus 27:30; Deuteronomy 14:2), the animals (Leviticus 27:32), and new wine, oil, and honey (2 Chronicles 31:5). When people withheld their tithes and offerings from God, they were robbing from Him (Malachi 3:8-10).

Despite the heavy emphasis on tithing in the Old Testament, many

Bible expositors today do not believe that tithing is intended for the New Testament church—at least as a commandment from the law. In fact, the New Testament does not include a single verse where God specifies that believers should give 10 percent of their income to the church. This should not be taken to mean, however, that church members should not support the church financially. The New Testament emphasis seems to be on what might be called "grace giving." We are to freely give as God has freely given to us. And we are to give as we are able (2 Corinthians 8:12). For some, this will mean less than 10 percent. For others whom God has materially blessed, this will mean much more than 10 percent.

To give to the church with a right attitude, we must first give ourselves to the Lord. The early church is our example: "They gave themselves first to the Lord and then to us in keeping with God's will" (2 Corinthians 8:5). Only when we have given ourselves to the Lord will we have a proper perspective on money.

We also read in Romans 12:1, "Offer your bodies as living sacrifices, holy and pleasing to God—this is your spiritual act of worship." The first sacrifice we make to God is not financial. Our first sacrifice is that of our own lives. As we give ourselves unconditionally to the Lord for His service, our attitude toward money will be what it should be. God is not interested in our money until He first has our hearts.

The Sacraments of the Church

The New Testament speaks of two sacraments—the Lord's Supper and baptism. Some theologians prefer not to call them *sacraments* because this word seems to imply the conveyance of grace in participating in the rituals. These theologians prefer the word *ordinances.* Let's consider these in a bit more detail.

The Lord's Supper

Jesus instituted the Lord's Supper at the Last Supper, where He shared bread and wine with the disciples prior to His crucifixion (Mark

14:12-26). Four primary views of the significance of the Lord's Supper exist within the church:

The Roman Catholic view. The Catholic doctrine of transubstantiation teaches that the elements actually change into the body and blood of Jesus Christ at the prayer of the priest. This imparts grace to the recipient. Jesus is literally present. The appearance of the elements does not change, but the elements nevertheless change.

This view has a number of problems. First, note that Jesus was present with the disciples when He said the elements (bread and wine) were His body and blood (Luke 22:17-20). Obviously He intended for the disciples to take His words figuratively. Further, one must keep in mind the Scriptural teaching that drinking blood is forbidden to anyone (Genesis 9:4; Leviticus 3:17; Acts 15:29). Moreover, the idea that Jesus' body and blood are physically present in Roman Catholic churches all over the world each Sunday would imply the omnipresence of the physical (human) body of Christ. Scripturally, omnipresence is an attribute of Christ's divine nature only.

The Lutheran view. In the Lutheran doctrine of consubstantiation, Christ is present *in, with,* and *under* the bread and wine. Even though Christ is present, the elements do not change. Partaking of the elements after the prayer of consecration communicates Christ to the participant along with the elements.

The Reformed view. Christ is spiritually present at the Lord's Supper. It is a means of grace. The dynamic presence of Jesus in the elements becomes effective when the believer partakes. This partaking of His presence involves an inner communion with His person.

The memorial view. My view is that the elements do not change. The ordinance is not intended as a means of communicating grace to the participant. The bread and wine are symbols and reminders of Jesus in His death and resurrection (1 Corinthians 11:24-25). Communion also reminds us of the basic facts of the gospel (11:26), our anticipation of the second coming (11:26), and our oneness as the body of Christ (10:17).

Baptism

Christians hold at least three views regarding the significance of baptism. The first of these is the sacramental view espoused by Roman Catholics and Lutherans. In this view, God conveys grace to the believer through the sacrament of baptism. As a result of this ritual, the believer's sins are allegedly remitted and he is given a new nature.

A second view is the covenantal view, which holds that New Testament baptism is essentially a counterpart to Old Testament circumcision as a sign of the covenant. Contrary to the sacramental view, this view does not see baptism as a means of salvation. Rather, baptism is a sign of God's covenant to save humankind and a means of entering into that covenant (and enjoying its benefits).

A third view (my view) is the symbolic view. This view says that baptism does not produce salvation and does not convey grace but rather is a symbol pointing to the believer's complete identification with Jesus Christ. It is a public testimony that shouts to the world that a change in status has occurred in the person's life: Formerly, the person was identified with the world and was lost, but now the person is identified with Jesus Christ. The immersion into the water and the coming up out of it symbolizes death to the old life and resurrection to the new life in Christ (Romans 6:1-4).

Immersion or sprinkling. Christians are divided as to whether baptism should be by immersion or sprinkling. Those who argue for sprinkling point out that a secondary meaning of the Greek word *baptizo* is "to bring under the influence of." This fits sprinkling better than immersion. Moreover, they say, baptism by sprinkling better pictures the coming of the Holy Spirit upon a person.

Also, immersion may have been impossible in some of the baptisms portrayed in Scripture. In Acts 2:41, for example, the apostles would have struggled to immerse all 3000 people who were baptized. The same may be true in regard to Acts 8:38; 10:47; and 16:33.

Those who hold to the immersion view, as I do, respond by pointing out that the primary meaning of the Greek word *baptizo* is "to immerse." And the prepositions normally used in conjunction with *baptizo* (such as *into* and *out of* the water) clearly picture immersion and not sprinkling. The Greek language has perfectly acceptable words for *sprinkling* and *pouring*, but these words are never used to describe baptism in the New Testament.

History reveals that the ancient Jews practiced baptism by immersion. The Jewish converts to Christianity—including the apostles—would probably have followed this precedent.

Certainly baptism by immersion best pictures the significance of death to the old life and resurrection to the new life in Christ (Romans 6:1-4). And, despite what sprinkling advocates say, every instance of water baptism recorded in the New Testament was by immersion. Arguments that not enough water was available to accomplish immersion are weak and unconvincing. Archaeologists have uncovered ancient pools all over the Jerusalem area.

Though immersion is the biblical norm of baptism, it is not necessarily an inflexible norm. God accepts believers on the basis of their faith in Christ and their desire to obey Him, not on the basis of how much water covers the body at the moment of baptism.

Infant baptism. Some Christians say infant baptism is analogous to circumcision in the Old Testament, which was done to infant boys (see Genesis 17:12). They add that household baptisms in the New Testament must have included infants (Acts 16:33). As well, Jesus Himself clearly blessed the children in Mark 10:13-16 and said that to such belong the kingdom of God.

Other Christians (myself included) disagree with this view and point out that the biblical pattern is that a person always get baptized following his or her conversion experience (see, for example, Acts 2:37-41; 8:12; 10:47; 16:29-34; 18:8; 19:4-5). Moreover, household baptisms such as described in Acts 16:33 do not specify the presence of any infants. Having said that, it is certainly permissible and right for young children who have trusted in Christ to get baptized.

The Sabbath and the Lord's Day

The Hebrew word for *Sabbath* means "cessation." The Sabbath was a holy day and a day of rest for both man and animals (Exodus 20:8-11). This day commemorated God's rest after His work of creation (Genesis 2:2). God set the pattern for living—working six days and resting on the seventh. The Sabbath thus finds its ultimate origins in the creation account.

At Mount Sinai, the Sabbath—already in existence—formally became a part of the law (its observance is one of the Ten Commandments) and a sign of God's covenant relationship with Israel (Exodus 20:8-11). Keeping the Sabbath was a sign that showed submission to God, and honoring it brought great blessing (Isaiah 58:13-14). By contrast, to break the Sabbath law was to rebel against Him, and this was a sin that warranted the death penalty (see Exodus 31:14). God provided detailed instructions for Sabbath observance in Leviticus 25; Numbers 15:32-36; and Deuteronomy 5:13-15.

By the time of Jesus, Jewish legalists had added all kinds of new rules and regulations for properly keeping the Sabbath. The Sabbath thus became a burden instead of a blessing. These legalistic Jews put their own laws in place of divine law (see Matthew 15:9). Jesus stood against such legalism.

Keeping the Sabbath is the only one of the Ten Commandments not repeated after the Day of Pentecost (Acts 2). The early church made Sunday (the first day of the week) the day of worship for several reasons:

- New Testament believers are not under the Old Testament law (Romans 6:14; 2 Corinthians 3:7,11,13; Galatians 3:24-25; Hebrews 7:12).

- Jesus rose and appeared to some of His followers on the first day of the week (Sunday) (Matthew 28:1).

- Jesus continued His appearances on succeeding Sundays (John 20:26).

- The descent of the Holy Spirit took place on a Sunday (Acts 2:1-4).

- The early church was thus given the pattern of Sunday worship, and this they continued to do regularly (Acts 20:7; 1 Corinthians 16:2).

- Sunday worship was further hallowed by our Lord, who appeared to John in that last great vision on "the Lord's Day" (Revelation 1:10).

- In Colossians 2:16 we read, "Therefore do not let anyone judge you by what you eat or drink, or with regard to a religious festival, a New Moon celebration or a Sabbath day." This verse indicates that the distinctive holy days of the Old Testament are no longer binding on New Testament believers.

What About the Role of Women?

The question of whether women should be in leadership roles in the church today is extremely controversial, and discussions on the subject often generate more heat than light. The following chart illustrates the case for and the case against women in leadership roles in church:

THE CASE FOR	THE CASE AGAINST
Jesus considered men and women equal (Luke 10:38-42).	Men and women are equal in worth, but the male-female authority structure still exists (1 Corinthians 11:3).
Jesus first appeared to a woman after the resurrection (Mark 16:9).	Jesus called all-male disciples and Paul instituted all-male elders in the church.
Female subordination is a result of the fall. Christ ended the curse brought by sin.	Male headship is established in Genesis 2— before the fall ever occurred.
Galatians 3:28 speaks of the equality of men and women.	Positional equality does not negate the male-female authority structure.

THE CASE FOR	THE CASE AGAINST
Ephesians 5:21-24 instructs both men and women to submit to each other.	The woman was created from Adam's rib to be his helper (Genesis 2:22). Adam named the woman, showing his authority over her (Genesis 2:23). God gave instructions to Adam alone, showing his headship (Genesis 2:16-17).
Verses about women not being in authority over men reflect only a first-century culture.	The apostle Paul argued *theologically*, not *culturally*, for male leadership (1 Timothy 2:11-14).

I believe we gain perspective on this issue by recognizing that God sovereignly designed an ordered universe to function in a particular way. Romans 13:1 tells us that God is the source not simply of all authority but of the very concept of authority. Theologian Duane Litfin emphasizes this:

> That the universe should be ordered around a series of over/under hierarchical relationships is His idea, a part of His original design. He delegates His authority according to His own pleasure to those whom He places in appropriate positions and it is to Him that His creatures submit when they acknowledge that authority.[9]

Within that authority structure, both men and women are given the privilege of serving God—but in different ways. Simply because Scripture says women can't teach men in a position of authority does not mean that their ministries are unimportant. To Paul, all ministries were significant: "The eye cannot say to the hand, 'I don't need you!' And the head cannot say to the feet, 'I don't need you!' On the contrary, those parts of the body that seem to be weaker are indispensable, and the parts that we think are less honorable we treat with special honor" (1 Corinthians 12:21-23).

Women are not prohibited from teaching men on an individual basis—as apparently Priscilla, with her husband Aquila, taught Apollos

(Acts 18:26). (Priscilla was evidently teaching under the headship of Aquila, to whom the authority belonged.) Nor are women forbidden to personally address fellow believers, male and female, to their "edification, and exhortation, and comfort" (1 Corinthians 14:3 KJV). Nor are women forbidden to teach women (Titus 2:3-4) or children (2 Timothy 1:5; 3:14-15), or take part in other fruitful ministries (for example, Romans 16:3,6,12). In short, women are privileged to serve God in many different ways within the authority structure He designed.

So, should women be involved in ministry in the church? Absolutely! "That women are gifted for and called to service in the church is plain," says J.I. Packer, "and gifted persons are gifts that the churches must properly value and fully use."[10] However, this call to service, according to Scripture, is not to involve ecclesiastical authority over men.

In this chapter, I have touched on a number of issues related to the church in which Christians have different opinions. Christians must agree to disagree in an agreeable way on such issues.

The areas of agreement are the most important. We all agree that the church is a place of equipping, teaching, and discipleship. It is a place of worship, a place of fellowship, a place where the ministry of comfort takes place, and a place of involvement where every Christian's role is important.

Are you a member of such a church?

Discussion Questions

1. Has your perspective on the church changed since reading this chapter? How so?

2. Would you say that the church you are presently attending is faithful to the New Testament criteria for a church?

3. Do you think "seeker-sensitive" churches are biblical churches? Why or why not?

4. Do you agree with the position taken in this chapter regarding the role of women in the church? Why or why not?

5. Do you agree with the position taken in this chapter regarding the proper day of worship (the Lord's Day)? Why or why not?

6. In what way are you contributing to the ministry of your church?

12
Angels Among Us

We are living in an age of celestial quackery. Over the past decade, all kinds of strange ideas about angels have surfaced in our society—even in Christian churches. For example, a popular belief today is that angels can be contacted by various means, including praying to them, writing letters to them, and meeting them during deep meditation. Contrary to such absurd views, the biblical pattern is that angels always show up among people unexpectedly. We never once witness anyone in the Old or New Testaments seeking to contact an angel.

Other people today are making extravagant claims regarding the alleged benefits of angel contact. Some say angels can introduce us to entirely new religious experiences. Others say angels are cheerleaders for our "higher selves" and are here to guide us into a new age of enlightenment and harmony. Still others say angels can act as "brain program editors," getting rid of all our bad thoughts and helping us to have healthy, positive thoughts. The problem is that not a single verse in the entire Bible gives credence to such fanciful views.

The Bible—God's Word—is the only authoritative source of reliable information about angels. In this chapter, we will take a brief journey through Scripture to uncover some fascinating facts about these celestial creatures.

Angels Are Created Beings

Colossians 1:16 tells us that Jesus Christ created the entire company of angels. One moment they did not exist. The next moment they did exist. As their consciousness first sprang into being, their first sight was of their Creator, Jesus Christ (John 1:3; Hebrews 1:2,10; see also Isaiah 44:24). How awesome a moment that must have been!

The angels were apparently all created simultaneously (Hebrews 2:22; Revelation 5:11). As theologian Louis Berkhof puts it, "Their full number was created in the beginning; there has been no increase in their ranks."[1] Unlike human beings, who are conceived and born at different times in history, all the angels were created at a single moment. Matthew 22:30 would seem to confirm this, in that angels do not marry and thus do not procreate. We find no biblical basis for the idea of little baby angels (Raphael angels) that we often see in gift shops.

Most theologians believe God created angels sometime prior to the creation of earth, and good evidence supports this view. Job 38:7 (NASB), for example, makes reference to the "sons of God" singing at the time earth was created. Scholars largely agree that these "sons of God" are angels. After all, the term "sons of God" is used elsewhere in Job in reference to angels (Job 1:6; 2:1).

James Montgomery Boice is representative of contemporary theologians in saying that "if Job 38:7 is to be taken as referring to angels, as there is every reason for it to be, then even before the creation of the material universe [that is, the planets and stars], there was a vast world of spirit beings."[2] These angelic spirit beings sang as a massive choir when God created the earth.

Elect and Evil Angels

When God created the angels, they were all good and holy (Jude 6; see also Genesis 1:31; 2:3). For God to create anything wicked—such as evil angels—would be inconsistent with His holy character. God did not create Satan and the fallen angels (demons) in a state of wickedness.

Though all the angels were originally created in a state of holiness, we can infer from Scripture that they were subjected to a period of probation. Some of the angels retained their holiness and did not sin, while others—following Lucifer's lead—rebelled against God and fell into great sin (Isaiah 14:12-17; Ezekiel 28:12-16; Revelation 12:9).

Once the angels were put to the test to remain loyal to God or to rebel with Lucifer, their decision seems to have been made permanent in its effect. As theologian Charles Ryrie put it, "Those who successfully passed the probationary test will always stay in that original holy state. Those who failed are now confirmed in their evil, rebellious state."[3]

The good angels are called *elect* angels in 1 Timothy 5:21. They are not elect because they sinned and then were elected for redemption (remember, these angels never sinned during the probationary period). Rather they are elect because God intervened to permanently confirm (or "elect") them in their holiness so they could not possibly sin in the future. Louis Berkhof explains: "They evidently received, in addition to the grace with which all angels were endowed, and which was sufficient to enable them to retain their position, a *special grace of perseverance*, by which they were confirmed in their position."[4] Good angels are therefore now incapable of sinning. The lines have been drawn, and the lines are now absolute.

In keeping with this, the evil angels who rebelled against God are nonredeemable. Those that followed Satan's rebellion fell decisively and are permanently locked in their evil state without recourse or even the possibility of redemption. Theologian Henry Thiessen suggests that "because the angels are a company and not a race, they sinned *individually,* and not in some federal head of the race [as was true with humanity's fall in the person of Adam]. It may be that because of this, God made no provision of salvation for the fallen angels."[5] The evil angels are destined for eternal suffering (Matthew 25:41).

The Abode of the Holy Angels

Though angels apparently have access to the entire universe, and though God sends them on specific errands or assignments on earth (Daniel 9:21), Scripture indicates that they actually live in heaven:

- Micaiah makes reference to "the LORD sitting on his throne with all the host of heaven standing on his right and on his left" (2 Chronicles 18:18). The "host of heaven" refers to the angelic realm.

- Daniel 7:10 speaks of "thousands upon thousands" of angels attending God in heaven, and "ten thousand times ten thousand" (one hundred million) angels standing before Him.

- Isaiah 6:1-6 pictures angels hovering around God's throne, proclaiming, "Holy, holy, holy is the LORD Almighty."

- Jesus speaks of angels "ascending and descending" to and from heaven in John 1:51.

- Hebrews 12:22 exhorts believers, "You have come to...the city of the living God. You have come to thousands upon thousands of angels in joyful assembly."

- John the apostle, author of the book of Revelation, said, "Then I looked and heard the voice of many angels, numbering thousands upon thousands, and ten thousand times ten thousand. They encircled the throne and the living creatures and the elders" (Revelation 5:11).

The natural habitat of angels would seem to be in heaven in the very presence of God. When they have an assigned task to perform, they leave the realm of heaven, complete their task on earth (or wherever God sends them), and then return to heaven.

This, of course, is not to discount the possibility that some angels have prolonged assignments on earth. Several Scriptural passages indicate that God has assigned certain angels to guard and protect believers during their earthly sojourns (Psalm 91:9-11).

The Nature of Angels

As we peruse the pages of Scripture, we discover numerous fascinating facts about the nature of angels:

Angels are personal beings. Angels are persons (spirit persons) with all the attributes of personality:

- *Intelligence:* Angels possess great wisdom (2 Samuel 14:20) and great discernment (2 Samuel 14:17), and they use their minds to look into matters (1 Peter 1:12).

- *Emotions:* Angels are in joyful assembly in God's presence in heaven (Hebrews 12:22). They shouted for joy at the creation (Job 38:7) and rejoice in heaven whenever a sinner repents (Luke 15:7).

- *Will:* Angels give evidence of having a moral will in the many moral decisions they make. For example, an angel exercised his moral will in forbidding John to worship him, acknowledging that worship belongs only to God (Revelation 22:8-9).

Beyond having the attributes of personality, angels engage in personal actions. For example, angels love and rejoice (Luke 15:10), they desire (1 Peter 1:12), they contend (Jude 9; Revelation 12:7), they worship (Hebrews 1:6), they talk (Luke 1:13), and they come and go (Luke 9:26).

Angels are incorporeal and invisible. The word *incorporeal* means "lacking material form or substance." Angels, then, are not material, physical beings; they are spiritual beings and are invisible (Hebrews 1:14). (This doesn't contradict the fact that angels can appear to humans.)

Because angels are invisible, you and I are generally unaware of their activities behind the scenes. We cannot know just how many times angels have intervened on our behalf without our knowledge.

So angels are able to appear visibly to people, but they are normally not visible to the human eye. Recall from the Old Testament that the Lord had to open Balaam's eyes before he could see an angel standing in his way (Numbers 22:31). The prophet Elisha had to ask the Lord to open his servant's eyes; only then was the young man able to see

ANGELS

Scripture reveals many interesting facts about the nature of angels.

Invisible *Hebrews 1:14*	**Powerful** *Psalm 103:20*
Obedient *Matthew 6:10*	**Localized** *Daniel 9:22-23*
Many have wings *Isaiah 6:1-5*	**The Nature of Angels**	**Holy** *Job 5:1*
Can appear as men *Hebrews 13:2*	**Persons** *Revelation 22:8-9*
Innumerable *Revelation 5:11*	**Immortal** *Luke 20:36*

a multitude of angelic beings on the mountainside, protecting them from their enemies (2 Kings 6:17).

Billy Graham has some great insights on man's normal inability to see angels:

> While angels may become visible by choice, our eyes are not constructed to see them ordinarily any more than we can see the dimensions of a nuclear field, the structure of atoms, or the electricity that flows through copper wiring. Our ability to sense reality is limited: The deer of the forest far surpass our human capacity in their keenness of smell. Bats possess a phenomenally sensitive built-in radar system. Some animals can see things in the dark that escape our attention. Swallows and geese possess sophisticated guidance systems that appear to border on the supernatural. So why should we think it strange if men fail to perceive the evidences of angelic presence?[6]

God may have chosen to keep people from normally perceiving angels because of the human tendency to worship and venerate the creation instead of the Creator. Remember what happened to the apostle John? When he was receiving his revelation from the Lord and beheld a mighty angel, his first inclination was to bow down and worship the angel. The angel immediately instructed John to cease and to render worship only to God (Revelation 22:8-9). Perhaps as a safeguard, God purposefully designed man with the inability to perceive His glorious angels.

Angels are localized beings. Despite the fact that angels are spirit beings, they nevertheless seem to have spatial limitations. This seems clear because Scripture portrays them as having to move from one place to another. The angel Gabriel engaged in "swift flight" to travel from heaven to Daniel's side (Daniel 9:21-23). Then, in Daniel 10:10-14, we read about another angel that was delayed on his errand by an evil spirit—apparently a demon (a fallen angel).

After some angels appeared visibly to the shepherds in the field to announce Christ's birth, the angels left them and went back into heaven (Luke 2:15). Angels can only be in one place at a time and must engage in spatial travel in order to go from one place to another. In keeping with this, Christ speaks of angels "ascending and descending" from heaven (John 1:51).

Many angels have wings. Angels are commonly depicted on postcards, cartoons, magazines, and other literature as having wings. But do all angels have wings?

Scripture is clear that at least many angels have wings. For example, the seraphim described in Isaiah 6:1-5 have wings, as do the cherubim Ezekiel saw in his vision (Ezekiel 1:6) and the angels the apostle John saw in his vision (Revelation 4:8). But many other Bible verses about angels make no mention of wings (for example, Hebrews 13:2). What can we conclude from this?

Though all of God's angels could possibly have wings, this is not a necessary inference. Theologian Millard Erickson explains:

> The cherubim and seraphim are represented as winged (Exod. 25:20; Isa. 6:2)...However, we have no assurance that what is true of cherubim and seraphim is true of angels in general. Since there is no explicit reference indicating that angels *as a whole* are winged, we must regard this as at best an inference, but not a necessary inference, from the biblical passages which describe them as flying.[7]

Angels can appear as men. Though angels are by nature incorporeal and invisible, they can nevertheless appear as men (Matthew 1:20; Luke 1:26; John 20:12). Their resemblance to men can be so realistic that the angel is actually taken to *be* a human being (Hebrews 13:2).

Recall from the Old Testament that Abraham welcomed three "men" in the plains of Mamre (Genesis 18:1-8). These "men" walked, talked, sat down, and ate—just like normal men—but they were not men; they were angels (Genesis 18:22; 19:1). We have no scriptural evidence that angels need food for sustenance. But they can apparently appear as men and eat like men while fulfilling their assigned task on earth.

A person who helped you during a time of need could possibly have been an angel that *appeared* as a human. We have no reason to suppose that such appearances cannot occur today just as they did in biblical times.

Angels are powerful. The Scriptures portray the angels as extremely powerful and mighty beings. Psalm 103:20 calls them "mighty ones who do his bidding." Second Thessalonians 1:7 makes reference to God's "powerful angels."

In Matthew 28:2-7 we read that an angel rolled away the giant stone at Jesus' sepulcher. A large wheel of granite would weigh at least two tons (4000 pounds).

Scripture seems to indicate that some angels are more powerful than others. As noted previously, Daniel 10:13 explains that an angel that had been sent by God to accomplish a task was detained by a more powerful fallen angel (a demon). Only when the archangel Michael showed up to render aid was the lesser angel freed to carry out his task.

Angels are not all-powerful. Despite the fact that the angels are very powerful, none of them—the archangel Michael included—are all-powerful like God. They are creatures with creaturely limitations. This is important because angels are not replacements for God, as some angel enthusiasts imply in their writings today. Angels' power is derived from and dependent on God. They exercise their power on God's behalf, never to achieve their own ends.

Angels are holy. The angels who passed their probationary test and did not sin were confirmed in their holiness (1 Timothy 5:21). The word *holy* comes from a root that means "set apart." God's angels are set apart from sin and are set apart to God, to serve Him and carry out His assigned tasks.

Many times Scripture refers to the angels as God's "holy ones" (Job 5:1; 15:15; Psalm 89:7; Daniel 4:13,17,23; 8:13; Jude 14). They are set apart to God in every way. Their commitment to God is complete. Their joy is to please their Creator.

In contrast, the fallen angels (demons) are *un*holy in every way. They are set apart from righteousness and set apart to the devil, to do his unholy bidding. They are against everything related to God. Their time is limited, and their ultimate destiny is the lake of fire (Matthew 25:41).

Angels are obedient. God's holy ones are obedient to Him. In Psalm 103:20, the psalmist exults, "Praise the LORD, you his angels, you mighty ones who do his bidding, who obey his word."

This angelic obedience is reflected in Matthew 6:10. In this part of the Lord's Prayer, we find the words: "Your kingdom come, your will be done on earth as it is in heaven." On the surface, this may seem an unlikely verse in support of the obedience of angels. But many scholars believe this verse carries this idea: "May God's will be done among people on earth as it is already being done by the holy angels in heaven." If this interpretation is correct, then the angels set an example for us of unwavering obedience to God.

Angels have greater knowledge than do human beings. Though angels are not all-knowing (as God is), they nevertheless possess great wisdom and intelligence. God created the angels as a higher order than humans (Psalm 8:5). Therefore, they innately possess a greater knowledge than man.

Angels also gain ever-increasing knowledge through long observation of human activities. Unlike human beings, angels do not have to study the past; they have experienced it. They know from firsthand experience how others have acted and reacted in situations and can predict with greater accuracy how we may act in similar circumstances. The experience of longevity gives angels greater knowledge.

Angels are immortal. Once created, angels never cease to exist. Scripture is clear that angels are not subject to death (Luke 20:36). We read in Daniel 9:21 that the angel Gabriel appeared to the prophet Daniel. More than 500 years later, this same (unaged) Gabriel appeared to Zacharias, the father of John the Baptist (Luke 1).

Because angels are immortal and do not die—and because they do not propagate baby angels (Matthew 22:30)—we can infer that the number of angels has been, is now, and always will be the same.

Angels are innumerable. Scripture refers to "a great company of the heavenly host" (Luke 2:13) and "tens of thousands and thousands of thousands" of angels (Psalm 68:17). The Bible elsewhere describes their number as "myriads of myriads" (Revelation 5:11 NASB). (The word *myriad* means "vast number," "innumerable.") Daniel 7:10, speaking of God, says that "ten thousand times ten thousand stood before him." The number "ten thousand times ten thousand" is 100,000,000 (one hundred million). This is a number almost too vast to fathom. Job 25:3 understandably asks, "Can his forces be numbered?"

The Ranks of Angels

I noted in a previous chapter that our God is a God of order. In keeping with this, Scripture indicates that the angels are organized by rank:

- In Colossians 1:16 we read, "For by [Christ] all things were created: things in heaven and on earth, visible and invisible, whether thrones or powers or rulers or authorities; all things were created by him and for him."

- Colossians 2:10 speaks of Christ, "who is the head over every power and authority."

- First Peter 3:22 refers to Christ, "who has gone into heaven and is at God's right hand—with angels, authorities and powers in submission to him."

- Ephesians 1:21 says that Christ's authority is "far above all rule and authority, power and dominion, and every title that can be given, not only in the present age but also in the one to come."

In the rabbinic (Jewish) thought of the first century, the terms *principalities, powers, thrones,* and *dominions* pointed to the hierarchical organization in the angelic realm. These appellations point to differences of rank.

Defining the various ranks of angels is difficult, but theologians have suggested some likely interpretations. *Thrones* may be angelic beings whose place is in the immediate presence of God—in the immediate vicinity of His glorious throne. They may even sit on their own lesser thrones, demonstrating their derived authority under the greater authority of God. These beings may be invested with regal power to carry out God's sovereign bidding.

Dominions are apparently next in dignity. These angels exercise authority over specific domains as God's agents.

Rulers are next in line and exercise rule as God assigns. We are not told what their rule consists of. But like the other angels in authority, the "ruler angels" reflect the fact that God governs the universe with order and organization.

Authorities are possibly subordinates that serve under one of the other orders of angels. Again, we are not told any specifics, but these angelic beings also carry out imperial responsibility.

Beyond these specific angelic ranks, Scripture also speaks of other angels who have varying levels of authority and dignity—including the archangel Michael, the cherubim, the seraphim, and Gabriel. Let us briefly consider each of these.

The archangel Michael. The word *archangel* implies the highest rank among angels. Apparently Michael is in authority over all the other angels—including the thrones, dominions, rulers, and authorities. The term *archangel* occurs just twice in the New Testament, and in both instances it is singular and is preceded by the definite article ("the" archangel—1 Thessalonians 4:16; Jude 9). Some scholars conclude from this that the term is restricted to a single archangel—Michael.

Even if more than one archangel exists, Michael is undeniably the prominent archangel. He is called one of the "chief princes"

(Daniel 10:13) and "the great prince" (Daniel 12:1), and he seems to lead the other angels (Revelation 12:7). The word *prince* is a title of authority and, when used of angels, refers to beings in authority over a host of angels in battle. Michael, as a chief prince and great prince (and especially as the archangel) would be in authority over all the "prince angels."

Michael's name means "Who is like God?" This name humbly points to God's incomparability. It speaks of Michael's complete and unwavering devotion to God and is in stark contrast with Satan, who in his pride declared, "I will be like the most High" (Isaiah 14:14 KJV).

The cherubim. Scripture depicts the cherubim as powerful and majestic angelic creatures who surround God's throne and defend His holiness from any contamination by sin (Genesis 3:24; Exodus 25:18,20; Ezekiel 1:1-18). They are indescribably beautiful and powerful spirit-beings of the highest order (Ezekiel 1:5-14; 28:12-13,17).

The cherubim guarded Eden after Adam and Eve's expulsion (Genesis 3:24). Figures of cherubim adorned the ark of the covenant, positioned to gaze on the mercy seat (Exodus 25:17-22.). Cherubim also adorned Solomon's temple (1 Kings 6:23-35.). They were represented on the veil that barred the entrance to the holy of holies. As well, the Old Testament portrays cherubim as the chariot on which God descends to the earth (2 Samuel 22:11; Psalm 18:10).

The word *cherubim* apparently means "to guard." This meaning fits well with their function of guarding the entrance of Eden (Genesis 3:24). This meaning also fits with the cherubim on the temple veil that barred entrance into the holy of holies (1 Samuel 4:4; Psalm 80:1). Here the cherubim are apparently guardians of the holiness of God.

The seraphim. The Hebrew term for *seraphim* literally means "burning ones." This speaks of their consuming devotion to serving God. They are afire with devotion to and adoration of God in His unfathomable holiness. They continually proclaim the perfect holiness of God (Isaiah 6:1-5).

Gabriel. The name *Gabriel* literally means "mighty one of God."

The name speaks of the incredible power God entrusted to him. Gabriel stands in the very presence of God (Luke 1:19), evidently in some preeminent sense. His high rank in the angelic realm is obvious from both his name and his continuous standing in God's presence. When carrying out God's bidding, Gabriel apparently has the ability to fly "swiftly"—perhaps faster than any other angel (Daniel 9:21).

In Scripture, Gabriel brings revelation to God's people regarding God's purpose and program. For example, in the Old Testament he appeared to the prophet Daniel and revealed the future by interpreting a vision for Him (8:16-17). In the New Testament, some 500 years later, Gabriel brought the message to Zacharias about the birth of John the Baptist, and he announced Jesus' birth to the virgin Mary (Luke 1:18-19,26-38).

The Ministry of Angels

Hebrews 1:14 reveals that angels are "ministering spirits sent to serve those who will inherit salvation." How do angels minister to the heirs of salvation? Here are a few ways they may serve:

- bringing messages to people (Luke 1:13)
- answering a believer's prayer (Acts 12:7; see also Daniel 10:13)
- giving encouragement in times of danger (Acts 27:23-24)
- restraining evil among humans (Genesis 18:22; 19:1,10-11)
- taking care of believers at the moment of death (Luke 16:22; Jude 9)
- executing judgment (Acts 12:22-23)

The angels' ministry to believers is wide and varied.

One of the angels' key ministries among Christians is to act as guardians. Many Christians wonder whether Christians have their own personal guardian angels that remain with them throughout life. This is a much debated issue. Two primary verses in the New Testament relate to the idea of guardian angels. Matthew 18:10, speaking of little children, says, "See that you do not look down on one of these little ones. For I tell you that their angels in heaven always see the face of my Father in heaven." Then, in Acts 12:15, we find a woman named Rhoda who recognized Peter's voice outside the door of the house, and the others inside—thinking Peter was in jail (where he had been thrown by Jewish authorities)—said, "You're out of your mind...It must be his angel."

A number of theologians have concluded from these two verses that every Christian must have his or her own guardian angel. This view is possible, but many theologians argue that these two verses constitute flimsy support for such an idea. (For example, the angels of the little ones in Matthew 18:10 are in heaven, not with the little ones.) These theologians argue that Scripture seems to indicate that many multitudes of angels are always ready and willing to render help and protection to each individual Christian whenever a need arises.

For example, we read in 2 Kings 6:17 that Elisha and his servant were surrounded by many glorious angels. Luke 16:22 indicates that several angels helped carry Lazarus's soul to Abraham's bosom. Jesus could have called on 12 legions of angels to rescue Him if He had wanted (Matthew 26:53). Psalm 91:9-11 tells us, "If you make the Most High your dwelling—even the LORD, who is my refuge—then no harm will befall you, no disaster will come near your tent. For he will command his angels concerning you to guard you in all your ways." Scripture seems to indicate that the whole company of angels may be involved in protecting all Christians.

Because angels are so active in believers' lives, evangelist Billy Graham says, "Every true believer in Christ should be encouraged and strengthened! Angels are watching; they mark your path. They superintend the events of your life and protect the interest of the Lord God, always working to promote His plans and to bring about His highest will for you."[8] Indeed, Graham says, if we "would only realize how close His ministering angels are, what calm assurance we could have in facing the cataclysms of life. While we do not place our faith directly in angels, we should place it in the God who rules the angels; then we can have peace."[9]

A Thought to Ponder

One day, in heaven, we will join our voices with the voices of angels in worship and praise to our eternal God. The book of Revelation describes this glorious scene in detail:

> After this I looked and there before me was a great multitude that no one could count, from every nation, tribe, people and language, standing before the throne and in front of the Lamb. They were wearing white robes and were holding palm branches in their hands. And they cried out in a loud voice:
>
> > "Salvation belongs to our God,
> > who sits on the throne,
> > and to the Lamb."
>
> All the angels were standing around the throne and around the elders and the four living creatures. They fell down on their faces before the throne and worshiped God, saying:
>
> > "Amen!
> > Praise and glory
> > and wisdom and thanks and honor
> > and power and strength
> > be to our God for ever and ever.
> > Amen!" (Revelation 7:9-12).

Imagine what this will be like—over 100 million angels (Revelation 5:11) and untold millions of the redeemed (7:9) will sing praise to God in unity and harmony. I shiver when I hear a good choir of a few dozen people sing a great anthem. But to have more than a hundred million angels and believers singing in unison...*incredible!*

Discussion Questions

1. Has this chapter changed the way you view angels? How so?

2. Do you think you have experienced angelic assistance in your past—particularly in a time of danger? Explain.

3. How do you reconcile the existence of guardian angels with the fact that Christians still suffer and experience some bad things in life?

4. What impression do you think God's angels have of you as they watch over your life?

Satan
Against Us

Many people in our society today, including some who claim to be Christians, believe Satan is not a real person—an idea no doubt inspired by Satan himself. After all, if we don't believe we have an enemy to contend with, we will not prepare for defense. And if we don't prepare for defense, the enemy can attack at will and work his evil while remaining incognito.

The biblical evidence for the existence and activity of Satan and demons is formidable. Seven books in the Old Testament specifically teach that Satan is real (Genesis, 1 Chronicles, Job, Psalms, Isaiah, Ezekiel, and Zechariah). All of the New Testament writers and 19 of the books talk about him (for example, Matthew 4:10; 12:26; Mark 1:13; 3:23,26; 4:15; Luke 11:18; 22:3; John 13:27). Jesus refers to Satan some 25 times.

The Scriptures are just as certain of Satan's existence as of God's existence. The Scriptures reveal that Satan, formerly named Lucifer, is both a fallen angel and a genuine person. How do we know he is a person? For one thing, Satan has all the attributes of personality—including mind (2 Corinthians 11:3), emotions (Revelation 12:17), and will (Isaiah 14:12-14; 2 Timothy 2:26). The Bible uses personal pronouns to describe him (Matthew 4:1-12), and he performs personal actions (John 8:44; 1 John 3:8; Jude 9).

The Scriptures portray Satan as a created being who, though powerful, has definite limitations. Satan does not possess attributes that belong to God alone, such as being everywhere-present, all-powerful, and all-knowing.

Though Satan possesses creaturely limitations, he is nevertheless extremely powerful and influential in the world. He is the "prince of this world" (John 12:31), "the god of this age" (2 Corinthians 4:4), and the "ruler of the kingdom of the air" (Ephesians 2:2). He deceives the whole world (Revelation 12:9; 20:3). He has power in the governmental realm (Matthew 4:8-9; 2 Corinthians 4:4), the physical realm (Luke 13:11,16; Acts 10:38), the angelic realm (Jude 9; Ephesians 6:11-12), and the ecclesiastical (church) realm (Revelation 2:9; 3:9). Clearly, Christians should be very concerned about Satan.

Satan's Fall

Many scholars believe Ezekiel 28 and Isaiah 14 provide evidence that Lucifer led a rebellion against God, at which time his name was changed to Satan. Ezekiel 28 (NASB) describes a being who was full of wisdom and perfect in beauty and who had the seal of perfection (verse 12). He also had the nature of a cherub angel (verse 14), was initially blameless and sinless (verse 15) on the holy mount of God (verses 13-14), and was cast out of the mountain of God and thrown to the earth in judgment (verse 16). Such things cannot describe a mere human being, so many conclude this is a reference to Lucifer.

One theologian has suggested that Lucifer...

> awoke in the first moment of his existence in the full-orbed beauty and power of his exalted position; surrounded by all the magnificence which God gave him. He saw himself as

above all the hosts in power, wisdom, and beauty. Only at the throne of God itself did he see more than he himself possessed...Before his fall he may be said to have occupied the role of prime minister for God, ruling possibly over the universe but certainly over this world.[1]

Lucifer was created in a state of perfection, and he remained perfect in his ways until iniquity was found in him (Ezekiel 28:12,15). What was this iniquity? We read in verse 17, "Your heart became proud on account of your beauty, and you corrupted your wisdom because of your splendor." Lucifer apparently became so impressed with his own beauty, intelligence, power, and position that he began to desire for himself the honor and glory that belong to God alone. The sin that corrupted Lucifer was self-generated pride. Isaiah 14:12-17 confirms this and describes Lucifer's five boastful "I wills..."

"I will ascend to heaven" (Isaiah 14:13). Apparently Lucifer wanted to abide in heaven and desired equal recognition alongside God Himself.

"I will raise my throne above the stars of God" (Isaiah 14:13). The "stars" likely refer to the angels of God. Lucifer apparently desired to rule over the angelic realm with the same authority as God.

"I will sit enthroned on the mount of assembly, on the utmost heights of the sacred mountain" (Isaiah 14:13). Scripture elsewhere indicates that the "mount of assembly" is the center of God's kingdom rule (Isaiah 2:2; Psalm 48:2). So we may say that Satan desired to rule over human beings in place of the Messiah.

"I will ascend above the tops of the clouds" (Isaiah 14:14). The Bible often uses clouds to metaphorically represent God's glory (Exodus 13:21; 40:28-34; Job 37:15-16; Matthew 26:64; Revelation 14:14). Apparently Lucifer sought a glory equal to that of God Himself.

"I will make myself like the Most High" (Isaiah 14:14). Scripture says God possesses heaven and earth (Genesis 14:18-19). Apparently Lucifer sought the supreme position of the universe for himself.

God rightfully judged this mighty angelic being: "I threw you to the earth" (Ezekiel 28:17). As a result of Lucifer's heinous sin, God banished him from heaven (Isaiah 14:12). He became corrupt, and his name changed from Lucifer ("morning star") to Satan ("adversary"). His power became completely perverted (Isaiah 14:12,16-17).

Lucifer's rebellion represents the actual beginning of sin in the universe—preceding Adam and Eve's fall by an indeterminate time. Sin originated when Lucifer freely chose to rebel against the Creator—with full understanding of the issues involved.

Apparently, one-third of the angels freely chose to follow Lucifer in his rebellion. Many scholars believe the first five verses of Revelation 12 contain a mini-history of Satan, with verse 4 referring to the fall of the angels who followed him: "His [Satan's] tail swept a third of the stars out of the sky and flung them to the earth." The word *stars* is sometimes used of angels in the Bible (Job 38:7). If *stars* refers to angels in Revelation 12:4, then after Lucifer rebelled against God, he evidently was able to draw a third of the angelic realm after him in this rebellion. The New Testament calls these fallen angels *demons*.

The demons are highly committed to their dark prince, Satan. Theologian Merrill Unger draws attention to this:

> These spirits, having [made] an irrevocable choice to follow Satan, instead of remaining loyal to their Creator, have become irretrievably confirmed in wickedness, and irreparably abandoned to delusion. Hence, they are in full sympathy with their prince, and render him willing service in their varied ranks and positions of service in his highly organized kingdom of evil.[2]

Scripture designates demons as "unclean spirits" (Matthew 10:1 NASB), "evil spirits" (Luke 7:21), and "spiritual forces of evil" (Ephesians 6:12). These terms point to the demons' immoral nature. This may help explain why many people involved in the occult are involved in immorality.

Satan's Names

We learn much about Satan and his work from his various names and titles. Here is a sampling of these names:

- *Accuser of our brethren* (Revelation 12:10 NASB). The Greek of this verse indicates that accusing God's people is Satan's continuous, ongoing work. He never lets up. Satan accuses God's people "day and night." He opposes God's people in two ways. First, he brings

SATAN'S NAMES

Satan is known by many names in Scripture:

Devil
Matthew 4:1

God of this age
2 Corinthians 4:4

Roaring lion
1 Peter 5:8

Evil one
1 John 5:19

Adversary
1 Peter 5:8

Satan's Names

Prince of this world
John 12:31

Murderer
John 8:44

Enemy
Matthew 13:39

Beelzebub
Matthew 12:24

Father of lies
John 8:44

Serpent
Genesis 3:1

Tempter
Matthew 4:3

Accuser of the brethren
Revelation 12:10

charges against believers before God (Zechariah 3:1). Second, he accuses believers to their own conscience.

- *Devil* (Matthew 4:1). This word carries the idea of an adversary as well as a slanderer. The devil was and is Christ's adversary; he is the adversary of all who follow Christ. Satan slanders God to man (Genesis 3:1-7) and man to God (Job 1:9; 2:4). (A slanderer is a person who uses false reports to injure someone else's reputation.)

- *Enemy* (Matthew 13:39). This word comes from a root meaning "hatred." It characterizes Satan's attitude in an absolute sense—he hates both God and those who follow Him.

- *Adversary* (1 Peter 5:8 NASB). This word indicates that Satan opposes us and stands against us in every way he can.

- *Beelzebub* (Matthew 12:24). This word literally means "lord of the flies," carrying the idea of "lord of filth." The devil corrupts everything he touches. He is no doubt behind the filth of pornography, which tempts not only unbelievers but believers as well.

- *Evil one* (1 John 5:19). He opposes all that is good and promotes all that is evil. He is the very embodiment of evil.

- *Father of lies* (John 8:44). The word *father* is used here metaphorically of the originator of a family of deceitful people. Satan was the first and greatest liar.

- *Roaring lion* (1 Peter 5:8-9). This graphic simile depicts Satan's strength and destructiveness. He seeks to mutilate Christians.

- *Tempter* (Matthew 4:3). Theologian Henry Thiessen says, "This name indicates his constant purpose and endeavor to incite man to sin. He presents the most plausible excuses and suggests the most striking advantages for sinning."[3]

- *Serpent* (Genesis 3:1; Revelation 12:9). This word symbolizes the origin of sin in the Garden of Eden. The serpent is treacherous, deceitful, venomous, and murderous.

- *Murderer* (John 8:44). This word literally means "man killer" (1 John 3:12,15). Hatred is the motive that leads one to commit murder. Satan hates both God and His children, so he has a genuine motive for murder.

- *God of this age* (2 Corinthians 4:4). This does not mean Satan is deity. It simply means that this is an evil age, and Satan is its god in the sense that he is the head of it.

- *Prince of this world* (John 12:31). The key word here is *world.* This word refers not to the physical earth but to a vast anti-God system that Satan has promoted and that conforms to his wicked ideals, aims, and methods.

From this brief survey of names, we can see that Satan's purpose is to thwart God's plan in every area and by every means possible.

Satan's Vast Experience

Satan has vast experience bringing people down. In fact, his experience is far greater than any human's has ever been. As theologian Charles Ryrie put it...

> By his very longevity Satan has acquired a breadth and depth of experience which he matches against the limited knowledge of man. He has observed other believers in every conceivable situation, thus enabling him to predict with accuracy how we will respond to circumstances. Although Satan is not omniscient, his wide experience and observation of man throughout his entire history on earth give him knowledge which is far superior to anything any man could have.[4]

Because of his vast experience, Satan knows the best way to foul you up. He is a master tempter, with thousands of years of practice of luring people into sin. Christian, beware!

Satan as the "Ape" of God

Augustine called the devil *Simius Dei*—"the ape of God." Satan is the great counterfeiter. He mimics God in many ways. "The principal tactic Satan uses to attack God and His program in general is to offer a counterfeit kingdom and program."[5] Second Corinthians 11:14 hints at this by saying Satan masquerades as an angel of light.

In what ways does Satan act as the ape of God? Consider the following:

- Satan has his own church—the "synagogue of Satan" (Revelation 2:9).

- Satan has his own ministers—ministers of darkness who bring false sermons (2 Corinthians 11:4-5).

- Satan has formulated his own system of theology called "doctrines of demons" (1 Timothy 4:1 NASB; Revelation 2:24).

- His ministers proclaim his gospel—"a gospel other than the one we preached to you" (Galatians 1:8).

- Satan has his own throne (Revelation 13:2) and his own worshippers (13:4).

- Satan inspires false Christs and self-constituted messiahs (Matthew 24:4-5).

- Satan employs false teachers who bring in "destructive heresies" (2 Peter 2:1).

- Satan sends out false prophets (Matthew 24:11).

- Satan sponsors false apostles who imitate the true apostles of Christ (2 Corinthians 11:13).

One theologian has concluded that "Satan's plan and purposes have been, are, and always will be to seek to establish a rival rule to God's kingdom. He is promoting a system of which he is the head and which stands in opposition to God and His rule in the universe."[6]

Fallen Angels Among Unbelievers

Second Corinthians 4:4 indicates that Satan blinds the minds of unbelievers to the truth of the gospel. This passage indicates that

Satan inhibits the unbeliever's ability to think or reason properly about spiritual matters. One of the ways Satan seems to do this is by leading people to think that any way to heaven is as acceptable as another. In other words, Satan promotes the idea that one does not need to believe in Jesus as the only means to salvation.

Satan also seeks to snatch the Word of God from the hearts of unbelievers when they hear it (Luke 8:12). Demons, under Satan's lead, seek to disseminate false doctrine (1 Timothy 4:1). As well, they influence false prophets (1 John 4:1-4) and entice men to worship idols (Leviticus 17:7; Deuteronomy 32:17; Psalm 106:36-38). In short, fallen angels do all they can to spread spiritual deception.

Scripture also portrays demons as inflicting physical diseases on people, such as muteness (Matthew 9:33), blindness (Matthew 12:22), and epilepsy (Matthew 17:15-18). Further, they afflict people with mental disorders (Mark 5:4-5; 9:22; Luke 8:27-29; 9:37-42), promote self-destructive behavior (Mark 5:5; Luke 9:42), and are even responsible for some people's deaths (Revelation 9:14-19).

Of course, we must be careful to note that even though demons can cause physical illnesses, Scripture distinguishes natural illnesses from demon-caused illnesses (Matthew 4:24; Mark 1:32; Luke 7:21; 9:1; Acts 5:16). Theologian Millard Erickson notes that numerous healings don't mention demons:

> In Matthew, for example, no mention is made of demon exorcism in the case of the healing of the centurion's servant (8:5-13), the woman with the hemorrhage of twelve years' duration (9:19-20), the two blind men (9:27-30), the man with the withered hand (12:9-14), and those who touched the fringe of Jesus' garment (14:35-36).[7]

We must not presume we are being afflicted by a demon every time we get sick.

Fallen Angels Among Believers

Fallen angels are also very active opposing believers in various ways:

- Satan tempts Christians to sin (Ephesians 2:1-3; 1 Thessalonians 3:5).

- Satan tempts Christians to lie (Acts 5:3).

- Satan tempts Christians to commit sexually immoral acts (1 Corinthians 7:5).

- Satan accuses and slanders Christians (Revelation 12:10).

- Satan sows tares among Christians (Matthew 13:38-39).

- Satan incites persecutions against Christians (Revelation 2:10).

- Satan plants doubt in believers' minds (Genesis 3:1-5).

- Satan fosters spiritual pride in Christians' hearts (1 Timothy 3:6).

- Demons instigate jealousy and division among Christians (James 3:13-16).

- Demons hinder answers to believers' prayers (Daniel 10:12-20).

Discernment on Difficult Issues

Discussions about the devil and demons often lead to controversy, even among churchgoing Christians. Let's take a discerning look at some of these difficult issues.

Can Christians Be Demon Possessed?

A demon-possessed person has a demon residing within and exerting direct control and influence. This is not the same as mere demon influence. The work of the demon in the latter case is external; demon possession is from within.

A demon-possessed person may manifest unusual, superhuman

strength (Mark 5:2-4). He may act in bizarre ways such as going nude and living among tombs rather than in a house (Luke 8:27). The possessed person often engages in self-destructive behavior (Matthew 17:15). These are just a few of the biblical signs of demon possession.

I often encounter churchgoers who believe Christians themselves can be demon possessed. According to our definition, however, a Christian cannot be possessed by a demon since he is indwelt by the Holy Spirit (1 Corinthians 6:19). I like the way my old friend Walter Martin put it. He said that when the devil knocks on the door of the Christian's heart, the Holy Spirit opens it and says, "Get lost!"

Scripture does not include a single reference to a Christian being demon possessed. Christians are certainly afflicted by the devil but not possessed by him.

God has delivered Christians from Satan's domain. As Colossians 1:13 puts it, God "has rescued us from the dominion of darkness and brought us into the kingdom of the Son he loves." Furthermore, we must remember that "the one who is in you is greater than the one who is in the world" (1 John 4:4). This statement would not make much sense if Christians could be possessed by the devil.

Having said this, however, we must acknowledge that even though a Christian cannot be possessed, he can nevertheless be oppressed or influenced by demonic powers. But the oppression or influence is always external to the Christian, not internal.

Does the Devil Still Have Access to Heaven?

Many Christians wonder whether the devil still has access to heaven. I believe that he does. The events that took place in the book of Job make clear that Satan has the freedom to appear before God and engage in discourse with Him (Job 1:6; 2:1). Revelation 12:10 tells us that Satan is the "accuser of our brothers," indicating that he goes before God's throne and makes slanderous statements about the saints. In the future tribulation period, however, God will decisively cast the devil out of heaven (Revelation 12:9). Some time later God will throw Satan into the lake of fire (Revelation 20:10 NASB). Our enemy's time is definitely limited.

Can Satan Read Our Minds?

I'm not sure why, but I'm often asked if Satan can read our minds. I personally do not think he can. Scripture indicates that only God has the ability to "know the hearts of all men" (1 Kings 8:39). God is all-knowing (Matthew 11:21), and He certainly knows our thoughts: "Before a word is on my tongue you know it completely, O LORD" (Psalm 139:4). Satan, by contrast, is a creature with creaturely limitations.

Nevertheless, Satan is a highly intelligent being (Ezekiel 28:12) who has had thousands of years of experience dealing with human beings, and so he may give the appearance of knowing our thoughts. Satan is also the head of a vast network of demonic spirits who answer to him (Revelation 12:4,7), and this too may give the appearance of Satan being all-knowing. But again, he is just a creature with creaturely limitations. Scripture never indicates that he can read our minds.

Can Christians Bind the Devil?

Christians often claim that references to binding and loosing in the New Testament indicate that we have authority over the powers of darkness (Matthew 18:18). This is a common misconception.

God has certainly given us all we need to have victory over the devil (see Ephesians 6:11-18), but the New Testament verses that speak of binding and loosing have nothing whatsoever to do with spiritual warfare.

In Matthew 18:18, for example, Jesus said, "Whatever you bind on earth will be bound in heaven, and whatever you loose on earth will be loosed in heaven." The terms *bind* and *loose* were Jewish idioms indicating that what is announced on earth has already been determined in heaven. To bind meant to forbid, refuse, or prohibit; to loose meant to permit or allow. We can announce the prohibition or allowance of certain things on earth because heaven (or God) has already made an announcement on these matters.

In Matthew 18 Jesus was speaking only about church discipline. Those members of the church who sin but then repent are to be "loosed" (that is, they are to be restored to fellowship), while those who are unrepentant are to be "bound" (that is, they are to be removed from fellowship). We can make these pronouncements on earth because heaven (God) has already made them.

The context of this passage has nothing to do with spiritual warfare, so we cannot conclude that God has given Christians the power to bind demons.

The Christian's Defense

We as Christians should be very thankful that God has made provision for our defense against Satan and his fallen angels. What is this defense?

Christ's intercession. To begin, we must ever keep in mind that twice the New Testament tells us the Lord Jesus lives in heaven to make intercession for us (Romans 8:34; Hebrews 7:25). In other words, Jesus prays for us on a regular basis. Certainly Christ's intercession for us includes the kind of intercession He made for His disciples in John 17:15, where He asked the Father to keep them safe from the evil one.

Spiritual armor. God has provided us with spiritual armor for our defense (Ephesians 6:11-18). Each piece of armor is important and serves its own special purpose. But you and I must choose to put on this armor. God doesn't force us to dress in it. We do it by choice. Without wearing this spiritual armor—the belt of truth, the breastplate of righteousness, the shield of faith, and the like—you and I don't stand a chance against the forces of darkness. But with the armor on, victory is ours. Wearing this armor includes such things as living in righteousness and obedience to God's will, having faith in God, and using the Word of God effectively. These are the things that spell defeat for the devil in your life.

The Word of God. Using of the Word of God effectively is especially important for spiritual victory. Jesus used the Word of God to defeat the devil during His wilderness temptations (Matthew 4). We must learn to do the same. The greater exposure we have to Scripture, the more the Spirit can use this mighty sword in our lives. If we never read or study our Bibles, we are terribly exposed to defeat and despair. Reading our Bibles regularly helps ensure our safety.

Knowledge. Scripture specifically instructs us that each believer must be informed and alert to Satan's attacks (1 Peter 5:8). To defeat an enemy, you need to know as much as you can about him—including his tactics. The apostle Paul says, "We are not [to be] ignorant of his schemes" (2 Corinthians 2:11 NASB). We find all the information we need about this enemy and his schemes in the Word of God.

Resistance. The Bible encourages us to take a decisive stand against Satan. James 4:7 says, "Resist the devil, and he will flee from you." This is not a one-time resistance. Rather, we must steadfastly resist the devil on a day-to-day basis. And when we do, he will flee from us. Ephesians 6:13-14 tells us to stand firm against the devil. We can't do this in our own strength, but in the strength of Christ we can. After all, Christ "disarmed the rulers and authorities…[and] made a public display of them, having triumphed over them" (Colossians 2:15 NASB).

Reconciliation. We must not give place to the devil by letting "the sun go down while you are still angry" toward someone (Ephesians 4:27). Permitting unrighteous anger to dwell in our hearts gives the devil a chance to work in our lives.

The Holy Spirit. We are instructed to rely on the indwelling spirit of God, remembering that "the one who is in you is greater than the one who is in the world" (1 John 4:4).

Prayer. We should pray for ourselves and for each other. Jesus set an example for us in the Lord's Prayer by teaching us to pray, "Deliver us from the evil one" (Matthew 6:13). This should be a daily prayer. Jesus also showed us how to pray for others when He prayed for Peter: "Simon, Simon, Satan has asked to sift you as wheat. But I have prayed for you, Simon, that your faith may not fail" (Luke 22:31-32). We should pray for each other that we will maintain a strong faith in the face of adversity.

Avoiding the occult. Of course, the believer should never dabble in the occult, for this gives the devil opportunity to work in our lives (Deuteronomy 18:10-11; Romans 16:19).

Assurance in God. Finally, we must remember that Satan is on a leash. He cannot go beyond what God will allow him (the book of Job makes this abundantly clear). We should rest secure in the fact that God is in control of the universe and realize that Satan cannot simply do as he pleases in our lives.

By following these disciplines, we will have victory over Satan and his host of demons. And remember, above all, that successfully defeating the powers of darkness rests not on what you can do in your own strength but on what Christ has already done. Indeed, you are more than a conqueror through Him who loved us (Romans 8:37).

Discussion Questions

1. What would you say to a person who told you he or she believes that Satan is just a biblical myth?

2. What do you think are the most important things we learn about Satan from his names?

3. Do you feel that Satan or any of his demons are targeting you in any area of your life? How so?

4. Do you struggle with pride? Sexual temptations? Jealousy? Lying? Have you considered the possibility that Satan or his demons may be actively seeking your downfall in these areas?

5. Do you think a Christian can be demon possessed? Why or why not?

6. Summarize the Christian's defense against the devil.

14

God's Prophecies
of the End Times

I noted earlier that in the New Testament, Jesus fulfilled hundreds
of specific Old Testament messianic prophecies—including that He
would be born in Bethlehem (Micah 5:2), be born of a virgin (Isaiah
7:14), and be pierced for our sins (Zechariah 12:10). The Bible also
contains many specific prophecies of end-time events and persons
that will be fulfilled just as literally. These include prophecies of the
rapture, the tribulation period, the Antichrist and his false prophet,
God's two prophetic witnesses, Armageddon, the second coming,
the millennial kingdom, and the new heavens and new earth. As we
ponder these events and persons, we can only respond with awe at
God's sovereign control over human history.

The Rapture

The rapture is that glorious event in which the dead in Christ
will rise and living Christians will be instantly translated into their

resurrection bodies—and both groups will be caught up to meet Christ in the air and taken back to heaven (1 Thessalonians 4:13-17). This means one generation of Christians will never pass through death's door. They will be alive on earth one moment; the next moment they will be instantly translated into their resurrection bodies and caught up to meet Christ in the air. What a moment that will be!

Christians seem to love to debate end-time issues. Perhaps the hottest debate is about the timing of the rapture. Four primary views have surfaced:

- *Partial rapturism* is the view that only spiritual Christians will be raptured when Christ returns. Carnal Christians will be left behind. Throughout the tribulation period, as more Christians become spiritual, they too will be raptured. Such raptures may continue to occur throughout the tribulation period. (Hardly anyone holds to this view anymore.)

- *Pretribulationism* is the view that Christ will rapture the entire church before any part of the tribulation begins. This means the church will not go through the judgments prophesied in the book of Revelation (chapters 4–18).

- *Posttribulationism* is the view that Christ will rapture the church after the tribulation at the second coming of Christ. This means the church will go through the time of judgment prophesied in the book of Revelation, but believers will be kept safe through the judgments.

- *Midtribulationism* is the view that Christ will rapture the church in the middle of the tribulation period. The two witnesses of Revelation 11, who are caught up to heaven, represent the church.

Most Christians today are either "pretribs" or "posttribs." I believe the pretrib position, the majority view among evangelicals, is most consistent with the biblical testimony. Revelation 3:10 indicates that believers will be kept from the actual hour of testing that is coming on the whole world. Further, no Old Testament passage on the tribulation mentions the church (Deuteronomy 4:29-30; Jeremiah 30:4-11; Daniel 8:24-27; 12:1-2), and no New Testament passage on the tribulation mentions the church (Matthew 13:30,39-42,48-50; 24:15-31; 1 Thessalonians 1:9-10; 5:4-9; 2 Thessalonians 2:1-12; Revelation 4-18).

Granted, Scripture does say Christians will live during the tribulation period (for example, Revelation 6:9-11). But pretribs believe these people become Christians sometime after the rapture. Perhaps they become convinced of the truth of Christianity after witnessing millions of Christians supernaturally vanish off the planet at the rapture. Or perhaps they become Christians as a result of the ministry of the 144,000 Jewish Christians introduced in Revelation 7 (who themselves apparently come to faith in Christ after the rapture). Many may become Christians as a result of the miraculous ministry of the two witnesses of Revelation 11, prophets who apparently have the same powers as Moses and Elijah.

In any event, Scripture assures us that the church is not appointed to wrath (Romans 5:9; 1 Thessalonians 1:9-10; 5:9). This means the church cannot go through the "great day of wrath" in the tribulation period (Revelation 6:17).

All throughout Scripture, God protects His people before judgment falls (see 2 Peter 2:5-9). Enoch was transferred to heaven before the judgment of the flood. Noah and his family were in the ark before the judgment of the flood. Lot was taken out of Sodom before judgment was poured out on Sodom and Gomorrah. The firstborn among the Hebrews in Egypt were sheltered by the blood of the Paschal lamb before judgment fell. The spies were safely out of Jericho and Rahab was secured before judgment fell on Jericho. So too will the church be secured safely (by means of the rapture) before judgment falls in the tribulation period.

In addition to recognizing this substantial theological support for the pretrib view, I believe the posttrib view has some significant theological problems. One problem is, who will populate the millennial kingdom in mortal bodies?

Scripture is clear that when Christ comes again at the end of the tribulation period (the second coming), some Christians will enter His millennial kingdom in their mortal bodies. We know this to be true because they will continue to be married to their spouses (Isaiah 4:1-3), they will continue to bear children (Isaiah 65:20-23; Jeremiah 23:3-6; 30:19-20), and even though longevity will be extended, aging and death will occur among them (Isaiah 65:20-23). These people will clearly not yet be glorified with resurrection bodies.

The problem for posttribs, then, is this: How can mortal Christians enter the millennial kingdom if the rapture occurs at the end of the tribulation period? Once raptured (and resurrected), Christians are no longer married to spouses and can no longer have babies. No mortal believers would be left to enter the millennial kingdom.

This is obviously not a problem for the pretrib view, which holds that the rapture occurs before the tribulation period. In this view, other people become Christians during the tribulation period, and these Christians enter the millennial kingdom in their mortal bodies.

Another problem for posttribulationism is, who are the participants in the judgment of the nations (Matthew 25:31-46)? Scripture tells us that after Christ returns at the second coming, He will separate the sheep from the goats (still on earth) according to the way they treated Christ's "brothers"—feeding them, clothing them, and visiting them in prison.

The problem is, if all believers are raptured (and resurrected) at the end of the tribulation, then who are the sheep and the brothers? No separation of the sheep from the goats could occur on earth because all of the sheep (and the brothers) would have just been raptured and be up in the air with Christ. They would thus already be separated from unbelievers. Matthew 25:31-46 just can't be made to fit in a posttrib scenario.

A third problem for posttribulationism has to do with John 14:1-3:

> Do not let your hearts be troubled. Trust in God; trust
> also in me. In my Father's house are many rooms; if it were

not so, I would have told you. I am going there to prepare a place for you. And if I go and prepare a place for you, I will come back and take you to be with me that you also may be where I am.

In the posttrib scenario, all believers are raptured and meet Christ in the air, only to return back to the earth with Christ. But John 14:1-3 says that Christ will take believers from the earth to the place Christ has prepared for them. This passage is not a problem for the pretrib view, which says that Christ will rapture the church before the tribulation period begins and take them to the place He has prepared in heaven.

I believe a pretrib rapture fits best with all the scriptural facts. Let me hasten to add, though, that the exact timing of the rapture is not worth fighting about. Let's keep in mind that the different views of the rapture may disagree over the precise timing of end-time events, but they all agree on the big picture:

- A rapture will occur.
- Judgment will also occur.
- Christians will live forever with Jesus in heaven.

In the long haul—after we've been with Christ for billions of years in heaven—the question of whether the rapture happened before or after the tribulation period will truly seem insignificant.

The Tribulation

Scripture reveals that the tribulation will be a definite time of great travail at the end of the age (Matthew 24:29-35). It will be so severe that no period in history, past or future, will equal it (Matthew 24:21). The Bible calls it the time of Jacob's trouble, for it is a judgment on Messiah-rejecting Israel (Jeremiah 30:7; Daniel 12:1-4). God will also judge the nations for their sin and for rejecting Christ

(Isaiah 26:21; Revelation 6:15-17). The period will last seven years (Daniel 9:24,27).

This will be a period of wrath (Revelation 11:18), judgment (Revelation 14:7), indignation (Isaiah 26:20-21), trial (Revelation 3:10), trouble (Jeremiah 30:7), destruction (Joel 1:15), darkness (Amos 5:18), desolation (Daniel 9:27), overturning (Isaiah 24:1-4), and punishment (Isaiah 24:20-21). The term *tribulation* is quite appropriate. No passage alleviates to any degree the severity of this time that will come upon the earth.

The tribulation is the focus of Revelation 4 through 18. In this book, we read about the seal judgments, the trumpet judgments, and the bowl judgments that God will pour out on humankind in steadily increasing intensity. The suffering will be immense; the death toll immeasurable.

Notable Persons of the Tribulation Period

During the seven-year tribulation period, notable persons will emerge—some as Satan's instruments, others as God's:

The Antichrist. The apostle Paul warned of a "man of lawlessness," who is the Antichrist (2 Thessalonians 2:3,8-9). This individual will perform counterfeit signs and wonders and deceive many people during the tribulation period (2 Thessalonians 2:9-10). The apostle John describes this anti-God individual in the book of Revelation as a beast (Revelation 13:1-10). This demon-inspired individual will rise to political prominence in the tribulation period, seek to dominate the world, attempt to destroy the Jews, persecute all true believers, set himself up as God in a rebuilt Jewish temple, and set up his own kingdom (Revelation 13). He will glorify himself with arrogant and boastful words (2 Thessalonians 2:4). He is destined for the lake of fire (Revelation 19:20 NASB).

The false prophet. The false prophet—an assistant to the Antichrist—will entice the world to worship the Antichrist (Revelation 13:11-12). He too will perform great signs and wonders, even causing fire to come down from heaven (13:13). He will force people all over the world to receive the mark of the Antichrist on their right hand or forehead, without which they cannot buy or sell (13:16-17). To receive this mark, however, ensures one of receiving God's wrath. Many Christians will be martyred for refusing to receive the mark. At Jesus' second coming, He will defeat and destroy this false prophet (19:11-20).

The 144,000. Revelation 7:4 makes reference to 144,000 Jews—12,000 from each tribe of Israel—who supernaturally become Christians during the tribulation period and are divinely protected for service to God. The Bible doesn't specifically tell us their function, but many theologians believe they may engage in evangelism all over the earth.

I believe this group may fulfill God's original call of Israel to be "a light to the Gentiles." God originally called the Jews to tell the other nations of the earth the good news about God (Isaiah 42:6; 49:6). Obviously, Israel failed at this task. The Jews didn't even recognize the true Messiah when He showed up! The 144,000 Jews of Revelation 7 may be the ones who will fulfill God's original calling on Israel by witnessing all over the earth during the tribulation period. Innumerable conversions will apparently occur during this time, even among the Jews (Zechariah 13:8-9; Romans 11:26-27).

The two witnesses. The two witnesses mentioned in Revelation 11:3 receive power from God in much the same way that Moses and Elijah did. They wear sackcloth, a style of clothing that often signifies repentance. They will prophesy for 1260 days, and their message will no doubt be a call to repent. Scripture tells us this about them:

> If anyone tries to harm them, fire comes from their mouths and devours their enemies. This is how anyone who wants to harm them must die. These men have power to shut up the sky so that it will not rain during the time they are prophesying; and they have power to turn the waters into blood and to strike the earth with every kind of plague as often as they want.

Now when they have finished their testimony, the beast that comes up from the Abyss will attack them, and overpower and kill them. Their bodies will lie in the street of the great city, which is figuratively called Sodom and Egypt, where also their Lord was crucified. For three and a half days men from every people, tribe, language and nation will gaze on their bodies and refuse them burial. The inhabitants of the earth will gloat over them and will celebrate by sending each other gifts, because these two prophets had tormented those who live on the earth.

But after the three and a half days a breath of life from God entered them, and they stood on their feet, and terror struck those who saw them. Then they heard a loud voice from heaven saying to them, "Come up here." And they went up to heaven in a cloud, while their enemies looked on (Revelation 11:5-12).

What a moment this will be. Here the ungodly people of the earth are having a party, giving each other gifts to celebrate the death of the two prophets. Suddenly, they stand up alive, and terror overtakes everyone. Then God transports them up to heaven. What a powerful witness this will be of God's awesome power.

Armageddon

Human suffering will steadily escalate during the tribulation period. First are the seal judgments: bloodshed, famine, death, economic upheaval, a great earthquake, and cosmic disturbances (Revelation 6). Then come the trumpet judgments: hail and fire mixed with blood, the sea turning to blood, water turning bitter, further cosmic disturbances, affliction by demonic scorpions, and the death of a third of humankind (Revelation 8:6-9:21). Then come the bowl judgments: horribly painful sores on people, more bodies of water turning to blood, the death of all sea creatures, people being scorched by the sun, total darkness engulfing the land, a devastating earthquake, and much more (Revelation 16). Worse comes to worst, however, when these already traumatized human beings find themselves engaged in a catastrophic series of battles called Armageddon.

The word *Armageddon* literally means "Mount of Megiddo" and refers to a location about 60 miles north of Jerusalem. This is the location of Barak's battle with the Canaanites (Judges 4) and Gideon's battle with the Midianites (Judges 7). This will be the site for the final horrific battles of humankind just prior to the second coming (Revelation 16:16).

Napoleon is reported to have once commented that this site is perhaps the greatest battlefield he had ever seen. Of course, the battles Napoleon fought will dim in comparison to Armageddon. So horrible will Armageddon be that no one would survive if not for Christ coming again (Matthew 24:22).

The Second Coming of Jesus Christ

Explaining away the second coming of Jesus Christ is fashionable in our day. Some liberal Christians claim the second coming is a symbolic reference to finding God again in our hearts. Some cultists believe the second coming is a spiritual event (that is, Jesus is not coming physically and visibly). Still others try to argue that the second coming refers not to Jesus but to some other religious leader who will guide the world into a new age of enlightenment.

In reality, the second coming is that event when Jesus Christ—the King of kings and Lord of lords—will return to earth in glory at the end of the present age and set up His kingdom. The very same Jesus who ascended into heaven will come again at the second coming (Acts 1:11).

The second coming will be a visible, physical, bodily return of the glorified Jesus. One key Greek word used to describe the second coming of Christ in the New Testament is *apokalupsis*. This word carries the basic meaning of "revelation," "visible disclosure," "unveiling," and "removing the cover" from something that is hidden. The word is used of Christ's second coming in 1 Peter 4:13 (NASB): "To the degree that you share the sufferings of Christ, keep on rejoicing; so that also at the *revelation* of his glory, you may rejoice with exultation."

Another Greek word used of Christ's second coming in the New Testament is *epiphaneia,* which means "to appear," "to shine forth." In Titus 2:13 (NASB) Paul is "looking for the blessed hope and the *appearing* of the glory of our great God and Savior, Christ Jesus." In 1 Timothy 6:14 (NASB) Paul urges Timothy to "keep the command-ment without stain or reproach until the *appearing* of our Lord Jesus Christ."

The second coming will be a universal experience; every eye will witness the event. Revelation 1:7 says, "Look, he is coming with the clouds, and every eye will see him, even those who pierced him; and all the peoples of the earth will mourn because of him." Moreover, at the time of the second coming, magnificent signs will appear in the heavens (Matthew 24:29-30). Christ will come as the King of kings and Lord of Lords with many crowns on His head—crowns that represent absolute sovereignty. His eyes will be like blazing fire (Revelation 19:11-16).

What an awesome spectacle this will be. I can't wait!

The Millennial Kingdom

Following the second coming of Christ, Jesus will personally set up His kingdom on earth. In theological circles, this is known as the millennial kingdom. This is another doctrine that Christians seemingly love to debate, and three theological views prevail.

Premillennialism teaches that following the second coming, Christ will institute a kingdom of perfect peace and righteousness on earth that will last for one thousand years. After this reign of true peace, the eternal state begins (Revelation 20:1-7; see also Isaiah 65:17-25; Ezekiel 37:21-28; Zechariah 8:1-17). The reason I subscribe to this view is that it recognizes that just as Christ literally fulfilled the Old Testament messianic prophecies at His first coming, so He will literally fulfill the prophecies of His second coming and millennial kingdom.

Amillennialism, a more spiritualized view, teaches that when Christ comes, eternity will begin with no prior thousand-year (millennial) reign on earth. Amillennialists generally interpret the thousand-year reign of Christ metaphorically and say it refers to Christ's present (spiritual) rule from heaven.

The *postmillennial* view, another spiritualized view, teaches that through the church's progressive influence, the world will be "Christianized" before Christ returns. Immediately following this return, eternity will begin (no thousand-year kingdom). Of course, a practical problem for postmillennialism is that the world seems to be getting worse and worse instead of being "Christianized."

A literal and plain reading of Scripture leads effortlessly to premillennialism. A basic rule of thumb for interpreting the Bible is this: When the plain sense of Scripture makes good sense, seek no other sense. In view of this basic rule, I see no reason to spiritualize Bible prophecies relating to the millennium. The Bible plainly teaches a literal thousand-year kingdom over which Christ will rule on planet earth (Revelation 20:4,6).

Following the millennial kingdom, God promises us a new heaven and a new earth. That is a glorious time to look forward to.

The New Heaven and New Earth

The Scriptures say the old heaven and earth will pass away. In the book of Revelation we read, "Then I saw a new heaven and a new earth, for the first heaven and the first earth had passed away, and there was no longer any sea...He who was seated on the throne said, 'I am making everything new!'" (Revelation 21:1,5).

The Greek word used to designate the newness of the cosmos is *kainos.* This word means "new in nature" or "new in quality." So the phrase "a new heaven and a new earth" refers not to a cosmos that is totally other than the present cosmos. Rather, the new cosmos will stand in continuity with the present cosmos, but it will be utterly renewed and renovated.

Matthew 19:28 (NASB) calls this "the regeneration." Acts 3:21 (NASB) mentions the "restoration of all things." The new earth, being a renewed and an eternal earth, will be adapted to the vast moral and physical changes that the eternal state necessitates. The new heaven and new earth will conform with all that God is—in a state of fixed bliss and absolute perfection. The new earth will actually be a part of heaven itself.

I will discuss heaven and the eternal state in greater detail in chapter 15. First, however, allow me to put to rest a few common misconceptions people have about Bible prophecy.

Common Misconceptions About Prophecy

People have a number of misconceptions about Bible prophecy today. These include claims of mistaken and unfulfilled prophecies in the Bible, of prophecies manufactured after the fact, and of clearly set dates for Christ's second coming. Let us briefly consider these misconceptions.

Mistaken and Unfulfilled Prophecies?

Some people today challenge the veracity of the Bible by claiming it includes mistaken and unfulfilled prophecies. They often point to Jesus' "failed prophecy" in Matthew 24:34 that the end would come in His lifetime.[1]

In Matthew 24:34, Jesus states, "I tell you the truth, this generation will certainly not pass away until all these things have happened." Evangelical Christians have generally held to one of two interpretations of this verse. One is that Christ is simply saying that those people who witness the signs stated earlier in Matthew 24 (all of which deal with the future tribulation period) will see the coming of Jesus Christ within that very generation. In other words, the generation alive when such events as the abomination of desolation (verse 15), the great tribulation (verse 21), and the sign of the Son of Man in heaven (verse 30) begin to come to pass will still be alive when these prophetic judgments are completed. Since the tribulation is a period of seven years (Daniel 9:27; Revelation 11:2), then Jesus would be saying that the generation alive at the beginning of the tribulation will still be alive at the end of it, at which time the second coming of Christ occurs.

Other evangelical Christians say the word *generation* in this verse is to be taken in its secondary meaning of "race," "kindred," "family," "stock," or "breed." Jesus' statement could mean that the Jewish race would not pass away until all things are fulfilled. Since many divine promises were made to Israel, including the eternal inheritance of the land of Palestine (Genesis 12; 14-15; 17) and the Davidic kingdom (2 Samuel 7), Jesus could be referring to God's preservation of the nation of Israel in order to fulfill His promises to the nation. This would go along with the apostle Paul's words about a future for the nation of Israel when the Jews will be reinstated in God's covenantal promises (Romans 11:11-26).

Either way, this verse certainly does not represent a mistaken prophecy, as some try to argue.

Prophecies Manufactured After the Fact?

Some people today argue that the biblical prophecies are not impressive because they were manufactured after the event that was prophesied. One critic argues, "The Bible as we have it today is the result of much editing and interpolation...There is considerable reason to suppose that many alleged prophecies...were manufactured after the fact in question."[2]

Let's consider Old Testament prophecies as we seek to answer this objection. Scholars are practically unanimous that the prophetic books of the Old Testament were completed at least 400 years before Christ was even born, many of them dating as early as the eighth and ninth centuries BC. The exception to this is the book of Daniel, which some scholars date at 167 BC. However, whether a prophetic book dates 167 years before Christ or 800 years before Christ, it requires prophetic revelation from God, who knows the end from the beginning.

Consider the book of Isaiah. Our earliest manuscript copy of Isaiah was dated at AD 980, but following the discovery of the Dead Sea Scrolls in 1947, scholars could examine a manuscript copy of Isaiah dated at 150 BC. This manuscript is but a *copy* of an original document that dates back to the seventh century BC. So the specific prophecies of the coming divine Messiah recorded in Isaiah—including the facts that Jesus would be born of a virgin (7:14), be called Immanuel (7:14), be anointed by the Holy Spirit (11:2), have a ministry in Galilee (9:1-2), have a ministry of miracles (35:5-6), be silent before His accusers (53:7), be crucified with thieves (53:12), accomplish a sacrificial atonement for humankind (53:5), and then be buried in a rich man's tomb (53:9)—could not have been recorded after the fact, as some people try to argue. These prophecies were recorded hundreds of years before the fact, and their literal fulfillment in the first century (along with hundreds of other Old Testament messianic prophecies) proves the divine inspiration of Scripture.

The Date of the Second Coming

Every few years or so, someone writes a book suggesting a particular date when the rapture and/or second coming of Christ will occur. Such books quickly sell a lot of copies, but when the suggested date passes with no fanfare, people forget about it. Here are ten reasons why Christians should not fall for date-setting schemes:

1. Over the past 2000 years, the track record of those who have predicted the end within their lifetimes have been 100 percent wrong. The history of doomsday predictions is a history of dashed expectations. Though we could possibly be living in the last days, Christ's second coming could also possibly be a long way off. We must therefore be discerning.

2. Those who succumb to the date-setting mentality may end up making harmful decisions for their lives. Selling one's possessions

and heading for the mountains, purchasing bomb shelters, stopping education, leaving family and friends—these destructive actions can ruin lives.

3. Christians who succumb to the date-setting mentality may damage their faith with failed expectations.

4. If one loses confidence in the prophetic portions of Scripture, biblical prophecy ceases to be a motivation to holiness (Titus 2:12-14).

5. Christians who succumb to the date-setting mentality may damage the faith of new and immature believers when predicted events don't happen.

6. Setting dates may lead to "prophetic agnosticism." People may develop an attitude that we can't be sure of what the future holds.

7. Date-setters tend to be sensationalistic, and sensationalism is unbefitting to a follower of the Lord Jesus. Christ calls His followers to live soberly and alertly as they await His coming (Mark 13:32-37).

8. Christians who get caught up in the date-setting mentality can potentially do damage to the cause of Christ. Humanists, skeptics, and atheists love to mock Christians when their dates fail. Why give ammunition to the enemies of Christianity?

9. Christians who succumb to the date-setting mentality may get sidetracked from their first priority—living righteously and in holiness in daily fellowship with the Lord Jesus Christ.

10. The timing of end-time events is completely in God's hands (Acts 1:7), and we haven't been given the precise details. As far as the second coming is concerned, we should live as if Jesus were coming today and yet prepare for the future as if He were not coming for a long time. Then we will be ready for time and eternity.

My friend, an exciting future awaits all Christians. We should be excited about this future, but God gave us prophecy for more than just excitement. He gave it to us so we'd be motivated to purify our lives (see Titus 2:12-14). So this is my challenge: Live your life in such a way that when the rapture occurs, you won't be embarrassed to see your Lord face-to-face. Let us live to please Him every single day.

Discussion Questions

1. What is your position regarding when the rapture will occur? Can you defend your position biblically?

2. How do the rapture and second coming relate to the way you live your life in the present? Are you ready for Christ to return today?

3. What's the problem with settings dates for the rapture or second coming? Have you ever postponed a long-range project because you thought Christ's coming might be near?

4. God knows the end from the beginning and is in control over human history. What does this mean for you personally?

15

The Wonder of Heaven and the Afterlife

The doctrine of the afterlife involves four fundamental issues: the reality of death, the future judgment, heaven, and hell. Every human being—Christians *and* unbelievers—will face death and a judgment. Christians will spend eternity with Christ in heaven. Unbelievers will be consigned to hell for all eternity. Let's consider the details.

Death and Dying

The New Testament word for death carries the idea of separation. At the moment of physical death, man's spirit separates or departs from his body (2 Corinthians 5:8). This is why, when Stephen was being stoned to death, he prayed, "Lord Jesus, receive my spirit" (Acts 7:59). At the moment of death "the spirit returns to God who gave it" (Ecclesiastes 12:7). Such verses indicate that at death, the believer's spirit departs from the physical body and immediately goes into the presence of the Lord in heaven. Death for the believer leads to a supremely blissful existence (Philippians 1:21).

For the unbeliever, however, death holds grim prospects. At death the unbeliever's spirit departs from the body and goes not to heaven but to a place of great suffering (Luke 16:19-31).

Both believers and unbelievers remain as disembodied spirits until the future day of resurrection. Believers' resurrection bodies will be specially suited to dwelling in heaven in the direct presence of God—the perishable will be made imperishable and the mortal will be made immortal (1 Corinthians 15:53). Unbelievers will also be resurrected, but they will spend eternity apart from God (John 5:29).

The Judgment of Humankind

John Wesley, in one of his famous sermons, commented, "Every man shall give an account of his own works, a full and true account of all that he ever did while alive, whether it was good or evil."[1]

We need to hear such words in times like these. Few people today—even among Christians—govern their actions as if they will be held accountable for them at a future judgment. Though many prefer to ignore any mention of the subject, the fact remains that every human being—Christian and non-Christian—will face a judgment.

Scripture reveals that the purpose of the Christian's judgment is altogether different from that of the unbeliever's judgment. The Christian is judged not in relation to salvation (which is absolutely secure) but in relation to receiving or losing rewards from God. The unbeliever, however, is judged as a precursor to being cast into the lake of fire. We will examine both judgments below.

The Judgment of Christians

All Christians will one day stand before the judgment seat of Christ (Romans 14:8-10). At that time God will examine the deeds each believer has done. He will also weigh our personal motives and the intents of our hearts.

The idea of a judgment seat comes from the athletic games of the apostle Paul's day. When the races and games were over, a dignitary would sit on an elevated throne in the arena. Then, one by one, the winning athletes would come up to the throne to receive a reward—usually a wreath of leaves, a victor's crown. In the case of Christians, each of us will stand before Christ the Judge and receive—or lose—rewards.

Christ's judgment of us will not be in a corporate setting—like a teacher praising or scolding a big class. Rather, it will be individual and personal. "We will all stand before God's judgment seat" (Romans 14:10).

This judgment has nothing to do with whether or not the Christian will remain saved. Those who have placed faith in Christ *are* saved, and nothing threatens that. Believers are eternally secure in their salvation (Romans 8:30; Ephesians 4:30). Nevertheless, as noted previously, believers will either receive or lose rewards depending on how they lived their lives as Christians.

Scripture indicates that some believers at the judgment may have a sense of deprivation and suffer some degree of forfeiture and shame. Indeed, certain rewards may be forfeited that otherwise might have been received, and this will involve a sense of loss. The fact is, Christians differ radically in holiness of conduct and faithfulness in service. God, in His justice and holiness, takes all this into account. For this reason, 2 John 8 warns us, "Watch out that you do not lose what you have worked for, but that you may be rewarded fully." In 1 John 2:28 John wrote about the possibility of a believer actually being ashamed at Christ's coming.

We must keep all this in perspective, however. The prospect of living eternally with Christ in heaven is something that should give each of us joy. And our joy will last for all eternity. How then can we reconcile this eternal joy with the possible loss of reward and perhaps even some level of shame at the judgment seat of Christ?

I think theologian Herman Hoyt's explanation is the best I have seen:

> The Judgment Seat of Christ might be compared to a commencement ceremony. At graduation there is some measure of disappointment and remorse that one did not do better and work harder. However, at such an event the overwhelming emotion is joy, not remorse. The graduates do not leave the auditorium weeping because they did not earn better grades. Rather, they are thankful that they have been graduated, and they are grateful for what they did achieve. To overdo the sorrow aspect of the Judgment Seat of Christ is to make heaven hell. To underdo the sorrow aspect is to make faithfulness inconsequential.[2]

Christ's judgment of our actions will be infallible. No issue will confuse Him. He will fully understand the circumstances in which we served Him on earth. As Wesley once put it, "God will then bring to light every circumstance that accompanied each word and action. He will judge whether they lessened or increased the goodness or badness of them."[3]

What kinds of rewards will believers receive at the judgment seat of Christ? Scripture often uses crowns to symbolize various achievements and awards in the Christian life.

The crown of life is given to those who persevere under trial, and especially to those who suffer to the point of death (James 1:12; Revelation 2:10). The crown of glory is given to those who faithfully and sacrificially minister God's Word to the flock (1 Peter 5:4). The crown incorruptible is given to those who win the race of temperance and self-control (1 Corinthians 9:25 NASB). The crown of righteousness is given to those who long for the second coming of Christ (2 Timothy 4:8).

In Revelation 4:10 we find believers casting their crowns before the throne of God in an act of worship and adoration. This teaches us something very important. Clearly we receive crowns (as rewards) not for our own glory but ultimately for the glory of God. Scripture tells us elsewhere that believers are redeemed in order to bring glory to God (1 Corinthians 6:20). Placing our crowns before the throne of God seems to be an illustration of this.

Here is something else to think about. The greater reward or crown a person has received, the greater capacity that person has to bring glory to the Creator. The lesser reward or crown a person has received, the lesser is his or her capacity to bring glory to the Creator. Because of the different rewards handed out at the judgment seat of Christ, believers will have differing capacities to bring glory to God.

Still, we should not take this to mean that certain believers will have a sense of lack throughout eternity. After all, each believer will be glorifying God to the fullness of his or her capacity in the next life. Each one of us, then, will be able to "declare the praises of him who called [us] out of darkness into his wonderful light" (1 Peter 2:9).

The Judgment of Unbelievers

Unlike Christians, whose judgment deals only with rewards and loss of rewards, unbelievers face a horrific judgment that leads to their being cast into the lake of fire. The judgment that unbelievers face is called the great white throne judgment (Revelation 20:11-15). Christ is the divine Judge, and those who are judged are the unsaved dead of all time. The judgment takes place at the end of the millennial kingdom, Christ's thousand-year reign on earth.

Those who face Christ at this judgment will be judged on the basis of their works (Revelation 20:12-13). We should understand that they actually get to this judgment because they are already unsaved. This judgment will not separate believers from unbelievers, for all who will experience it will have already made the choice during their lifetimes to reject salvation in Jesus Christ. Once they are before the divine Judge, they are judged according to their works not only to justify their condemnation but to determine the degree to which each person should be punished throughout eternity.

The destiny of the unsaved includes weeping and gnashing of teeth (Matthew 13:41-42), condemnation (Matthew 12:36-37), destruction

(Philippians 1:28), eternal punishment (Matthew 25:46), separation from God's presence (2 Thessalonians 1:8-9), and trouble and distress (Romans 2:9). The Scriptures also indicate that hell will have degrees of punishment.

Common observation shows that unsaved people vary as much in their quality of life as saved people do. Some saved people are spiritual and charitable (for example), and other saved people are carnal and unloving. Some unbelievers are terribly evil (like Hitler), while others—such as unbelieving moralists—are much less evil.

Just as believers respond differently to God's law and therefore have different rewards in heaven, so unbelievers respond differently to God's law and will experience different kinds of punishment in hell. Just as there are degrees of reward in heaven, so there are degrees of punishment in hell (see Matthew 10:15; 16:27; Luke 12:47-48; Revelation 20:12-13; 22:12).

Heaven: The Glorious Destiny of Christians

A common maxim of our day is that some Christians are so heavenly minded that they are of no earthly good. This is a lie deeply embedded in cultural religion. The truth is, heavenly minded Christians do the *greatest* earthly good by shining as lights in a world of darkness. Let us briefly consider what the Bible reveals about heaven.

Biblical Descriptions of Heaven

The city of glory. In Revelation 21 we find a description of the eternal city of God. This is a city of great glory which, I believe, is what Jesus was referring to during His earthly ministry when He told the disciples, "In my Father's house are many rooms; if it were not so, I would have told you. I am going there to prepare a place for you. And if I go and prepare a place for you, I will come back and take you to be with me that you also may be where I am" (John 14:2-3). Christ has personally prepared this glorious abode for His followers.

Revelation 21 presents to our amazed gaze a scene of such

transcendent splendor that the human mind can scarcely take it in. This is a scene of ecstatic joy and fellowship of sinless angels and redeemed glorified human beings. The voice of the Alpha and the Omega, the beginning and the end, utters a climactic declaration: "Behold, I am making all things new" (Revelation 21:5 NASB).

Theologian Millard Erickson comments on the glorious splendor of this city: "Images suggesting immense size or brilliant light depict heaven as a place of unimaginable splendor, greatness, excellence, and beauty...It is likely that while John's vision employs as metaphors those items which we think of as being most valuable and beautiful, the actual splendor of heaven far exceeds anything that we have yet experienced."[4] Truly, as the apostle Paul said, "No eye has seen, no ear has heard, no mind has conceived what God has prepared for those who love him" (1 Corinthians 2:9).

The statement in Revelation 21:23 that "the city does not need the sun or the moon to shine on it, for the glory of God gives it light, and the Lamb is its lamp" is in keeping with Isaiah 60:19: "The sun will no more be your light by day, nor will the brightness of the moon shine on you, for the LORD will be your everlasting light, and your God will be your glory."

The heavenly country. Hebrews 11 is faith's hall of fame in the Bible. In this pivotal chapter we read of the eternal perspective of many of the great faith warriors in biblical times:

> All these people were still living by faith when they died. They did not receive the things promised; they only saw them and welcomed them from a distance. And they admitted that they were aliens and strangers on earth. People who say such things show that they are looking for a country of their own. If they had been thinking of the country they had left, they would have had opportunity to return. Instead, they were longing for a better country—a heavenly one (Hebrews 11:13-16).

This passage tells us that the biblical heroes were not satisfied with earthly things. They looked forward to a better country. And what a glorious country heaven is. Eighteenth-century Bible expositor John Gill contemplates how the heavenly country…

> is full of light and glory; having the delightful breezes of divine love, and the comfortable gales of the blessed Spirit; here is no heat of persecution, nor coldness, nor chills of affection; here is plenty of most delicious fruits, no hunger nor thirst; and here are riches, which are solid, satisfying, durable, safe and sure: many are the liberties and privileges here enjoyed; here is a freedom from a body subject to diseases and death, from a body of sin and death, from Satan's temptations, from all doubts, fears, and unbelief, and from all sorrows and afflictions.[5]

The holy city. In Revelation 21:1-2 we find heaven described as "the holy city." This is a fitting description, for this city will not know sin or unrighteousness of any kind. Only the pure of heart will dwell there.

This doesn't mean you and I must personally attain moral perfection in order to dwell there. Those of us who believe in Christ have received the very righteousness of Christ. Because of what Christ accomplished for us at the cross, taking our sins on Himself, we have been made holy (Hebrews 10:14). That is why we will have the privilege of living for all eternity in the holy city.

The home of righteousness. Second Peter 3:13 tells us that "in keeping with his promise we are looking forward to a new heaven and a new earth, the home of righteousness." What a perfect environment this will be to live in. During our earthly lives, we have to lock up our houses, fearful that intruders might break in. Unrighteousness is all around us. But heaven will be the home of righteousness. It will therefore be a perfect living environment for those who have been made righteous by Christ.

The kingdom of light. Colossians 1:12 refers to heaven as "the kingdom of light." Christ, of course, is the light of the world (John

8:12). The eternal kingdom thus takes on the character of the King. Christ, the light of the world, rules over the kingdom of light. Moreover, Christ's own divine light illumines the holy city of light (Revelation 21:23). How glorious it will be!

The paradise of God. The word *paradise* literally means "garden of pleasure" or "garden of delight." Revelation 2:7 calls heaven the "paradise of God." The apostle Paul in 2 Corinthians 12:4 said he "was caught up to paradise" and "heard inexpressible things, things that man is not permitted to tell."

Apparently this paradise of God is so resplendently glorious, so ineffable, so wondrous, that Paul was forbidden to say anything about it to those still in the earthly realm. But what Paul saw gave him an eternal perspective that enabled him to face the trials that lay ahead of him.

The new Jerusalem. Perhaps the most elaborate description of the heavenly city is in Revelation 21, where we read of the new Jerusalem. The city measures approximately 1500 miles by 1500 miles by 1500 miles. The eternal city is so huge that it would measure approximately the distance between the Mississippi River and the Atlantic Ocean. It could be shaped either like a cube or like a pyramid. A pyramid shape would explain how the river of the water of life can flow down its sides as pictured in Revelation 22:1-2. John's description of the new Jerusalem reveals a series of contrasts with the earth. Theologian Bruce Shelley summarizes them:

> In contrast to the darkness of most ancient cities, John says heaven is always lighted. In contrast to rampant disease in the ancient world, he says heaven has trees whose leaves heal all sorts of sicknesses. In contrast to the parched deserts of the Near East, he pictures heaven with an endless river of crystal-clear water. In contrast to a meager existence in an arid climate, John says twelve kinds of fruit grow on the trees of heaven. In a word, heaven is a wonderful destiny, free of the shortages and discomforts of this life.[6]

The Blessings of Heaven

As we explore what the Scriptures say about the blessing of heaven for believers, let's remember what this information means to each of us personally. Heaven is not just a doctrine. Our forward gaze of heaven has everything to do with how we live as vibrant Christians in the present.

The absence of death. The Old Testament promises that in the heavenly state death will be swallowed up forever (Isaiah 25:8). Paul speaks of this same reality in his description of the future resurrection: "When the perishable has been clothed with the imperishable, and the mortal with immortality, then the saying that is written will come true: 'Death has been swallowed up in victory'" (1 Corinthians 15:54). Revelation 21:4 tells us that God "will wipe every tear from their eyes. There will be no more death or mourning or crying or pain, for the old order of things has passed away."

What an awesome blessing this is—no more fatal accidents, no more incurable diseases, no more funeral services, no more final farewells. Death will be gone and done with, never again to trouble those who dwell in heaven. Life in the eternal city will be painless, tearless, and deathless.

Intimate fellowship with God and Christ. Can anything be more sublime and more utterly satisfying for the Christian than to enjoy the sheer delight of unbroken fellowship with God and have immediate and completely unobstructed access to the divine glory (John 14:3; 2 Corinthians 5:6-8; Philippians 1:23; 1 Thessalonians 4:17)? We shall see him face-to-face in all His splendor and glory. We will gaze upon His countenance and behold His resplendent beauty forever.

Surely our greatest joy and most exhilarating thrill will be to see our divine Creator's face and fellowship with Him forever. He "who alone possesses immortality and dwells in unapproachable light" (1 Timothy 6:16 NASB) shall reside intimately among His own, and "they shall be His people, and God Himself will be among them" (Revelation 21:3 NASB).

To fellowship with God is the essence of heavenly life, the fount and source of all blessing: "You will fill me with joy in your presence, with eternal pleasures at your right hand" (Psalm 16:11). We may be confident that the crowning wonder of our experience in the eternal city will be the perpetual and endless exploration of that unutterable beauty, majesty, love, holiness, power, joy, and grace that is God Himself.

Reunion with Christian loved ones. One of the most glorious aspects of our lives in heaven is that we will be reunited with Christian loved ones. The Thessalonian Christians were apparently very concerned about their Christian loved ones who had died. They expressed their concern to the apostle Paul. So in 1 Thessalonians 4:13-17, Paul teaches about the dead in Christ and assures the Thessalonian Christians that a reunion will indeed occur. And yes, believers will recognize their loved ones in the eternal state.

How do we know believers will recognize their loved ones? Besides the clear teaching of 1 Thessalonians 4, 2 Samuel 12:23 reveals that David knew he would be reunited with his deceased son in heaven. He had no doubt about recognizing him. As well, when Moses and Elijah (who had long passed from earthly life) appeared to Jesus on the Mount of Transfiguration (Matthew 17:1-8), all who were present recognized them. Furthermore, in Jesus' story of the rich man and Lazarus in Luke 16:19-31, the rich man, Lazarus, and Abraham all recognized each other in the intermediate state.

Satisfaction of all needs. In our present life on earth, we sometimes go hungry and thirsty. Our needs are not always met. But in the eternal state, God will abundantly meet each and every need. As we read in Revelation 7:16-17, "Never again will they hunger; never again will they thirst. The sun will not beat upon them, nor any scorching heat. For the Lamb at the center of the throne will be their shepherd; he will lead them to springs of living water. And God will wipe away every tear from their eyes."

Serene rest. The Scriptures indicate that a key feature of heavenly life is rest (Revelation 14:13). No more deadlines to work toward. No more overtime work in order to make ends meet. No more breaking one's back. Just sweet, serene rest. And our rest will be especially sweet because it is in the very presence of God, who meets our every need.

Sharing in Christ's glory. In the heavenly state believers will actually share in the glory of Christ. Romans 8:17 tells us, "Now if we are children, then we are heirs—heirs of God and co-heirs with Christ, if indeed we share in his sufferings in order that we may also share in his glory." Likewise, Colossians 3:4 informs us that "when Christ, who is your life, appears, then you also will appear with him in glory."

This, of course, does not mean that we become deity. But it does mean that you and I as Christians will be in a state of glory, sharing in Christ's glory, wholly because of what Christ has accomplished for us. We will have glorious resurrection bodies and be clothed with shining robes of immortality, incorruption, and splendor.

A Top-Down Perspective

The incredible glory of the afterlife should motivate each of us to live faithfully during our relatively short time on earth. Especially when difficult times come, we must remember that we are but pilgrims on our way to another land—to the final frontier of heaven, where God Himself dwells.

J.I. Packer once said that the "lack of long, strong thinking about our promised hope of glory is a major cause of our plodding, lackluster lifestyle."[7] Packer points to the Puritans as a much-needed example for us, for they believed that "it is the heavenly Christian that is the lively Christian." The Puritans understood that we "run so slowly, and strive so lazily, because we so little mind the prize...So let Christians animate themselves daily to run the race set before them by practicing heavenly meditation."[8]

I have come to appreciate the Puritans, and I personally seek to imitate their example. The Puritans "saw themselves as God's pilgrims, traveling home through rough country; God's warriors, battling the world, the flesh, and the devil; and God's servants, under orders to worship, fellowship, and do all the good they could as they went along."[9] We should all have this attitude.

I am particularly impressed with the writings of Puritan Richard Baxter. He certainly had some habits worthy of imitation. His first habit was to "estimate everything—values, priorities, possessions, relationships, claims, tasks—as these things will appear when one actually comes to die."[10] In other words, he weighed everything in terms of eternal benefit. After all, our life on earth is short; our life in heaven is forever. If we work only for the things of this earth, what eternal benefit will all of it have?

Baxter's second habit was to "dwell on the glory of the heavenly life to which one was going."[11] Baxter daily practiced "holding heaven at the forefront of his thoughts and desires."[12] The hope of heaven brought him joy, and joy brought him strength. Baxter once said, "A heavenly mind is a joyful mind; this is the nearest and truest way to live a life of comfort...A heart in heaven will be a most excellent preservative against temptations, a powerful means to kill thy corruptions."[13]

Christian apologists Gary Habermas and J.P. Moreland have come up with a term I like a lot: "a 'top-down' perspective." That's precisely what we need during our earthly pilgrimage as we sojourn toward our heavenly destiny:

> The God of the universe invites us to view life and death from his eternal vantage point. And if we do, we will see how readily it can revolutionize our lives: daily anxieties, emotional hurts, tragedies, our responses and responsibilities to others, possessions, wealth, and even physical pain and death. All of this and much more can be informed and influenced by the truths of heaven. The repeated witness of the New Testament is that believers should view all problems, indeed, their entire existence, from what we call the "top-down" perspective: God and his

kingdom first, followed by various aspects of our earthly existence.[14]

Hell: The Infernal Destiny of the Wicked

The Scriptures assure us that hell is a real place. But hell was not part of God's original creation, which He called "good" (Genesis 1:31). Hell was created later to accommodate the banishment of Satan and his fallen angels who rebelled against God (Matthew 25:41). People who reject Christ will join Satan and his fallen angels in this infernal place of suffering.

A variety of Bible words either refer to or relate to the doctrine of hell:

Sheol. In the Old Testament the word *hell* translates the Hebrew word *Sheol. Sheol* can have different meanings in different contexts. Sometimes the word means "grave" (Psalm 49:15). Other times it refers simply to the place of departed people. The Old Testament often characterizes this place as being full of horror (Psalm 30:9), weeping (Isaiah 38:3), and punishment (Job 24:19).

Hades. Hades is the New Testament counterpart to Sheol. The rich man, after he died, endured great suffering in Hades (Luke 16:19-31). Hades, however, is a temporary abode and will one day be cast into the lake of fire (hell). In the future, God will raise the wicked evildoers in Hades and judge them at the great white throne judgment. He will cast them into the lake of fire, which will be their permanent place of suffering throughout all eternity (Revelation 20:14-15).

Gehenna. Another word related to the concept of hell is Gehenna (Matthew 10:28; 2 Kings 23:10). This word has an interesting history. For several generations in ancient Israel, atrocities were committed in the Valley of Ben Hinnom—atrocities that included human sacrifices, even the sacrifice of children to the false Moabite god Molech (2 Chronicles 28:3; 33:6; Jeremiah 32:35). Eventually the valley came to be used as Jerusalem's public rubbish dump. Not only garbage but also the bodies of dead animals and the corpses of criminals were thrown on the heap where they—like everything else in the dump—would perpetually burn. The fires in the valley never stopped burning.

This place was originally called (in the Hebrew) *Ge[gen]hinnom* (the valley of the son[s] of Hinnom). It was eventually shortened to the name *Ge-Hinnom*. The Greek translation of this Hebrew phrase is *Gehenna*. It became an appropriate and graphic metaphor for the reality of hell.

Eternal fire. Jesus often referred to the eternal destiny of the wicked as "eternal fire" (Matthew 25:41). What precisely is the fire of hell? Some believe it is literal. And indeed, that may very well be the case. Others believe fire is a metaphor of the great wrath of God. Scripture tells us, "The LORD your God is a consuming fire, a jealous God" (Deuteronomy 4:24). "God is a consuming fire" (Hebrews 12:29). "His wrath is poured out like fire" (Nahum 1:6). "Who can stand when he appears? For he will be like a refiner's fire" (Malachi 3:2). God said, "My wrath will break out and burn like fire because of the evil you have done—burn with no one to quench it" (Jeremiah 4:4). How awful is the fiery wrath of God!

Fiery furnace. Scripture sometimes refers to the destiny of the wicked as the "fiery furnace." Jesus said that at the end of the age the holy angels will gather all evildoers and "throw them into the fiery furnace, where there will be weeping and gnashing of teeth" (Matthew 13:42). This weeping will be caused by the environment, the company, the remorse and guilt, and the shame that are all part and parcel of hell.

Destruction. Second Thessalonians 1:8-9 tells us that unbelievers "will be punished with everlasting destruction and shut out from the presence of the Lord and from the majesty of his power." The Greek word translated *destruction* carries the meaning "sudden ruin," or "loss of all that gives worth to existence." The word refers not to annihilation but rather to separation from God and a loss of everything worthwhile in life.

Eternal punishment. Jesus affirmed that the wicked "will go away to eternal punishment, but the righteous to eternal life" (Matthew 25:46). Notice that the punishment of the wicked is just as eternal as the eternal life of the righteous. One is just as long as the other.

Exclusion from God's presence. The greatest pain suffered by those in hell is that they are forever excluded from God's presence. If His presence brings ecstatic joy (Psalm 16:11), then the eternal absence of His presence will bring utter dismay.

The various horrific terms used to describe hell throughout Scripture highlight the tremendous significance of Christ coming into the world to provide salvation (John 3:16-17). Only by receiving His gift of salvation are we redeemed from the infernal destiny of hell.

Controversial Questions About the Afterlife

The afterlife is a fascinating topic for many people today. Understandably, debate has emerged among churchgoers over a number of issues related to the afterlife—including near-death experiences, purgatory, reincarnation, and the question of whether the wicked really suffer for all eternity or are simply annihilated. We now turn our attention to these issues.

Near-Death Experiences

Researchers have suggested a variety of explanations for so-called near-death experiences, in which people who have died allegedly leave their bodies, go through a tunnel, and encounter a being of light. Here is a summary of four possible explanations:

1. Some scholars explain these experiences as a result of a lack of oxygen to the brain. This is known as hypoxia. They say this lack of oxygen to the brain accounts for sensations like going through a tunnel and seeing a bright light. The problem with this view, however, is that medical tests reveal that people who have gone through near-death experiences did not have less oxygen in their blood gases than other people.

2. Some scholars have suggested that going through a dark tunnel and then seeing a bright light are actually deeply embedded memories of the birth experience. The late astronomer and scientist Carl Sagan held to this view. Critics respond by saying that a memory of birth would be traumatic, not pleasant (like a near-death experience). Further, in the birth experience the baby's face is pressed against the birth canal, conflicting with the rapid transit of going through a dark tunnel. As well, some suggest that the baby's brain is not developed enough to retain such memories.

3. Other suggested explanations include trauma or injury to the brain, severe psychological stress that may cause the release of chemicals in the brain that could induce certain experiences, or perhaps hallucinations caused by various medications. Such alternative theories, however, do not really explain the various details of the typical near-death experience. For example, these theories cannot explain how people who were brain-dead at the time are later able to describe in vivid detail the medical personnel's attempts to resuscitate them.

4. Christian researchers note the strong possibility that many of these experiences are actually caused by the evil one—Satan, the father of lies, who has the ability to perform counterfeit miracles (2 Thessalonians 2:9). The "being of light" people encounter during these experiences often expresses openness to all the world religions, denies the sin problem, and tells people not to worry about hell—all anti-biblical ideas that Satan would be likely to promote. Further, many researchers have noted that many who have near-death experiences later develop psychic powers.

What kinds of psychic powers are we talking about? Some people who have had a near-death experience later claim to engage in astral travel or out-of-body experiences—the soul allegedly leaves the body and travels around the so-called astral realm. Some people develop clairvoyance—the ability to perceive things that are outside the natural range of human senses. Some people develop telepathic abilities to mystically communicate by means of thoughts alone. And many people come into contact with spirit guides, who allegedly stay with them for the rest of their lives.

Here's an important point: In Scripture, God condemns occultism and psychic phenomena. Anyone who doubts this should meditate on Deuteronomy 18:10-13. Much of what is going on in so-called near-death experiences is clearly not of God. Reader beware!

Does Purgatory Exist?

The Roman Catholic church teaches that Christians who are perfect at death are admitted to heaven. Christians who are not perfectly cleansed and are still tainted with the guilt of venial sins, however, do not go to heaven but rather go to purgatory, where they allegedly go through a process of cleansing (or "purging").

Purgatory is clearly not a scriptural doctrine. We are cleansed not by an alleged fire of purgatory but by the blood of Jesus Christ (Hebrews 9:14). Jesus "Himself is the propitiation for our sins" (1 John 2:2 NASB). Solely through Jesus' work on the cross are we made righteous (2 Corinthians 5:21). The apostle Paul spoke of his life as "not having a righteousness of my own derived from the Law, but that which is through faith in Christ, the righteousness which comes from God on the basis of faith" (Philippians 3: 9 NASB). Through this wonderful work of Christ on the cross, believers are blameless and therefore do not need purgatory (Jude 24 NASB; see also Ephesians 1:4).

When Jesus died on the cross, He said, "It is finished" (John 19:30). Jesus completed the work of redemption at the cross. In His high priestly prayer to the Father, Jesus said, "I have brought you glory on earth by completing the work you gave me to do" (John 17:4). Hebrews 10:14 declares, "By one sacrifice he has made perfect forever those who are being made holy." No further purging is necessary. First John 1:7 says, "The blood of Jesus, his Son, purifies us from all sin." Romans 8:1 says, "Therefore, there is now no condemnation for those who are in Christ Jesus."

What About Reincarnation?

The word *reincarnation* literally means to "come again in the flesh." It involves the belief that the soul passes into another body after death. A person is born again and again and again, life after life after life. The cycle is based on the law of karma. This law says that if we do good things in this life, we will build up good karma, which will cause us to be born in a better condition in the next life. Conversely, if we do bad things in this life, we will build up bad karma, which will cause us to be born in a worse condition in the next life. Through this process, karma allegedly brings healing to the soul and rids humanity of all selfish desires.

Some churchgoers claim that reincarnation is compatible with Christianity. Indeed, 21 percent of Protestants and 25 percent of professing Catholics say they believe in reincarnation.[15] But the salvation-by-works doctrine of reincarnation has many practical problems:

- Why punish people for something they cannot remember having done in a previous life? And how does punishment for sins people don't remember make them better people?

- If the purpose of karma is to rid humanity of its selfish desires, why hasn't human nature improved after all the millennia of reincarnations?

- If reincarnation and the law of karma are so beneficial on a practical level, how do advocates of this doctrine explain the immense and ever-worsening social and economic problems—including widespread poverty, starvation, disease, and horrible suffering—in India, where reincarnation has been systematically taught for centuries?

- Reincarnation makes people socially apathetic. Belief in reincarnation serves as a strong motivation *not* to be a good neighbor and lend a helping hand. After all, if people suffer precisely because they have not yet paid off their prescribed karmic debt, helping such suffering people will only short-circuit the process. People will be born in a worse state in the next life to pay off the karmic debt that they were supposed to pay off in the present life. Further, the good neighbor would also accumulate more bad karmic debt for interfering with the law of karma in suffering people's lives. It is a no-win scenario.

Reincarnation also has many biblical problems. For example, in 2 Corinthians 5:8 the apostle Paul states, "We are confident, I say, and would prefer to be away from the body and at home with the Lord." At death, the Christian immediately goes into the presence of the Lord, not into another body. Likewise, Luke 16:19-31 tells us that unbelievers at death go to a place of suffering, not into another body. Further, Hebrews 9:27 assures us that "man is destined to die once, and after that to face judgment." Each human being lives once as a mortal on earth, dies once, and then faces judgment. He does not have a second chance by reincarnating into another body.

Eternal Punishment or Annihilation?

Some Christians today hold to a doctrine known as annihilationism. This doctrine teaches that man was created immortal. However, those who continue in sin and reject Christ are, by a positive act of God, deprived of the gift of immortality and are ultimately destroyed in hell. Consciousness is snuffed out. They are annihilated and do not suffer eternally.

Annihilationism is answered by Matthew 25:46, which tells us that the wicked "will go away to eternal punishment, but the righteous to eternal life." By no stretch of the imagination can the punishment spoken of in Matthew 25:46 be defined as a nonsuffering extinction of consciousness. If actual suffering is lacking, so is punishment. Punishment entails suffering. Suffering necessarily entails consciousness. Certainly one can exist and not be punished; but no one can be punished and not exist. Annihilation means the obliteration of existence and anything that pertains to existence, such as punishment. Annihilation avoids punishment rather than encountering it.

Matthew 26:46 uses the same word for *eternal* when referring to the eternal life of the righteous and to the conscious punishment of the wicked. The word comes from the adjective *aionion,* meaning "everlasting," "without end." The wicked will be consciously punished everlastingly and without end, not annihilated out of existence.

Notice that there are no degrees of annihilation. People are either annihilated or they aren't. The Scriptures, by contrast, describe degrees of punishment on the day of judgment (Matthew 10:15; 11:21-24; 16:27; Luke 12:47-48; John 15:22; Hebrews 10:29; Revelation 20:11-15; 22:12). The fact that people will suffer varying degrees of punishment in hell shows that annihilation, or the extinction of consciousness, counters Matthew 25:46 and the rest of Scripture. Moreover, for one who is suffering excruciating pain, extinction would actually be a blessing—not a punishment (see Luke 23:30-31; Revelation 9:6). Any honest seeker after truth must admit that one cannot define "eternal punishment" as an extinction of consciousness.

In this chapter, I have covered some wondrous facts about heaven, some horrific facts about hell, and a number of controversial issues. As interesting as all this is, I want to close with a more sobering thought, worthy of our most focused reflection and meditation.

People often refer to death as "the great equalizer." Whether male or female, black or white, rich or poor, fat or thin, short or tall...all people eventually die.

The logical response to this ever-present reality is to make preparations for what lies beyond death's door. And the single wisest decision you can make to prepare for death is to develop a personal relationship with the only person who has ever defeated death—Jesus Christ. He alone can give you eternal life.

If you haven't done so already, I urge you to trust in Him today for salvation. Now is the day of salvation (2 Corinthians 6:2).

Discussion Questions

1. Has the reality of a future judgment been a motivation for you to live righteously? Do you need to make any changes in your life as you anticipate this judgment?

2. What do you most look forward to in heaven?

3. What dangers do you see in regard to the near-death experiences that so many people speak of?

4. What are the big problems with believing in reincarnation?

5. Do you think unbelievers will suffer for all eternity in hell? Why or why not?

6. Do you presently have a top-down perspective?

Postscript

In this book I have tried to show that modern cultural religion accepts many ideas that are not Christian at all and are, in fact, patently unbiblical. Here are just a few examples:

- Cultural religion weds religion with evolutionary theory. Biblical Christianity teaches that God created all things—including human beings.

- Cultural religion teaches that the problem of evil proves that God cannot be all-powerful and all-knowing. Biblical Christianity portrays God as being infinite in perfections, including being all-powerful and all-knowing. Surely this all-powerful and all-knowing God has a sovereign purpose for allowing evil to exist temporarily.

- Cultural religion downplays sin in favor of a "feel good" Christianity. Biblical Christianity reveals the true ugliness of sin, clearly delineating its damning effects.

- Cultural religion downplays and sometimes even denies the deity of Jesus Christ. Biblical Christianity teaches that He is absolute deity.

- Cultural religion has exalted angels, sometimes focusing on these celestial creatures to the exclusion of God. Biblical Christianity portrays angels as servants of the living God who do only His bidding.

- Cultural religion teaches that everyone will be saved in the end. Biblical Christianity delineates two groups of people in the end—the saved and the unsaved—with two very different destinies (heaven and hell).

Perhaps now you understand why, in the introduction of this book, I asked these questions:

> Have you ever wondered if the Christianity you believe in is the genuine, bona fide Christianity of the Bible? Have you ever pondered the possibility that even though most of your Christian beliefs are biblical, others may find more support in other traditions? Have you ever secretly asked whether your view of salvation is rooted more in the official position of your denomination than the Bible?

These are important questions that deserve thoughtful answers. My hope is that this book has helped you to see clearly on these very important issues. And my prayer is that God will continue to illumine your mind so that you will daily be able to discern the wide divide between cultural religion and biblical Christianity (John 16:12-15; 2 Corinthians 2:9-12).

Notes

Christianity According to the Bible

1. The Barna Update, November 29, 2005. www.barna.org.
2. J.I. Packer, *Knowing Christianity* (Wheaton: Harold Shaw, 1995), p. 60.
3. Ibid., p. 138.
4. Edythe Draper, *Draper's Book of Quotations for the Christian World* (Wheaton: Tyndale, 1992), p. 66.
5. Ibid., p. 66.
6. *More Gathered Gold,* electronic media, HyperCard stack for Macintosh.
7. Ibid.

Chapter 1—God Communicates to Us

1. J.I. Packer, *Knowing Christianity* (Wheaton: Harold Shaw, 1995), p. 10.
2. John Calvin, *Institutes of the Christian Religion,* ed. John McNeill (Philadelphia: Westminster, 1960), I:53.
3. Packer, p. 16.
4. Norman Geisler and William Nix, *A General Introduction to the Bible* (Chicago: Moody, 1986), p. 28.
5. E.J. Young, *Thy Word Is Truth* (Grand Rapids: Eerdmans, 1957), p. 113.
6. Cited in Chuck Colson, *Against the Night* (Ann Arbor: Servant, 1989), p. 152.
7. Cited in Norman Geisler, *Christian Apologetics* (Grand Rapids: Baker, 1976), p. 322.
8. Nelson Glueck, *Rivers in the Desert* (Philadelphia: Jewish Publications, 1969), p. 31.
9. Cited in Josh McDowell, *Evidence That Demands a Verdict* (San Bernardino: Campus Crusade for Christ, 1972), p. 68.
10. Lee Strobel, *The Case for Christ* (Grand Rapids: Zondervan, 1998), p. 97.
11. Cited in Josh McDowell, *The New Evidence that Demands a Verdict* (Nashville: Nelson, 1999), p. 63.
12. Norman Geisler and Frank Turek, *I Don't Have Enough Faith to Be an Atheist* (Wheaton: Crossway, 2004), p. 256.
13. Gary Habermas, *Ancient Evidence for the Life of Jesus* (Nashville: Nelson, 1984), p. 65.
14. Ibid., p. 66.
15. Data on Justin Martyr, Polycarp, and Irenaeus is derived from Geisler and Nix, p. 190.
16. Strobel, pp. 79-80.
17. Cited in Gary Habermas, *The Historical Jesus* (Joplin: College Press, 1996), p. 203.

18. Cited in Habermas, *The Historical Jesus,* p. 199.

19. Tacitus, *Annals* 15.44, cited in Strobel, p. 82.

20. Julius Africanus, cited in McDowell, *The New Evidence That Demands a Verdict,* pp. 57-58.

Chapter 2—The Right Way to Interpret the Bible

1. Norman Geisler, *Explaining Hermeneutics* (Downers Grove: InterVarsity, 1988), pp. 14-15.

2. Graham Stanton, "Presuppositions in New Testament Criticism," in *New Testament Interpretation,* ed. Howard Marshall (Grand Rapids: Eerdmans, 1977), p. 68.

3. Bernard Ramm, *Protestant Bible Interpretation* (Grand Rapids: Baker, 1978), p. 105.

4. J.I. Packer, *"Fundamentalism" and the Word of God* (Grand Rapids: Eerdmans, 1958), p. 102, italics added.

5. Cited in Bruce Milne, *Know the Truth* (Downers Grove: InterVarsity, 1982), p. 46.

6. *The American Heritage Dictionary of the English Language,* 4th edition.

Chapter 3—Our God Is an Awesome God

1. J.I. Packer, *Knowing God* (Downers Grove: InterVarsity, 1979), p. 29.

2. R.T. France, *The Living God* (Downers Grove: InterVarsity, 1972), p. 25.

3. Erich Sauer, *From Eternity to Eternity* (Grand Rapids: Eerdmans, 1979), p. 13.

4. Norman Geisler, Wayne House, and Max Herrera, *The Battle for God* (Grand Rapids: Kregel, 2001), p. 92.

5. Ibid., p. 24.

6. Robert Reymond, *Jesus, Divine Messiah: The New Testament Witness* (Phillipsburg: Presbyterian and Reformed, 1990), p. 84, inserts added.

Chapter 4—What a Wonder Is Jesus

1. Ronald Nash, "Was the New Testament Influenced by Pagan Religions?" Statement DB109, Christian Research Institute. www.equip.org. Inserted added.

2. Bruce Metzger, *Historical and Literary Studies: Pagan, Jewish, and Christian* (Grand Rapids: Eerdmans, 1968), p. 11. Insert added.

3. C.S. Lewis, *Mere Christianity* (New York: Macmillan, 1960), pp. 40-41.

4. Robert Reymond, *Jesus, Divine Messiah: The New Testament Witness* (Phillipsburg: Presbyterian and Reformed, 1990), p. 94.

5. Rob Bowman, *Jehovah's Witnesses, Jesus Christ, and the Gospel of John* (Grand Rapids: Baker, 1989), p. 99.

6. William Barclay, *The Gospel of John* (Philadelphia: Westminster, 1956), pp. 42-43.

7. S.E. Johnson, "Lord (Christ)," *The Interpreter's Dictionary of the Bible* (New York: Abingdon, 1976), 3:151.

8. William G.T. Shedd, *Romans* (New York: Scribner, 1879), p. 318.

9. Charles Ryrie, *Basic Theology* (Wheaton: Victor, 1986), p. 48.

10. Ibid., p. 28, insert added.

11. Reymond, pp. 121-22.

Chapter 5—God's Magnificent Creation

1. Henry Morris, *The Biblical Basis for Modern Science* (Grand Rapids: Baker, 1984), p. 156.

2. Ibid., p. 158.
3. Erich Sauer, *From Eternity to Eternity* (Grand Rapids: Eerdmans, 1979), p. 19.
4. John Whitcomb, Jr., *The Early Earth* (Grand Rapids: Baker, 1979), p. 58.
5. Robin Collins, "The Fine-Tuning Design Argument," *Reason for the Hope Within,* September 1, 1998, Discovery Institute. www.discovery.org.
6. Ibid.
7. Phillip Johnson, *Defeating Darwinism by Opening Minds* (Downers Grove: InterVarsity, 1997), p. 23.
8. William Dembski, *Intelligent Design: The Bridge Between Science & Theology* (Downers Grove: InterVarsity, 1999), p. 127.
9. Sauer, p. 30.

Chapter 6—Not the Way It's Supposed to Be: Human Sin

1. Cited in E.K. Simpson and F.F. Bruce, *Commentary on the Epistles to the Ephesians and Colossians* (Grand Rapids: Eerdmans, 1975), p. 50.
2. Billy Graham, *How to be Born Again* (Dallas: Word, 1989), p. 118.

Chapter 7—Jesus the Savior Became a Man

1. Robert Gromacki, *The Virgin Birth: Doctrine of Deity* (Grand Rapids: Baker, 1981), p. 102.
2. Ibid., p. 103.
3. Charles Ryrie, *Basic Theology* (Wheaton: Victor, 1986), p. 261.
4. John Walvoord, *Jesus Christ Our Lord* (Chicago: Moody, 1980), pp. 138-39.
5. Robert Lightner, "Philippians," in *The Bible Knowledge Commentary,* New Testament, eds. John F. Walvoord and Roy B. Zuck (Wheaton: Victor, 1983), p. 654.
6. Ibid., p. 654.
7. J.I. Packer, *Knowing God* (Downers Grove: InterVarsity, 1979), p. 50.
8. Walvoord, p. 115.
9. Robert Lightner, *Evangelical Theology* (Grand Rapids: Baker, 1986), p. 82.
10. Walvoord, p. 118.
11. Robert Reymond, *Jesus, Divine Messiah: The New Testament Witness* (Phillipsburg: Presbyterian and Reformed, 1990), p. 80.

Chapter 8—Bought with a Price: Human Salvation

1. Benjamin Warfield, *Biblical and Theological Studies* (Phillipsburg: Presbyterian and Reformed, 1968), p. 171.
2. Erich Sauer, *From Eternity to Eternity* (Grand Rapids: Eerdmans, 1979), p. 40.
3. Cited in J.I. Packer, *Knowing Christianity* (Wheaton: Harold Shaw, 1995), p. 94.
4. Bible Illustrations, electronic media, HyperCard stack.

Chapter 9—Jesus the Savior Is Risen

1. Quoted by Henry Thiessen, cited in Tim LaHaye, *Jesus: Who Is He?* (Sisters: Multnomah, 1996), p. 150.
2. J.P. Moreland and Kai Nielsen, *Does God Exist? The Great Debate* (Nashville: Nelson, 1990), p. 192.
3. Michael Green, *Man Alive!* (Downers Grove: InterVarsity, 1968), pp. 23-24.

4. Barry Leventhal, "Why I Believe Jesus is the Promised Messiah," in Norman Geisler and Paul Hoffman, *Why I Am a Christian* (Grand Rapids: Baker, 2001), p. 214.

5. Moreland and Nielsen, p. 42.

6. Gary Habermas, in Lee Strobel, *The Case for Christ* (Grand Rapids: Zondervan, 1998), p. 230.

7. William Lane Craig and Walter Sinnott-Armstrong, *God? A Debate Between a Christian and an Atheist* (Oxford: Oxford University Press, 2004), p. 70.

8. C.S. Lewis, *God in the Dock,* ed. Walter Hooper (Grand Rapids, MI: Eerdmans, n.d.), p. 26.

9. Ibid.

10. Craig and Sinnott-Armstrong, pp. 37-38.

11. Ibid., pp. 72-73.

12. Christian scholar Murray Harris espoused this view until he changed his mind in the early 1990s.

13. Robert Gundry, *Soma in Biblical Theology* (Cambridge: Cambridge Press, 1976), p. 168.

14. Canon Westcott, *The Gospel of the Resurrection,* Bible Illustrations, Logos Bible Software, electronic media.

15. Cited in John Stott, *Basic Christianity* (Downers Grove: InterVarsity, 1971), p. 47.

16. Cited in Wilbur Smith, *Sermons on the Christian Life,* Bible Illustrations, Logos Bible Software, electronic media.

Chapter 10—Power from on High: The Holy Spirit

1. William Arndt and Wilbur Gingrich, *A Greek-English Lexicon of the New Testament and Other Early Christian Literature* (Chicago: University of Chicago Press, 1957), p. 146.

2. R.A. Torrey, *Secret Power* (Ventura: Regal, 1987), p. 89.

Chapter 11—The Church—God's Forever Family

1. Charles Swindoll, *Growing Deep in the Christian Life* (Portland: Multnomah, 1986), p. 339.

2. Chuck Colson, *Christian Research Newsletter,* March 1993, p. 1.

3. Cited in John Blanchard, *More Gathered Gold* (Hertfordshire, England: Evangelical Press, 1986), p. 38.

4. Cited in Blanchard, p. 43.

5. Edythe Draper, *Draper's Book of Quotations for the Christian World* (Wheaton: Tyndale, 1992), p. 83.

6. Bible Illustrations, electronic media, HyperCard stack.

7. Draper, pp. 79-80.

8. Bible Illustrations.

9. Duane Litfin, "Evangelical Feminism," *Bibliotheca Sacra,* July-September 1979, p. 267.

10. J.I. Packer, "Let's Stop Making Women Presbyters," *Christianity Today,* 11 February 1991, p. 21.

Chapter 12—Angels Among Us

1. Louis Berkhof, *Systematic Theology* (Grand Rapids: Eerdmans, 1982), p. 146.

2. James Montgomery Boice, *Foundations of the Christian Faith* (Downers Grove: InterVarsity, 1981), p. 167.

3. Charles Ryrie, *Basic Theology* (Chicago: Moody, 1999), p. 127.

4. Berkhof, p. 145, emphasis added.
5. Henry Clarence Thiessen, *Lectures in Systematic Theology* (Grand Rapids: Eerdmans, 1981), p. 134, emphasis and insert added.
6. Billy Graham, *Angels: God's Secret Agents* (Garden City: Doubleday, 1975), p. 24.
7. Millard Erickson, *Christian Theology* (Grand Rapids: Baker, 1987), p. 440.
8. Graham, p. 92.
9. Ibid., p. 95.

Chapter 13—Satan Against Us

1. Donald Barnhouse, *The Invisible War* (Grand Rapids: Zondervan, 1965), pp. 26-27.
2. Cited in Henry Clarence Thiessen, *Lectures in Systematic Theology* (Grand Rapids: Eerdmans, 1981), p. 141.
3. Ibid., p. 142.
4. Charles Ryrie, *Balancing the Christian Life* (Chicago: Moody, 1978), p. 124.
5. Charles Ryrie, *Basic Theology* (Wheaton: Victor, 1986), p. 147.
6. Ryrie, *Balancing the Christian Life,* p. 124.
7. Millard Erickson, *Christian Theology* (Grand Rapids: Baker, 1987), p. 450.

Chapter 14—God's Prophecies of the End Times

1. George Smith, *Atheism: The Case Against God* (New York: Prometheus, 1989), pp. 209-10.
2. Smith, p. 207.

Chapter 15—The Wonder of Heaven and the Afterlife

1. John Wesley, *The Nature of Salvation* (Minneapolis: Bethany, 1987), p. 134.
2. Cited in Charles Ryrie, *Basic Theology* (Wheaton: Victor, 1986), p. 513.
3. Wesley, p. 135.
4. Millard Erickson, *Christian Theology* (Grand Rapids: Baker, 1987), p. 1229.
5. John Gill, "Hebrews 11:13-15," in The Online Bible (electronic media). Version 2.5.2.
6. Bruce Shelley, *Theology for Ordinary People* (Downers Grove: InterVarsity, 1994), p. 212.
7. J.I. Packer, ed. *Alive to God* (Downers Grove: InterVarsity, 1992), p. 162.
8. Ibid., p. 171.
9. Ibid., p. 163.
10. Ibid., p. 164.
11. Ibid., p. 165.
12. Packer, p. 165.
13. Cited in Packer, p. 167.
14. Gary Habermas and J.P. Moreland, *Immortality* (Nashville: Nelson, 1992), p. 185.
15. Norman Geisler and Yutaka Amano, *The Reincarnation Sensation* (Wheaton: Tyndale, 1987), p. 8.

Bibliography

Ankerberg, John, and John Weldon. *The Facts on Life After Death.* Eugene, OR: Harvest House, 1992.

Ankerberg, John, John Weldon, and Walter C. Kaiser. *The Case for Jesus the Messiah.* Chattanooga, TN: The John Ankerberg Evangelistic Association, 1989.

Berkhof, Louis. *Systematic Theology.* Grand Rapids: Eerdmans, 1982.

Blanchard, John. *Whatever Happened to Hell?* Durham, England: Evangelical Press, 1993.

Buell, Jon A., and O. Quentin Hyder. *Jesus: God, Ghost, or Guru?* Grand Rapids: Zondervan, 1978.

Buswell, James Oliver. *A Systematic Theology of the Christian Religion.* Grand Rapids: Zondervan, 1979.

Calvin, John. *Institutes of the Christian Religion.* Ed. John T. McNeill. Trans. Ford Lewis Battles. Philadelphia: The Westminster Press, 1960.

Chafer, Lewis Sperry. *Systematic Theology.* Wheaton: Victor Books, 1988.

Chafer, Lewis Sperry, and John F. Walvoord. *Major Bible Themes.* Grand Rapids: Zondervan, 1975.

Connelly, Douglas. *What the Bible Really Says: After Life.* Downers Grove, IL: InterVarsity Press, 1995.

Dickason, Fred. *Angels, Elect and Evil.* Chicago: Moody Press, 1978.

Douglas, J.D., ed. *The New Bible Dictionary.* Wheaton, IL: Tyndale House, 1982.

Elwell, Walter A., ed. *Topical Analysis of the Bible.* Grand Rapids: Baker Book House, 1991.

Enns, Paul. *The Moody Handbook of Theology.* Chicago: Moody Press, 1989.

Erickson, Millard J. *Christian Theology.* Unabridged one-volume edition. Grand Rapids: Baker Book House, 1987.

———. *The Word Became Flesh: A Contemporary Incarnational Christology.* Grand Rapids: Baker Book House, 1991.

France, R.T. *The Living God.* Downers Grove, IL: InterVarsity Press, 1972.

Geisler, Norman. *To Understand the Bible Look for Jesus.* Grand Rapids: Baker Book House, 1979.

Graham, Billy. *Angels: God's Secret Agents.* Garden City, NY: Doubleday & Co., 1975.

———. *How to be Born Again.* Dallas, TX: Word Publishing, 1989.

Gromacki, Robert G. *The Virgin Birth: Doctrine of Deity.* Grand Rapids: Baker Book House, 1984.

Habermas, Gary R., and J.P. Moreland. *Immortality: The Other Side of Death.* Nashville: Thomas Nelson, 1992.

Henry, Carl F. ed. *Basic Christian Doctrines.* Grand Rapids: Baker Book House, 1983.

Hodge, Charles. *Systematic Theology.* Abridged edition. Ed. Edward N. Gross. Grand Rapids: Baker Book House, 1988.

Hoekema, Anthony A. *The Bible and the Future.* Grand Rapids: Eerdmans, 1984.

Hoyt, Herman A. *The End Times.* Chicago: Moody Press, 1969.

Ice, Thomas, and Robert Dean. *Overrun by Demons?* Eugene, OR: Harvest House, 1994.

Keller, Phillip. *A Shepherd Looks at the Good Shepherd and His Sheep.* Grand Rapids: Zondervan, 1978.

Ladd, George Eldon. *The Last Things.* Grand Rapids: Eerdmans, 1982.

Lightner, Robert P. *Evangelical Theology.* Grand Rapids: Baker Book House, 1986.

Machen, J. Gresham. *The Virgin Birth of Christ.* New York: Harper, 1930.

McDowell, Josh, and Bart Larson. *Jesus: A Biblical Defense of His Deity.* San Bernardino, CA: Here's Life Publishers, 1983.

Morey, Robert A. *Death and the Afterlife.* Minneapolis: Bethany House, 1984.

Müller, George. *Autobiography of George Muller: The Life of Trust.* Grand Rapids: Baker Book House, 1984.

Pache, Rene. *The Future Life.* Chicago: Moody Press, 1980.

———. *The Inspiration and Authority of Scripture.* Chicago: Moody Press, 1978.

Packer, J.I. *Knowing God.* Downers Grove, IL: InterVarsity Press, 1979.

Pentecost, J. Dwight. *The Words and Works of Jesus Christ.* Grand Rapids: Zondervan, 1982.

———. *Things to Come.* Grand Rapids: Zondervan, 1974.

Reymond, Robert L. *Jesus Divine Messiah: The New Testament Witness.* Phillipsburg, NJ: Presbyterian and Reformed Publishing Co., 1990.

Rhodes, Ron. *Angels Among Us: Separating Truth from Fiction.* Eugene, OR: Harvest House, 1995.

———. *Christ Before the Manger: The Life and Times of the Preincarnate Christ.* Grand Rapids: Baker Book House, 1992.

———. *The Undiscovered Country: Exploring the Wonder of Heaven and the Afterlife.* Eugene, OR: Harvest House, 1996.

Ryrie, Charles C. *Basic Theology.* Wheaton: Victor Books, 1986.

———. *The Holy Spirit.* Chicago: Moody Press, 1965.

———. *The Ryrie Study Bible.* Chicago: Moody Press, 1986.

Sauer, Erich. *From Eternity to Eternity.* Grand Rapids: Eerdmans, 1979.

———. *The Dawn of World Redemption.* Grand Rapids: Eerdmans, 1977.

Shephard, J.W. *The Christ of the Gospels.* Grand Rapids: Eerdmans, 1975.

Smith, Jerome H. *The New Treasury of Scripture Knowledge.* Nashville: Thomas Nelson, 1992.

Smith, Wilbur M. *The Biblical Doctrine of Heaven.* Chicago: Moody Press, 1974.

Stedman, Ray C. *Spiritual Warfare.* Waco: Word Books, 1976.

Taylor, Rick. *When Life Is Changed Forever.* Eugene, OR: Harvest House, 1992.

Tenney, Merrill C., ed. *The Zondervan Pictorial Encyclopedia of the Bible.* Grand Rapids: Zondervan, 1978.

Thiessen, Henry Clarence. *Lectures in Systematic Theology.* Grand Rapids: Eerdmans, 1981.

Tozer, A.W. *The Pursuit of God.* Wheaton: Tyndale House, n.d.

Vine's Expository Dictionary of Biblical Words. Vine, W.E., Merrill F. Unger, and William White, eds. Nashville: Thomas Nelson, 1985.

Vos, Geerhardus. *Biblical Theology: Old and New Testaments.* Grand Rapids: Eerdmans, 1985.

Walvoord, John F. *Jesus Christ Our Lord.* Chicago: Moody Press, 1980.

———. *The Holy Spirit.* Grand Rapids: Zondervan, 1958.

Warfield, Benjamin B. *Biblical and Theological Studies.* Phillipsburg, NJ: Presbyterian and Reformed Publishing Co., 1968.

———. *The Lord of Glory.* Grand Rapids: Baker Book House, 1974.

Wesley, John. *The Nature of Spiritual Growth.* Minneapolis: Bethany House, 1977.

About the Author

Dr. Ron Rhodes
Reasoning from the Scriptures Ministries
P.O. Box 2526
Frisco, TX 75034

Web site: www.ronrhodes.org
E-mail: ronrhodes@earthlink.net
Free newsletter available upon request.

HARVEST HOUSE PUBLISHERS